Digital Media Effects

W. JAMES POTTER
University of California at Santa Barbara

ROWMAN & LITTLEFIELD
Lanham • Boulder • New York • London

Acquisitions Editor: Natalie Mandziuk
Acquisitions Assistant: Deni Remsberg
Sales and Marketing Inquiries: textbooks@rowman.com

Credits and acknowledgments for material borrowed from other sources, and reproduced with permission, appear on the appropriate pages within the text.

Published by Rowman & Littlefield
An imprint of The Rowman & Littlefield Publishing Group, Inc.
4501 Forbes Boulevard, Suite 200, Lanham, Maryland 20706
www.rowman.com

6 Tinworth Street, London SE11 5AL, United Kingdom

British Library Cataloguing in Publication Information Available

Library of Congress Cataloging-in-Publication Data
Names: Potter, W. James, author.
Title: Digital media effects / W. James Potter.
Description: Lanham : Rowman & Littlefield, 2021. | Includes bibliographical references and index.
Identifiers: LCCN 2020036675 (print) | LCCN 2020036676 (ebook) | ISBN 9781538140017 (hardcover) | ISBN 9781538141014 (paperback) | ISBN 9781538140024 (epub)
Subjects: LCSH: Mass media—Influence. | Digital media—Technological innovations. | Digital media—Social aspects. | Digital media—Psychological aspects.
Classification: LCC P94 .P66 2021 (print) | LCC P94 (ebook) | DDC 302.23/1—dc23
LC record available at https://lccn.loc.gov/2020036675
LC ebook record available at https://lccn.loc.gov/2020036676

♾️™ The paper used in this publication meets the minimum requirements of American National Standard for Information Sciences—Permanence of Paper for Printed Library Materials, ANSI/NISO Z39.48-1992.

Contents

Preface

Since the invention of movable type more than five centuries ago, mass media have been exerting an influence on individuals, institutions, cultures, and societies. Social scientists have been documenting the nature of that growing influence throughout the past century by producing a large body of literature that clearly shows that mass media are constantly influencing our beliefs, our behaviors, our emotions, and how we interact with information as well as with one another (Bryant & Oliver, 2009; Nabi & Oliver, 2009; Potter, 2012; Sparks, 2015).

While media influence has steadily grown as mass media have evolved with innovations in technology and marketing, that evolution has morphed into a revolution during the last several decades as **digitization** has changed the way information is generated, stored, and disseminated. This revolution is stimulating researchers to examine whether the effects of digital media are the same as they have found with **analog media** of print (books, newspapers, and magazines), audio recordings, film, radio, and television (broadcast and cable). If the effects of digital media are the same as the effects we have found from analog media, then we can continue to rely on what we know from the huge literature of media effects that has been generated over the past century. However, if the effects of exposure to digital media are very different than the effects of exposure to analog media, then the knowledge we have generated through research using analog media may be out of date and no longer useful to explain the nature of the current media effects.

Although the phenomenon of digital media is only a few decades old, researchers have already produced a substantial literature that documents its effects. Some of the findings in that literature demonstrate that the effects of digital media are the same as the effects of analog media. I refer to these as legacy effects. For example, legacy effects have been found in the way people are aware of their needs for specific kinds of information and entertainment that they use the media to satisfy. Also, the media have been successful in conditioning people into **exposure habits** that are reinforced over time.

Effects researchers have also found that exposure to digital media led to effects that had not been found with analog media. I refer to these as novel effects. For example, novel effects have been found as a result of the way people use digital media to interact with one another to address needs that analog media cannot satisfy, such as the need to compete against, as well as with, many people simultaneously and the need to connect with other individuals who share their exact same beliefs, problems, and desires for specific kinds of experiences.

While this book focuses on digital media and the effects that arise from exposure to their platforms and content, it also recognizes the significance of legacy effects. Both types are important. A treatment of media effects that limits itself to only the effects unique to digital media greatly underrepresents the power of digital media to influence us.

This book presents 12 chapters that are organized into five sections. The first three chapters present introductory issues that lay a foundation for the rest of the book. The first chapter creates a foundation for the book by delineating how digital media are different than analog media and how those differences open up entire new areas for exploring the nature of media effects. Chapter 2 introduces concepts that are needed to map the full variety of media effects. These concepts are then used throughout the book to help you comprehend the full range of media effects and understand how those individual effects differ from one another. In Chapter 3, I focus your attention on the research about how the media, especially digital media, attract user attention.

The next three chapters each focus on different kinds of media content that have been staples of analog media and brought forward as staples of digital media. These content types are news, advertising, and entertainment. The more recent research, which tests effects of these content types in digital media, typically finds legacy effects, that is, the patterns of influence of these content types have been found to be very similar regardless of whether the content is presented by analog or digital media.

The next four chapters focus on effects that can be attributed to the unique influence of digital media. Chapter 7 explains the development of social networking sites and how they have been affecting individuals. Chapter 8 focuses on the experience of living in virtual worlds as accessed through digital platforms. Chapter 9 is concerned with the effects of competing in digital games. And Chapter 10 reviews the research that has examined how digital media have been influencing institutions, especially the institutions of the economy, politics, and religion.

The book builds to a macro perspective on media effects. Chapter 11 lays out the broad effects that span across all types of digital experiences. These effects focus on how general exposure to digital media—regardless of type of content or experience—can shape how people concentrate, how they make choices, how they connect to others, how they can become disinhibited, and how they can become addicted. Finally, Chapter 12 explores two big-picture issues. One is the nature of privacy in the digital age. The other issue examined is the concept of control—from both a regulatory perspective and a personal perspective.

As you will see in these chapters, scholars have already come a long way in building understanding about digital effects in the several short decades since digital media have begun to emerge. A good deal of research has examined the nature of exposure to digital media and how effects arise from those exposures. But while there are still many gaps in our understanding, a relatively clear picture is developing that digital media are at least as powerful as analog media have been in consuming our resource of time and giving us a wide range of experiences that lead to an astonishing variety of effects.

Acknowledgments

I would like to thank those who offered feedback on the manuscript: Walter Gantz (Indiana University), Jeff Boone (Angelo State University), Chan L. Thai (University of Santa Clara), R. Glenn Cummins (Texas Tech University), Elise Assaf (California State University, Fullerton), Adam S. Kahn (California State University, Long Beach), Riva Tukachinsky (Chapman University), Kyle J. Holody (Coastal Carolina University), Kim Bissell (University of Alabama), Sarah G. Huxford (Point University), and Karrie A. Bowen (Penn State University Erie).

About the Author

W. James Potter, professor at the University of California at Santa Barbara, holds one PhD in communication studies and another in instructional technology. He has been teaching media courses for more than two decades in the areas of effects on individuals and society, content narratives, structure and economics of media industries, advertising, and journalism. He has served as editor of the *Journal of Broadcasting & Electronic Media* and is the author of many journal articles and several dozen books, including *Media Effects*; *Media Literacy* (10th ed.); *The 11 Myths of Media Violence*; *Major Theories of Media Effects*; *Becoming a Strategic Thinker: Developing Skills for Success*; and *7 Skills of Media Literacy*.

CHAPTER 1

The Current Media Environment

This chapter lays a foundation for the rest of the book by showing you how the media environment has been evolving from exposure experiences being provided exclusively by analog media to an expanded range of experiences being provided by digital media. We will first examine the key characteristics of analog media and contrast them with the key features that define digital media. Then I'll show you why it is extremely important to understand the nature of the influence that mass media are constantly exerting on all of us, and why this has grown significantly in importance with the rise of digital media.

Evolution of Mass Media

ANALOG MEDIA

Since the invention of movable type and the printing press almost six centuries ago, there has been a series of innovations in preserving messages and transmitting those

Table 1.1. Contrasting Analog and Digital Media

Analog Media	Digital Media
Channel bound	Fluid across channels
Continuous capture	Translation to binary code
Copy degradation	No copy degradation
Centralized decision-making	Dispersed decision-making
Very limited interaction	Widespread interaction
Messages as standard products	Messages customized
Relatively fixed	Continuous evolving

messages quickly and widely. These channels, which are sometimes called "traditional" or "old media," include print channels (books, newspapers, and magazines), audio recordings, film, broadcast (radio and television), and cable TV. While the most recognizable characteristic of analog media is that their messages are channel bound, they also differ in terms of how decisions are made regarding what messages get produced and distributed and the nature of those messages (see Table 1.1).

Channel Bound

The primary characteristic of analog media is that their messages are channel bound. This means that each form of analog media uses a different kind of technology to capture information, store it, and transmit it to audiences. For example, the channel of audio recording requires a certain kind of microphone that is sensitive to sound waves and translates them into electrical impulses. Those electrical impulses were first stored on vinyl discs by carving fluctuations into the groove that ran in a circular pattern on the surface of the vinyl disc. A needle was placed into the groove and the disc rotated so the needle could progress along the groove picking up the fluctuations and translating them back into electrical impulses that traveled to a speaker where they were then translated into sound waves so listeners could hear the recording. In contrast, the channel of broadcast television originally relied on cameras to capture images continuously and then imprint that information on electromagnetic waves that were sent wirelessly in a way that could be received by television sets that translated it into electrical impulses that were sent to a cathode ray tube that fired a stream of ions to a screen that was painted with pixels that glowed when ions hit it. The pattern of glowing pixels created images that appeared to move on the screen. As you can see from these two examples, each analog medium relies on a very different set of technologies to capture, store, and transmit its messages. Thus it requires considerable effort and technology to translate a message that was captured in one analog medium into a different analog medium.

Centralized Decision-Making

Analog media are also characterized by centralized decision-making. That is, they are controlled by hierarchically structured industries where experts at the top of those hierarchies make decisions about the creation and distribution of messages. This means that the creators of analog media messages must guess what audiences will want, then create their messages by assembling elements they think will appeal to those groups of people, and send their messages out hoping that those messages will attract relatively large numbers of users. Of course, even with analog media, there is feedback, but that feedback is seldom immediate; it takes a relatively long time to get this feedback—days or weeks rather than seconds or minutes. For example, feedback in book production is in the form of weekly sales data and reviews of those books published in magazines and newspapers. Feedback on audience sizes for prime-time television shows is provided the next day by Nielsen overnight reports. Nor is the feedback specific; producers of analog media messages do not get detailed feedback about why people exposed themselves to particular messages or their reactions to the particular elements they liked in those messages.

Messages as Standard Products

Analog media businesses produce standardized messages that they hope will attract large numbers of people. These message units (e.g., a daily newspaper, a Hollywood movie, an album of 12 song recordings, or a TV series) are produced by a team of professionals who have the skills to create a product that achieves high production value. These professionals create messages by adding characteristics that they believe will appeal to a wider range of individuals, thus increasing the probability that more consumers will expose themselves to their message. For example, a daily newspaper creates a product each day that includes a wide range of news stories (hard news, features, sports, recipes, horoscopes, comics, etc.) that it hopes will attract a large number of readers. While this is a good strategy for media businesses to use to increase the appeal of their messages, it also has a downside, which is that consumers must pay for the full package of messages when they may want only one particular message. Continuing with the daily newspaper example, people who want to read stories about local sports teams each day must pay for the entire newspaper, although they only read the sports page. Likewise subscribers to cable TV services are presented with several bundles of channels, but they cannot break the bundles apart and subscribe to individual cable channels. The products that analog media provide to audiences are units that contain a variety of elements that vary in interest to each audience member, but in order for an audience member to get access to that unit, he or she must pay for the entire bundle that makes up the product that the media business is selling.

DIGITAL MEDIA

The major characteristics that distinguish digital media from analog media are the fluidity across channels, the greater ability to customize messages, dispersed decision-making across more people, and ability to provide a wider range of experiences to users.

Fluidity Across Channels

With digital media, there is great fluidity across technological channels. When information is captured—whether through a microphone, a still image camera, a video camera, or a word processor—the information is immediately translated into binary code. That is, every element in a message is translated into either a 0 or a 1, and the message itself is expressed in a long string of those zeros and ones in order to capture all the elements in a message. This binary code is the language of computers and the **internet**, so any message that has been digitized can easily be transmitted across a very wide range of media channels and platforms.

All the devices we think about as being digital media rely on computers to receive and present messages (Balbi & Magaudda, 2018). "The digitization of just about everything—documents, news, music, photos, video, maps, personal updates, social networks, requests for information and responses to those requests, data from all kinds of sensors, and so on—is one of the most important phenomena of recent years" (Brynjolfsson & McAfee, 2014, p. 66). This is why the computer has been called the mother of all digital devices because the computer requires the use of digital code that is uniform so that information can be shared across all kinds of computers.

While the computer is essential to the digitization of messages, the internet has become essential to the distribution of those digitized messages. The internet is a worldwide network of circuits and packets of digitized data that connects countless billions of computerized devices and, thus, the people who use these devices (Blum, 2013). The internet has been called a network of networks because it makes it possible for an incredibly diverse range of networks to interact easily with one another by using shared protocols that link up different hardware and software (Balbi & Magaudda, 2018).

The digitization of messages and the use of the internet to share those digital messages have made it possible for the widespread use of mobile devices. These devices, particularly smartphones, tablets, and laptop computers, enable people to receive any kind of message (printed words, audio sounds, photographs, and video) wherever they can connect to the internet, which is virtually anywhere. This provides users of digital media a degree of convenience that is far superior than what analog media provide.

Dispersed Decision-Making

In contrast to analog media, digital media are organized horizontally rather than hierarchically. The interactive nature of digital media has forced decision-makers to rely less on their presumed expertise and be influenced much more by the emerging needs they perceive through interactions with potential audience members.

The interactive nature of digital media also allows every user to largely bypass authorities who used to function as gatekeepers and instead create any kind of content (e.g., texts, tweets, blog posts, email, photographs, recordings, and videos) and then distribute those messages widely by uploading content to internet platforms that make those messages instantly available to other people anywhere in the world.

Customized Messages

The interactive nature of digital media has made mass customization available. Producers of digital messages—whether industry professionals or everyday people—continually interact with potential audience members in order to progressively refine their messages to maximize their appeal to particular niche audiences. Even after they have crafted their messages and distributed them, producers monitor audience reactions so they can continue to produce messages that will satisfy specific audience needs. Producers pay a lot of attention to "likes" and ratings as well as engaging in conversations with those users while they are being exposed to those messages. Thus digital media allow for feedback that is more immediate, more widespread, and more detailed than the type of feedback generated by analog media.

Range of Experiences

Digital media offer an incredibly wide range of messages and experiences to users. Some of these are very popular and draw millions of users every day, and some are more specialized and appeal to only a handful of users. A useful way to organize all these experiences is to categorize them by the general type of experience they provide to users: those experiences that are primarily cooperative, those experiences that are primarily competitive, and those experiences where users are motivated primarily to acquire something they value.

Interactive media platforms that offer cooperative experiences have grown extremely popular. The most popular of these are called social networking sites (SNSs) such as Facebook (begun in 2004) and Twitter (begun in 2006). In 2008, 24% of the U.S. population were regular users of social media sites, and this percentage steadily increased to more than 81% by 2017 (Statistica, 2018). These experiences are examined in depth in Chapter 8.

Many interactive media platforms have been designed to attract users who want to compete against themselves, to compete against a computer, or to compete against one or many players. With the technology of computers, the internet, and mobile devices, **digital games** became part of mass media. These platforms offer users the opportunity to play simple games against a computer or to enter an exotic world where they can play complicated games with hundreds and even thousands of other players simultaneously around the globe. These experiences are examined in depth in Chapter 9.

People use interactive media platforms to acquire things of value directly from those platforms. These include information and entertainment experiences. People can also use internet platforms to shop and initiate purchases of physical goods. Of course people can acquire these kinds of things from brick-and-mortar stores, but interactive media platforms are typically easier to use. These digital platforms that provide acquisition experiences are examined in some detail in Chapters 4 through 6.

We are now experiencing a significant change as people are shifting their attention and time toward digital media. The reasons for this shift are that (a) digital media satisfy many audience needs better than analog media, and (b) digital media are able

Table 1.2. Timeline of Development of Communications Into Digital Media

350K–150K BCE	Formal languages begin to coalesce and spread
8K–5K BCE	Formal systems of writing begin to appear
1450 CE	Mechanical movable type and printing press (Gutenberg)
1837	First programmable mechanical computer (Babbage)
1850s	Invention of photography to capture still images
1880s	Invention of sound recordings and playback
1890s	Invention of motion picture recording and playback
1910s	Development of wireless transmission of audio signals (radio)
1930s	Modern age of computing begins with the design of machines to process large amounts of data
1930s	Development of wireless transmission of video signals (broadcast TV)
1946	Mobile phone technology first appears as bulky car phones
1965	Beginning of the internet by the U.S. Department of Defense in its DARPA (Defense Advanced Research Project Agency)
1969	ARPANET connects computers from five universities in a network
1970s	Small LANs (local computer networks) spring up everywhere
1970s	Rise of online gaming; development of virtual worlds in which large numbers of players compete simultaneously
1972	BITNET project begins to link computers at all U.S. universities
1972	First email message sent
1973	First successful personal computer is the Xerox Alto, which included two major innovations: the mouse and a graphical user interface (GUI) that managed the computer's desktop functions
1973	Motorola introduces first mobile cell phone (2.5 pounds)
1975	Microsoft founded by Bill Gates and Paul Allen
1976	Apple founded by Steve Jobs and Steve Wozniak
Late 1970s	Packet switching system allows exchanges internationally, and the internet goes global
1984	Apple markets first Macintosh with a GUI
1985	Microsoft introduces first version of Windows
1989	Development of WWW (World Wide Web) that digitized all information with hypertext, allowing for all computers to use same language
1990	Internet goes commercial, allowing for-profit companies to sell services and products
1994	Netscape is the first browser to allow users to surf the internet

1994	First search engine introduced (AltaVista)
1994	First blog (web log) where a college student begins posting online continuously about the details of his everyday life
1995	Internet allows commercial for-profit companies; Amazon.com launches as an online book retailer; eBay launches as an auction site
1997	Google made available to the public with page rank algorithm
Late 1990s	Beginning of social networking sites (SNSs) that allow users to present a personal profile and build a list of friends
1999	Napster allows peer-to-peer file sharing, especially music
2001	Birth of Wikipedia, which stimulates other wikis (i.e., open-source collaborative projects)
2001	iTunes launched by Apple to sell music; Apple launches iPod
2003	Myspace launched as a full-service SNS; quickly attracts millions of users
2004	Facebook launched as a Harvard-only SNS but then opens membership to everyone within 2 years and grows to 2 billion users
2005	YouTube begins as a service for sharing media, especially videos
2007	Apple introduces the iPhone, a hybrid between the mobile phone and a personal computer that connects to the internet and offers keyboards on touch screens
2007	Netflix and Hulu launched as media streaming on-demand services
2009	Bitcoin (untraceable digital currency) introduced
2013	Netflix starts to produce original content
2015	Google restructures, changing its name to Alphabet
2016	Apple introduces the iPhone X, which contains 6 CPU cores that work together and runs about 10,000 times faster than the Apollo guidance computer that landed men on the moon in 1969 (Brooks & Lasser, 2018)

Source: Adapted from Balbi & Magaudda, 2018; Chayko, 2018; and Potter, 2019.

to satisfy audience needs that analog media cannot. Therefore, it is likely this shift will continue and that the power of digital media to exert influence on individuals and institutions will continue to increase.

Why Study the Effects of Media?

We live in a society that is saturated with media messages, and the number of messages produced each year increases at an accelerating rate. Therefore, it is impossible to keep up with even a tiny fraction of this overwhelming amount of information that is aggressively competing for our attention. To survive, humans default to **automatic routines** of information filtering and processing to navigate their way through this flood of messages. While these automatic routines are necessary tools, their use increases the power of the media to influence us.

MESSAGE SATURATION

We live in a culture that is saturated with information. And much of that information comes to us through a flood of messages from the media. As Table 1.3 reveals, there will be 1 million book titles published in this one year in just the United States. Throughout the world, radio stations send out 65.5 million hours of original programming each year, and television adds another 48 million hours.

Table 1.3. Number of Media Vehicles

Medium	United States	World
Books (titles per year)	1 million	2.2 million
Radio stations	15,330	44,000
TV broadcast stations	7,890	27,831
Newspapers	1,286	22,643
Mass market periodicals	20,000	80,000
Scholarly journals	28,100	40,000
Newsletters	10,000	40,000
Archived office pages	3×10^9	7.5×10^9
Websites		1.5 billion

Source: Adapted from Potter, 2019.

Now with digital media, we have access to even more information than ever when we connect to the internet. By early 2012, there were more than 644 million registered host names for internet sites, and by December 2019, that number had grown to well over 1.7 billion. Almost all of these websites present multiple pages of information. Google said in 2008 that it was monitoring one trillion webpages regularly, and 5 years later it was monitoring 30 trillion pages or 100 million gigabytes of information.

ACCELERATING PRODUCTION OF INFORMATION

Not only is information easily available to almost anyone today, but also information keeps getting produced at an ever-increasing rate. Eric Schmidt, executive chairman of Google, points out that the amount of information that humans created from the dawn of civilization until 2003 was 5 exabytes (Schmidt & Cohen, 2013). By 2018, estimates claimed that internet users were generating 2.5 exabytes each day (Marr, 2018).

How is this possible? The answer is that there are more people producing information every day than ever before. It is estimated that 80% to 90% of all scientists who have ever lived on this planet are alive today and producing scientific information at an exponentially growing rate; there are now more than 100,000 scientific scholarly journals, and they publish more than 6 million articles each year (Shermer, 2002). That number has continued to grow along with the number of authors, artists, photographers, and so forth—all contributing information.

An even bigger reason for the growth of information is that digital devices make it easy for everyone to create messages in the form of print, photos, audio recordings, and video. The internet now has 4.4 billion regular users who send emails, texts, photos, and videos.

Perhaps the biggest reason for the growth of information is that much of it is generated by nonpeople. There is something called the **Internet of Things (IOT)**, which refers to inanimate objects (such as digital devices in cars, household appliances, and products in stores) that are constantly using the internet to share information. Some of these devices, such as cameras in public places and thermostats in buildings, can collect a megabyte of information per second. It was estimated that by 2020, there would be 25 billion things connected to the internet and sending 79.4 zettabytes of information in that year, which is 217 exabytes per day (Hernandez, 2019).

According to Cisco Systems, worldwide internet traffic increased by a factor of 12 in just the five years between 2006 and 2011, reaching 23.9 exabytes per month (Brynjolfsson & McAfee, 2014). "One estimate showed that 34 gigabytes of data and one hundred thousand words of information reach the average person's eyes and ears each waking day. By the time your head hits the pillow tonight, you will have been pitched 5,000 ads. As outlandish as this may sound, exposure to data continues to climb every few months as technology advances" (Napper & Rao, 2019, p. 40).

IMPOSSIBLE TO KEEP UP

There is now so much information already in our culture that it is impossible to keep up with even a small fraction of it. To illustrate this point, let's focus on just one medium: books. Until about two centuries ago, the majority of the population could not read, and even if they could, there were few books available. In the early 1300s, the Sorbonne Library in Paris contained only 1,338 books and yet was thought to be the largest library in Europe. Only elites had access to those books. By 2010, Google had estimated that there were about 130 million book titles in existence throughout the world, and almost all of them were accessible through the internet (Mashable, 2010). Because the internet has made a massive amount of information easily available to everyone, access is no longer a problem.

The problem has shifted from access to time. Each of us has only 24 hours each day, really limiting our ability to keep up with all the information available. For example, if you wanted to keep up with just the new books printed each year, you would need to read about two books every minute for 24 hours each day with no breaks over the entire year. All that effort would be needed just to keep up with the *new titles published in the United States alone*! You would have no time left to read any of the other 129 million book titles in existence worldwide. And this example is limited to only books!

We live in an environment that is far different from any environment humans have ever experienced before. And the environment changes at an ever-increasing pace. This is due to the accelerating generation of information and the sharing of that information through the increasing number of media channels and the heavy traffic of media vehicles traversing those channels. Messages are being delivered to everyone, everywhere, constantly. We are all saturated with information, and each year the media are more aggressive in seeking our attention. It is a hopeless expectation to keep up with all the information available. The most important challenge now lies in making good selections when the media are constantly offering us thousands of messages on any given topic.

THE CHALLENGE OF COPING

How do we meet the challenge of making selections from among the overwhelming number of messages in the constantly increasing flood of information? The answer to this question is, we put our minds on "automatic pilot" where our minds automatically filter out almost all message options. I realize that this might sound strange, but think about it. We cannot possibly evaluate every available message and consciously decide whether to pay attention to each one. There are too many messages to consider. So our minds have developed automatic routines that guide this filtering process very quickly and efficiently so we don't have to spend much, if any, mental effort.

To illustrate this automatic processing, consider what we do when we go to the supermarket to buy food. Let's say we walk into the store with a list of a dozen items we need to buy. We rush through the aisles, and 15 minutes later we walk out of the store with our dozen items. In this scenario, how many decisions have we made? Our first guess is to say 12 decisions, because we needed to make a decision to buy each of our dozen items. But what about all the items we *decided not* to buy? The average supermarket today has about 40,000 different products on its shelves. So we actually made 40,000 decisions in the relatively short time we were in the supermarket: 12 decisions to buy a product and 39,988 decisions not to buy a product. That is 45 decisions for each and every second we were in the store; that is indeed some fast thinking! Of course, we did not consider each product, weigh its merits relative to other products, and pick the best option. Instead, we relied on automatic programs running in our minds that guided us to certain products and brands, while ignoring all others. These automatic programs are what enable our minds to make so many decisions so quickly and efficiently.

Our culture is a grand supermarket of media messages. Those messages are everywhere whether we realize it or not, except that there are far more messages in our culture than there are products in any supermarket. To navigate our way efficiently day to day through our information-saturated culture, we rely on automatic processing. Psychologists refer to this automatic processing of information as automaticity. **Automaticity** is a state where our minds operate without any conscious effort from us. Thus the human mind is able to perform many mundane tasks routinely with remarkable efficiency. Once you have learned a sequence—such as tying your shoes, brushing your teeth, driving to school, or playing a song on the guitar—you can perform it over and over again with very little effort compared to the effort it took you to learn it in the first place. As we learn to do something, we are writing the instructions like a computer code in our minds. Once that code is written, it can later be loaded into our minds and run automatically to guide us through any previously learned task with very little thought.

In our everyday lives, the media offer us thousands of choices for exposures. With automatic processing, we experience a great deal of media messages without paying much attention to them. Every once in a while something in the message or in our environment triggers our conscious attention to a media message. To illustrate this, imagine yourself driving in your car with the car's sound system playing while you are talking to your friend. Your attention is on the conversation with your friend, instead of on the music coming from the speakers in your car. Then your favorite song starts playing, and your attention shifts from the conversation to the music. Or perhaps your conversation is interrupted when your friend notices that the sound system is playing her favorite song, and she starts singing along with the music. In both scenarios, you are being exposed to a stream of media messages from your car's sound system without paying conscious attention to them, but then something happens to trigger your conscious attention to the music.

The huge advantage of automatic processing of information is that it helps us get through a great many decisions with almost no effort. However, there are some serious disadvantages. When our minds are on automatic pilot, we may be missing a lot of messages that might be helpful or enjoyable to us. We might not have programmed all the triggers we need to help us get out of automatic processing when a useful message comes our way. Returning to the supermarket example from above, let's say you are very health conscious. Had you been less concerned with efficiency (getting through your shopping list as quickly as possible), you would have considered a wider range of products and read their labels for ingredients. Not all low-fat products have the same fat content; not all products with vitamins added include the same vitamins or the same amounts. Or perhaps you are very price conscious. Had you been less concerned with efficiency, you would have considered a wider variety of competing products and looked more carefully at the unit pricing, so you could get more value for your money. When we are *too* concerned with efficiency, we lose opportunities to expand our experience and to put ourselves in a position to make better decisions that can make us healthier, wealthier, and happier.

AUTOMATICITY INCREASES MEDIA INFLUENCE

Because we spend so much of our time with automatic processing of media messages, the media exert a continual influence on us without our conscious realization. We typically follow our habits day after day because it is easier to do that than to have to rethink everything every day. But this raises an important question: Who has programmed the computer code that governs our automatic routines?

The answer to this question is that *we* have programmed some of our code but that there are also other forces that have been programming our code. Those other influences include our parents, our friends, society in general with its social norms, and the educational system, along with a variety of other institutions (such as religion, politics, criminal justice system, and government). And given all the time we spend with media messages, mass media have programmed a great deal of our mental codes.

Each of these is constantly exerting an influence on how we think, how we feel, and how we behave. Some of this influence is obvious and easy to notice, but most of it occurs subtly and shapes our mental codes unconsciously. When we are not consciously paying attention to these influences, they quietly shape our mental codes without us being aware of it. This is especially the case with the media, because there are so many messages and because we open ourselves up to so much media exposure. Over time, this exposure becomes a habit that we rarely think about consciously. For many of us, we turn on the radio every time we get in our cars, turn on our computers when we get up in the morning, and keep checking our mobile devices constantly. When these channels are open, message producers are continually pumping messages into our subconscious minds.

The media are constantly programming and reprogramming our mental codes. They are adding information, altering our existing information structures, stimulating responses, and reinforcing certain patterns of thinking and acting. The media are thus exerting an influence on us whether we are aware of it or not.

The influence from the media does not stop when we cease exposing ourselves to media messages. As long as the media have an influence on programming our mental codes, their influence shapes how we think and act any time those mental codes are automatically running in our unconscious minds. So when you go into the supermarket to buy food, you may not be looking at coupons from newspapers or magazines; you may not be looking at TV monitors or watching the screen on your smartphone. But your purchasing decisions are being shaped by your "shopping code" running automatically in your mind, and much of your shopping code has been programmed by advertisers who have sent their messages to you through all kinds of media year after year—throughout your entire life.

Conclusions

The purpose of this book is to give you a map of the full range of digital media effects in a way that helps you recognize those effects in yourself as well as in other people.

In the next chapter, I will show you some tools—basic terms, definitions, and ways of thinking about media effects—to help you as a reader get ready to process all the upcoming information without losing sight of the big picture, which is the map of effects from digital media. These tools will help you navigate through all the detail in Chapters 3 through 12.

CHAPTER 2

What Is a Media Effect?

Table 2.1. Partial List of Media Effects	
• The Nature of Media Effects	▪ Acquiring Function
○ Time	▪ Triggering Function
○ Duration	▪ Altering Function
○ Change	▪ Reinforcing Function
○ Manifestation	○ Singular and Cascade Effects
○ Valence	• Big Picture
○ Intention	○ General Definition
○ Level	○ Media Effects Templates
○ Type	*Table 2.2. Media Effects Template: Individual Unit Effects*
• Nature of Media Influence	*Table 2.3. Media Effects Template: Macro Unit Effects*
○ Direct and Indirect	• Summary
○ Function	

The media effects literature has been produced by many researchers from a wide variety of scholarly fields. Most of these researchers have been trained in social scientific fields (especially psychology, sociology, political science, and economics), but also in the humanities (e.g., film studies, rhetoric, and literature) and applied fields (e.g., education, journalism, marketing, law, and health sciences).

Given the variety of interests of these scholars as well as the range of research tools they have used, we should expect that the literature they have produced would be very diverse. And indeed it is. A while ago, I conducted a content analysis of the media effects literature to identify the effects that were tested (Potter, 2009). In Table 2.1, I present a list of what I found. As you can see, the names of those listed effects suggest a great variety with some referring to narrow, specific effects and others referring to large classes of effects. If scholars were to conduct a content analysis of the media effects literature today, they would likely generate an even longer list displaying even more variety.

Table 2.1. Partial List of Media Effects

Advertising	Fraction of selection	Perception of hostile
Affluent society	Framing	media
Agenda building	Gatekeeping	Persuasion
Agenda setting	Global village	Play
Aggression	Gratification seeking	Pluralistic ignorance
Associative network	Gravitation	Political signification
building	Hegemony	Political socialization
Attitude construct	Heuristic processing	Polysemic interpretations
creation	Hidden persuaders	Power elite
Audience as	Homogenization	Priming
commodification	Imitation	Principled reasoning
Audience construction by	Indirect effects	Profit-driven logic of safety
media	Information flow	Program choice
Audience flow	Information seeking	Proteus effect
Audience polarization	Integrated response	Psychodynamics
Automatic activation	Interpretation by social	Pseudo-events blur reality
Availability-valence	class	Psychological
altering	Interpretive resistance	conditioning
Buffering	Knowledge gap	Rally effect
Capacity limits	Least objectionable	Reasoned action
Catharsis	programming	Reception
Channel repertoire	Levels of processing	Resource dependency
reinforcement	Limited-capacity	Revealed preferences
Character affiliation	information processing	Ritual reinforcement
Civic engagement	Marketplace alteration	Selective exposure
Coalition building	Mass audience	Selective gatekeeping
Cognitive dissonance	Media access	Selective perception
Cognitive response	Media as culture	Semiotic interpretations
Conservative/moralist	industries	Social cognitions
decision-making	Media culture	Social construction of
Consumer culture	Media enjoyment	meaning
creation and	Media enjoyment as	Social construction of
reinforcement	attitude	media technologies
Cue activation	Media entertainment	Social identity
Cultivation	Media flow	Social learning
Cultural imperialism	Media system	Social norms
Culture of narcissism	dependency	Sociology of news
Decision-making	Medium as message	Spiral of silence
Diffusion of innovations	Message construction	Synapse priming
Direct effects	Mood management	Technological
Disinhibition	Motivated attention and	determinism
Disposition altering	motivated processing	Television trivialization of
Distribution of knowledge	Neo-associationistic	public life
Double-action	thinking	Third-person effect
gatekeeping	Neo-mass audience	Transactional effects
Double jeopardy	Network political priming	Transmission of
Drench	News content	information
Elaboration likelihood	News diffusion	Transportation of
Elite pluralism	News factory	audiences
Empathy activation	News frame creation	Two-step flow
Encoding-decoding	News selection	Uses and dependency
Excitation transfer	News worker socialization	Uses and gratifications
Exemplification	One-dimensional man	Video malaise
Expectancy value	Parasocial interaction	

It is a considerable challenge to organize all these effects in a way that provides a map to help readers navigate through all the detail. In this chapter, I will first show you the major dimensions along which media effects can be arrayed, and then I will show you the major dimensions along which media influence can be arrayed. The chapter concludes with a focus on the big picture of media effects by presenting a general definition for all media effects and a Media Effects Template you can use as a map that will help you keep track of all the detail presented in Chapters 3 through 11.

The Nature of Media Effects

If you were to read through the large literature of media effects, you would see there are many dimensions that could be used to highlight the differences across those effects. For example, some researchers have designed experiments where they expose people to a media message and then immediately take measures to see if there is evidence for a particular effect. These researchers assume that effects occur immediately. In contrast, other researchers assume that effects take a longer time to occur, so they design experiments or surveys where people are measured repeatedly over time to be able to identify the point at which evidence for a media effect begins to show up and whether that effect changes in intensity or kind over time. Thus the timing of media effects is an important dimension to use when examining the differences across the many media effects documented in the literature. Other dimensions that are useful in arraying the variety of media effects are duration (temporary versus permanent), change (difference versus no difference), manifestation (observable versus latent), valence (positive, neutral, and negative), intention (or nonintention), the level of effect (micro versus macro), and type of effect (cognition, belief, attitude, affect, physiological, and behavior). Let's look closer at each of these eight dimensions that can be used to organize the media effects literature.

TIME

In everyday life, most people think that media effects are things that show up during a media exposure or immediately afterward. Of course some effects do show up immediately, but other effects may take a long time to manifest themselves. Let's say you see an ad for a product on a website and you click on a hot button to buy that product. This is an example of a media message triggering an immediate effect—a buying behavior—on you. But let's say you did not click on the hot button to buy the product; does this mean there was no media effect? Perhaps, but also perhaps not. If you continually expose yourself to ads in the media, you may gradually over time come to believe that you have more needs than you really have and that all of those needs can be easily satisfied by buying particular products. This is a long-term effect on what you believe; it cannot be attributed to any one media exposure but instead gradually builds up in a steady drip-drip-drip manner over time.

DURATION

Some effects last a short time and then go away, while other effects are permanent. For example, you may listen to the words of a new song and remember those words the rest of your life, or you may not be able to remember them an hour later.

CHANGE

When media researchers talk about effects, they typically characterize them as changes, that is, a change in behavior or a change in attitude. If there is no change, some scholars argue that there is no effect. But some effects—perhaps the most important and powerful media effects—show up as no change. For example, most advertising has as its purpose reinforcing existing habits among consumers. Advertisers do not want their brand-loyal customers to change; instead, they want to reinforce existing buying behaviors. If we ignore the reinforcement effect—where there is no change in behavior—then we will have too narrow a perspective on media effects.

MANIFESTATION

Some effects are easy to observe, such as when someone changes her or his behavior soon after being exposed to a particular media message. For example, Heather might be watching TV and see an ad for a special offer for a pizza. She grabs her phone, dials the number on the screen, and orders a pizza. But other effects are very difficult to observe; this does not necessarily mean they are not occurring or that the media are not exerting an influence.

VALENCE

In everyday life, people typically think of media effects as being negative, such as the antisocial behavior effect that arises from exposure to certain kinds of media content, particularly violence. But the media also exert positive effects. We frequently learn all kinds of useful things by exposing ourselves to information on websites and in books, newspapers, and magazines. We use music and stories from all kinds of media to shape our moods and trigger pleasant emotions. We use the media to interact with other people and make us feel part of interesting communities, both real and virtual.

The terms "negative" and "positive" are value laden. I am not drawing on any moral or ethical principles to make these value distinctions. Instead, I am simply regarding as positive those decisions, practices, and effects that somehow enhance a person's quality of life. Things that enhance quality of life are those that help people satisfy their needs, help them to achieve their goals better, and increase their feelings of happiness and well-being. In contrast, the decisions, practices, and effects that somehow reduce a person's quality of life are regarded as negative. When producers of digital media messages and platforms manipulate users to satisfy their own business goals at the expense of the users, especially when this is done unconsciously without the users' awareness and hence without their express permission, then this is regarded as a negative effect. Things that take away from a person's quality of life are those things that condition people to serve the needs of other entities as an unwanted sacrifice to the person.

There are times when a particular effect can be either negative or positive depending on the context. Let's take the desensitization effect as an example of an effect that can be either positive or negative. Desensitization can be positive when a therapist helps her patient overcome an irrational fear of flying in airplanes by showing her patient television shows about people happily boarding airplanes and enjoying air travel. But desensitization can be a negative effect when people lose their natural inclination to feel sympathy for other people after watching years of fictional characters being victimized by violence.

INTENTION

When the media industries are criticized for causing a negative effect, one of their defense strategies is to point out that they did not intend to create that negative effect. For example, when the media are criticized for presenting so much violence in Hollywood movies, producers of those movies will say that they are merely trying to entertain people, not teach them to behave violently. However, there are many effects that occur even though the producers of those media messages did not intend them to occur.

Intention can also be assessed from the audience point of view. For example, you may expose yourself to a website with the intention of getting information on a particular topic. But when you read that information, it triggers an emotional response of anger. You were not seeking this emotional response, so this was an unintentional effect.

LEVEL

Most of the research on media effects regards individuals as the targets of the effects. Scholars have produced a large amount of literature documenting a wide array of effects on individuals. But the media also exert influences on more macro-level things, such as the public, society, and institutions.

The research studies that examine individual-level effects differ fundamentally from the research studies that examine macro-level effects. These differences are not only in methods needed to measure the effects but also in the types of questions addressed and the types of conclusions presented. Typically, individual-level studies use an experiment or a survey as they focus on how individual people respond to different media messages. In contrast, macro-level studies gather aggregated data from institutions, such as the courts (rates of conviction and incarceration), education (rates of graduation, average scores on standardized achievement tests by school district, etc.), religion (size of memberships, attendances at various services, etc.), and politics (voting rates, public opinion polls on various issues and support for candidates, etc.).

Aggregates, at first, might seem to be the simple sum of effects on individuals. After all, isn't public opinion (which is an aggregate effect) really just the adding up of all individuals' attitudes? Mathematically that is correct. Public opinion is assessed in nationwide surveys of about a thousand or so individuals who are asked about their attitudes and beliefs, such as their approval of the way the president is doing his job. If, in such a survey, 600 individuals say they approve of the way the president is leading the country while the other 400 individuals say they disapprove, then public opinion is 60% approval. But conceptually the idea of public opinion is more than the sum of individual attitudes. It is something else. To illustrate this, ask yourself if you are particularly interested in the opinion of a random individual halfway across the country. Your answer is likely to be no. Why should you care about his or her one opinion? Now think about some social issue that you care about, such as changing the age for drinking, driving, voting, or military service. Would you be interested in hearing about what the public in America thinks about the issue? The answer to this question is likely to be yes, because that information would provide context for your own opinion. That aggregate opinion would also be far more illuminating to you. For example, if you knew that a random guy in Nebraska was in favor of making military service mandatory for all males and females ages 18 to 22, that would not likely concern you. But what if you were told that public opinion was strongly in favor of mandatory military service for all citizens aged 18 to 22? That would likely be of high interest to you. Also, other aggregates, such as institutions and society, seem to be entities that have a life of their own apart from individuals. Sociologists have known for a long time that studying aggregates is important (Mills, 1959).

TYPE

Most people have a perspective on media effects limited to only behaviors. But the media can also influence a person's physiology, affects, attitudes, beliefs, and cognitions. These six types differ in terms of the part of the person affected or the character of the experience of the effect within an individual.

Behaviors are typically defined as the overt actions of an individual (Albarracin, Zanna, Johnson, & Kumkale, 2005). Media effects researchers have conducted many studies where they observe people's media exposure behaviors to see which media they use and how they use those media. Researchers also expose people to particular media messages and then observe their subsequent behaviors for things like aggression, use of advertised products, and debating of political issues.

A physiological effect is an automatic bodily response. The body response can be either purely automatic (such as pupil dilation, blood pressure, and galvanic skin response) or quasi-automatic (heart rate, sexual responses, etc.). For example, when people watch an action/adventure movie, their heart rate and blood pressure typically increase. Their muscles tense and their palms sweat. They are experiencing a fight-or-flight response that has been hardwired into humans' brains. Threats trigger attention, and the body prepares itself to fight a predator or to flee. This fight-or-flight effect has enabled the human race to survive for thousands of years.

"Affect" refers to the feelings that people experience. This includes emotions and moods. The media can trigger emotions, especially fear, lust, anger, and laughter. The media also provide people with lots of opportunities to manage their moods, such that when we are feeling stressed with all the problems in our everyday lives, we can chill by listening to music, forget our problems by watching humorous videos, or lose ourselves in the experience of playing games on the internet.

Attitudes are judgments about something. For example, people see a fictional character in a video and make judgments about that character's attractiveness, hero status, likability, and so forth. When the media also present stories about real people, events, issues, and products, these stories often trigger the need for us to make our own judgments about controversial issues, political candidates, advertised products, and so on.

Beliefs have been defined as cognitions about the probability that an object or event is associated with a given attribute (Fishbein & Ajzen, 1975). Simply stated, a belief is faith that something is real or is true. The media continually create and shape our beliefs by showing us more of the world than we are able to see directly for ourselves. None of us have ever met George Washington, but we all believe he existed and was one of the founders of the United States as a country, because we have read about him in history books and websites and seen films about him. Each of us holds beliefs about the existence of a great many things we have never experienced directly in our lives; many of these beliefs have come from media messages.

A cognitive media effect occurs when media exposure influences a person's mental processes or the product of those mental processes. The easiest-to-document cognitive effect is the acquisition of factual information from media messages, particularly from books, newspapers, video news stories, and informational websites. The human mind can absorb this information through the process of memorization. However, the human mind can do far more than memorize; it can transform information into knowledge. This transformation of information can take the form of inferring patterns across media messages. The human mind can also group media messages in different ways to create new meanings. It can generalize beyond media messages to generate principles about real life. All of these mental activities illustrate cognitive effects on individuals.

Nature of Media Influence

The research literature of media effects does more than simply identify effects. It also provides tests of how the media exert their influence so that these effects occur. Therefore, the studies in the media effects literature each contain one effect variable and at least one explanatory variable. The way researchers design their studies tells us how they assume the media exert their influence. When we look across this large literature of media effects, there appear to be three major dimensions that can be used to reveal differences in the way researchers think about media influence. These are the dimensions of (a) whether the media influence is direct or indirect, (b) the function of that influence, and (c) whether the media influence results in only one particular effect or if it sets off a cascade of effects.

DIRECT AND INDIRECT

Sometimes the media exert a direct effect on individuals, while other times the effect is more indirect, such as through institutions. For example, a direct effect is when a person watches a political ad and is influenced to vote for a particular candidate. An indirect effect is when the media continually raise the prices for political advertising, so that candidates must spend much more time raising money, which makes them more beholden to organizations that give them the most money, which influences the policies they support most, which influences the services that governmental bodies provide, which influences us as individuals. Even people who are never exposed to political ads can still be affected by them—indirectly.

FUNCTION

Function refers to the way in which the media exert their influence in bringing about an effect. An analysis of the media effects literature reveals that researchers generally regard that influence being exhibited in four different functions. These four media-influenced functions are acquiring, triggering, altering, and reinforcing. The first two of these functions influence immediate effects that would show up either during the exposure or immediately after. The third—altering—has features that can show up immediately during exposure as an immediate effect, but it also has other features that may take a longer period of time to manifest themselves. And the fourth function is a long-term effect that would take at least weeks and perhaps years to manifest itself. Let's examine each of these functions some detail.

Acquiring Function

Every media message is composed of elements, and during exposure to these messages, individuals acquire and retain some of these elements. Message elements include things like facts, images, sounds, a pundit's attitude about something, the depiction of a sequence of events, and so forth. During media exposure, a person could pay attention to certain elements in a message and keep those elements in his or her memory. This is an immediate effect because the element is committed to memory during the exposure to the message.

In addition to acquiring factual information during media exposure, people also acquire beliefs, attitudes, affective information, and behavioral sequences in the same manner through memorization. With all of these types of effects, the media are creating a memory in a person's mind that was not there before the exposure. It is possible to argue that all of these effects are essentially cognitive, because they all require the cognitive skill of memorization and the retention of information in the individual's memory. And that is a valid point. However, while the process and the skill used may be the same across categories, the nature of what is retained is very different. Thus the function remains the same, but the effect itself is different and requires different categories of cognition, attitude, and belief.

Triggering Function

During exposures, the media can activate something that already exists in the individual. A media message could activate the recall of previously learned information, the recall of an existing attitude or belief, an emotion, a physiological reaction, or a previously learned behavioral sequence.

The media can also trigger a process that sets a person off on a task involving many steps. For example, when people read some news coverage about a political candidate they have never heard about before, they have no existing attitude about that candidate. During exposure to this news coverage, people can take the information from the news story and compare it to their standard for political candidates and create an attitude. This is different from simple acquisition, because the person is not memorizing someone else's attitude presented in the media but instead going through a construction process in the creation of his or her own attitude; in this case, the media message element (a new piece of information) triggered the construction of a new attitude.

The media can also trigger a reconstruction process. A media message might present information that does not conform to a person's existing knowledge structure, so the person must do something to incorporate the new information into his or her existing knowledge structure. For example, let's say that Mark has a very favorable attitude about a particular breakfast cereal but then is exposed to a media message that presents facts about the breakfast cereal using contaminated ingredients; this new information is likely to trigger a re-evaluation of his previously positive attitude about the cereal.

Altering Function

During an exposure, the media can alter something that is already present in the individual. For example, media messages can alter a person's knowledge structures with the addition of new facts. A belief can be altered when the media present a fact revealing that an individual's existing belief was faulty. The media can alter the standards that an individual uses to construct an attitude. Individuals who continually expose themselves to arousing elements in stories of horror and violence will have their naturally strong physiological response of fight or flight worn down to a weak level. By shifting content, the media can alter a person's mood. When individuals continually play interactive games, this practice serves to improve their hand–eye coordination and reduce reaction times to stimuli.

The alteration can show up immediately (i.e., during an exposure or immediately after the exposure to the media message) or it can take a long time to show up. The alteration can be temporary (and disappear after a few seconds) or it can last a long time. Most of the research on long-term media effects is based on assumptions of long-term media influence as a gradual shaping process. This is a kind of a drip-drip-drip process where each message in a series slowly alters a person's knowledge structure. Greenberg (1988) reminds us that there are also "drench" influences. He says that not all media messages have the same impact and that not all characters in media stories are equally influential in shaping our beliefs and attitudes. Some portrayals stand out because they "are deviant, are intense, and thus are more important viewing experiences" (p. 98).

Reinforcing Function

Through repeated exposures, the media gradually and continually add greater weight to something already existing in a person, thus making that something more difficult to change. The reinforcement function is applicable to all six types of effects. When the media continually present the same people in the news over and over, individuals' knowledge structures about those people become more rigid and less likely to be flexible enough to change. When the media present the same beliefs and attitudes, individuals' comfort level with those beliefs and attitudes becomes so strong that they are not able to change them. When the media present the same kinds of messages every day over the course of years, individuals' behavioral patterns of exposure become more weighty and harder to change.

SINGULAR AND CASCADE EFFECTS

Some media effects studies have relatively simple designs, where the study tests whether one potential factor of influence is associated with one particular media effect. To illustrate, researchers might conduct an experiment where they show their participants a media message and then measure their heart rate to see if the message has triggered an increase. This is an example of an immediate physiological effect. It is singular because researchers are not interested in seeing if other effects are clustered with it or if there is a cascade of other effects that follow from the elevation of a person's heart rate.

Other media studies will require more elaborate designs if the researchers are interested in testing a cascade of different types of effects. For example, researchers might be interested in testing for a sequence of effects where one type of effect occurs initially, in turn bringing about another type of effect in a cascade of influence. There are many such cascade-like effects in the social science literature. For example, we know that cognitions influence belief formation (Tversky & Kahneman, 1973; Wyer & Albarracin, 2005), affect (Isen, 2000), and attitude formation and change (Chaiken, Liberman, & Eagly, 1989; Petty & Cacioppo, 1986; Wegener & Carlston, 2005). Affect influences attitudes (Clore & Schnall, 2005; Zajonc, 1968) as well as behaviors (Johnson-Laird & Oatley, 2000). Beliefs influence attitudes (Fishbein & Ajzen, 1977; Kruglanski & Stroebe, 2005), and attitudes influence beliefs (Marsh & Wallace, 2005; McGuire, 1990) in a continuing reciprocal process. Behaviors influence attitudes (Festinger, 1957; Olson & Stone, 2005), and attitudes influence behavior (Ajzen & Fishbein, 1977, 2005), both consciously (Allport, 1935; Dulany, 1968) and unconsciously (Bargh, 1997).

The literature shows us that there are many cascading effects. For example, playing digital games typically does not result in a singular effect, but instead continual playing typically results in a cascade of different kinds of effects that reveal themselves over time. People who play a digital game for the first time will focus on learning its rules (acquiring cognitions). As they learn the rules, they begin to play better, and this triggers pleasure (affective effect), which motivates them to seek more pleasure by playing the game continually (behavior) and developing more elaborate game-playing strategies (cognitions), which leads them to believe they are becoming a good player, which triggers more pleasure. Over time with enough cycles, this cascade could lead to dependence on the game for rewards and eventually to addiction. This type of cascading effect is further illuminated in Chapter 11.

Big Picture

Now that you know about the ways scholars have thought about the differences across the many media effects as well as the ways scholars have thought about how the media exert their influence, it is important to return to the big picture. In this section I will provide you with a general definition of media effects that incorporates all these dimensions. Then I will provide a Media Effects Template that you can use to navigate through all the detail about effects that will be presented in Chapters 3 through 11.

GENERAL DEFINITION

Media effects are those things that occur as a result of—either in part or in whole—media influence. They can be positive as well as negative. They can occur whether the media have an intention for them to occur or not. They can occur immediately during exposure to a media message, or they can take a long time to occur after any particular exposure. They can last for a few seconds or an entire lifetime. They can show up clearly as a change, but they can also reinforce existing patterns. They can be easily observable, or they can be latent and therefore much more difficult to observe. They can affect individual people, or all people in the form of the public. They can also affect institutions and society. They can act directly on a target (a person, the public, an institution, or society), or they can exert their influence indirectly. They can exhibit a variety of functions (acquiring, triggering, altering, and reinforcing). And finally, they vary in complexity from a simple, singular effect to a cascade of effects with each one arising from a previous effect and leading to a subsequent effect.

Everything you will read in subsequent chapters of this book fits within the scope of this foundational definition of media effect. It is important to begin with a broad perspective on media effects in order to understand the incredibly wide range of influence the media exert and also to appreciate the truly wide range of effects research that has been produced by media scholars.

MEDIA EFFECTS TEMPLATES

To help organize all the ideas across all these dimensions, I have created two **Media Effects Templates**. One is for individuals, and the other is for aggregates. The Media Effects Template for individuals is displayed in Table 2.2. Notice that the template contains 20 boxes—each representing a different kind of media effect on individuals. These 20 boxes are the result of crossing the five types of media effects with the four types of media influences.

Table 2.2. Media Effects Template: Individual Unit Effects

		Media Influence Functions			
		Acquiring	Triggering	Altering	Reinforcing
Type of Effect	Cognitive	Memorize message element	Recall information Construction of a pattern	Change memory structure	Strengthen skills Reinforce skills
	Belief	Accept belief	Recall belief Construction of a belief	Change belief	Strengthen generalization
	Attitudes	Accept attitude	Recall attitude Construction of a new attitude	Change attitude	Strengthen evaluation
	Affects	Learn emotional information	Recall emotion Emotion	Change emotional sensitivity Mood change	Strengthen Reinforce mood
	Physiology		Automatic response	Reactions	Strengthen reaction

The Media Effects Template that was developed for individual-level effects has been modified a bit to be useful in organizing macro-level effects (see Table 2.3). Notice that the types of effects down the left side of that table are the same with the exception of physiological effects, which applies well to the human body but not to the public or other macro-level units. Also, the functions of acquiring, triggering, altering, and reinforcing were eliminated as column headings. These were important to classify the large literature of media effects on individuals. However, the literature of media effects on macro units is much smaller, and at this time it would not be useful to classify it by functions. Instead, the columns represent the three major kinds of macro units that have been examined in the media effects literature: the public, institutions, and the media themselves.

Table 2.3. Media Effects Template: Macro Unit Effects

		Media Influence On . . .		
		The Public	Institutions	Media
Type of Effect	Cognition/ knowledge	Public knowledge	Institutional knowledge	Media
	Beliefs/ norms	Public beliefs	Institutional beliefs/norms	Media norms
	Attitudes	Public opinion	Institutional attitudes	Media judgments
	Affect	Public mood	Institutional mood	Media mood
	Behavior	Public behavior	Institutional practices	Media practices

Summary

This chapter has provided you with a set of ideas to keep in mind as you encounter the information in the upcoming chapters. Use the broad definition to keep a wide perspective on the nature of media effects and how they arise.

Think about effects in terms of time, duration, change, manifestation, valence, intention, level, and type. Think about how the media are exercising their influence on you directly and indirectly, by their function (acquiring, triggering, altering, and reinforcing) and in terms of whether they account for a simple singular effect that is usually triggered immediately or whether they suggest a cascade of effects that play out over a longer period of time.

The ideas presented in this chapter at first might seem like a lot. However, this set of ideas is considerably smaller than the media effects literature. Regard the ideas presented in this chapter as a parsimonious set of tools that will provide you with great leverage in increasing your understanding of media effects—both digital and legacy effects. The more you use these ideas, the easier they will be to use. And even more important, the more you use these ideas in your everyday life, the more you will be able to perceive a greater range of media effects that are constantly occurring among your friends and with you.

CHAPTER 3

Attraction to Media

Exposure to messages is the most fundamental of all media effects. If there is no exposure, there cannot be any other kind of media effect. That is, if the media are not able to attract an audience, then there is no exposure, and without exposure, there is no media influence and no media effects.

From the media industry point of view, the exposure effect is always intentional, that is, the primary purpose of any media business is to construct audiences by attracting potential users and then conditioning them for repeat exposures. Thus the media are constantly trying to generate an exposure effect by first triggering an attraction to their messages and then triggering a pleasant experience that will satisfy users' needs in a rewarding way so the exposure will alter users' behavior into a long-term habit that the media continue to reinforce so that exposure habit grows stronger in those users over time.

From the media user point of view, the exposure effect typically begins intentionally, where people seek out messages and experiences they believe will satisfy their needs. But then over time people shift away from making decisions mindfully as their exposure habits grow, and subsequent exposures are triggered automatically by their conditioned habits. As long as people acquire pleasant experiences during media exposures, those habits get reinforced over time, making those habits more and more difficult to alter.

Media researchers have been examining the exposure effect for as long as there have been media researchers. Their curiosity about this effect has been primarily motivated by finding answers to four broad questions: (1) How much exposure is there? (2) Why are people attracted to media messages and experiences? (3) How do the media construct and reinforce exposure habits? (4) And does media exposure lead to addiction?

Broad Patterns of Exposure

The long history of research into media exposure shows that people expose themselves to an increasing number of media messages each year as indicated by the growing amount of time they spend with the media year after year (Hall, 2005; Himmelweit, Swift, & Jaeger, 1980; McIntosh, Schwegler, & Terry-Murray, 2000; Shah, McLeod, & Yoon, 2001; Sherry, 2001; Slater, 2003). As of now the average American is spending more than 11 hours per day with all forms of mass media, which is an increase of 90 minutes per day since 2015 (Fottrell, 2018).

The increase in media use has been largely driven by younger people. A Google search shows that, among children, the average time spent with all forms of mass media in the 1930s was 10 hours per week; this increased to 30 hours per week in the 1960s; 40 hours per week in the 1980s; 52 hours per week in the 1990s; and a whopping 75 hours per week in the 2000s.

The growth in exposure to the media had been driven exclusively by analog media until relatively recently. When the personal computer was introduced in the 1980s, people began accessing digital forms of the media. By 2012, 77% of all families in the developed world had a personal computer. Worldwide sales of personal computers reached a peak in 2012 when 351 million were sold; this was then followed by a decline to 269 million in 2016 as people began buying mobile devices to replace personal computers (Balbi & Magaudda, 2018). We are now in the post-PC age of digitization or the mobile age. Just as there was a shift from the mainframe computer age (mid-1930s to mid-1970s) to the personal computer age (mid-1970s to around 2012), we are now in the post-PC age (Balbi & Magaudda, 2018). The sales of mobile devices (such as tablets and especially smartphones) increased from 680 million in 2012 to 1.5 billion in 2016 (Balbi & Magaudda, 2018).

The amount of time people spend with media continues to grow, and most of that growth in the last few decades has come primarily from exposure to digital media. A 2006 study found that 42% of the most avid TV viewers (those watching at least 35 hours of TV per week) had also become the most intensive users of the internet (spending at least 30 hours or more a week online; Dawley, 2006).

Over the past decade, the amount of time people spend with analog media has started to decline for the first time in history. But the amount of time people spend with digital media has continued to grow so fast that the overall amount of time people spend with all media continues to increase. By 2008, the time spent with analog media of print (newspapers, magazines, and books) had dropped to 143 minutes per week, which was down 11% since 2004. Among young adults, the time spent reading print

Table 3.1. Exposure to Digital Media

In 1996, 70 million personal computers were sold worldwide, doubling to 134 million in 2000 and doubling again by 2007 (Balbi & Magaudda, 2018).

From 2000 to 2015, the number of people with access to the internet increased from 6.5% to 43% of the global population; now there are 3.2 billion people online (2016).

From 2005 to 2015, the number of people with cell phones increased from 2 billion to 7 billion. By 2015, for the first time in history, there was an average of one mobile phone for every person on earth.

Now 96% of U.S. adults own a mobile phone, and 68% own a smartphone; worldwide, 45% of the population owns a mobile phone.

Now 97% of smartphone users use their phones to regularly send text messages, 89% use it to access the internet, and 88% use it to send and receive email.

Usage studies show that U.S. adults and teens check their phones up to 150 times per day or every 6 to 7 minutes while they are awake, half of them check it first thing in the morning while they are still in bed, and 75% said they feel panic when they cannot immediately locate their phone.

The American population has shifted from talking on smartphones to texting; more than 75% of American teenagers text, with older teenagers sending an average of more than 100 texts per day.

One third of the world's population—2.5 billion people—use social media (Chayko, 2018).

Source: Compiled from Aiken, 2016; Balbi & Magaudda, 2018; Chayko, 2018; Gazzaley & Rosen, 2016.

media had declined to 49 minutes per week in 2008, which was a drop of 29% since 2004 (Carr, 2010). Now Americans are spending more time on their mobile devices than they spend watching television for the first time ever. According to eMarketer, the average adult will spend 3 hours and 43 minutes a day on a mobile device in 2019, compared with 3 hours and 35 minutes watching TV (He, 2019, May 31). For more information on this point, see Table 3.1.

The growth in exposure to digital media over the past few decades has been largely driven by younger people, just as the increases in exposure to analog media over the past century were driven by younger people. A report generated by the Kaiser Family Foundation in 2005 found that "the average schoolchild aged between eight and eighteen years spends a third of her life sleeping, a third at school, and a third engrossed in new media, from smartphones and tablets to TVs and laptops" (Alter, 2017, p. 237).

Also, computer use is especially high among college students. In the United States there are now 17.4 million college students, and more than half arrive on campus as freshmen with a laptop computer. The typical college student has been found to spend more than 3.5 hours a day on the computer emailing, instant messaging, and web surfing. And they likely spend an additional 7.5 hours every day engaged with other media, such as books, magazines, recordings, radio, film, and television (Siebert, 2006).

A major factor that explains the continual growth in the amount of time people spend with digital media is the growth in **multitasking**. People, especially younger people, frequently expose themselves to several media at the same time (Kaiser Family

Foundation, 2005). Gazzaley and Rosen (2016) point out that 95% of people report multitasking each day and that this multitasking consumes more than one third of their day. The typical teen and young adult believes that he or she can juggle six to seven different forms of media at the same time. Exposure numbers can increase quickly when an hour of clock time can be counted more than once because of multitasking. There are people who log more hours each day with the media than the number of hours they are awake.

In summary, the amount of time people spend with media has been increasing each year for the past century. For the majority of that time, those exposures were exclusively with analog media, but with the development of personal computers, the internet, and mobile devices over the past several decades, digital media have been driving—and even accelerating—the increases in media exposure.

Attraction

Because the media have been so successful in attracting all kinds of people year after year, this raises the question: Why are people so attracted to the media? Media scholars have been conducting research for almost a century to generate answers to this question. In general, the answers fall into two categories that differ a bit by whether you want to answer the question from the user's perspective or the media industry's perspective.

USER PERSPECTIVE

The user attraction research clearly shows that people believe they have needs that can be satisfied better through media exposures than through other means. While these needs vary across individuals, all people in general have continuing needs for information and for entertainment. For many decades, newspapers and magazines and then radio and television news programs have continuously provided people with information about their world. While many people can get information about what is happening at a very local level from talking to the people around them, they are limited in getting much information about what is happening in police stations, courts, meetings of municipal bodies, and athletic contests, so they rely on the media to satisfy this need for information. Also, people are limited to one geographical area, so they rely on the media to provide them with information about their region, nation, and planet. Thus the media satisfy individuals' needs for information with greater scope and richness. The media also provide a wide range of entertainment experiences with fictional stories of all kinds, such as novels, radio dramas, Hollywood films, and television series.

The above paragraph explains why people have been spending more time each year with the media, but it does not explain why there has been a shift away from analog media and toward digital media. The major reason for this shift is that digital media can satisfy people's need for information and entertainment *better* than analog media. When people connect to the internet, they have a much wider choice of sources of information and entertainment than analog media can provide them. And when people use a mobile device to connect to the internet, their access is more immediate and can occur anywhere and at any time the user wants.

Another reason for the shift is that digital media can satisfy needs that analog media cannot. Unlike analog media, digital media can satisfy users' needs to connect with other people. The interactive features of digital media give users the ability to establish a personal presence on a social networking platform and use it to build and maintain interpersonal networks by posting pictures, videos, and textual updates immediately at any time from anywhere. And they can easily stay in constant touch with friends anywhere in the world.

Digital media offer users a wide range of competitive experiences they cannot get when using analog media. Digital platforms provide a constant opportunity for anyone to compete against a computer, against one other person, or against a group of people scattered around the globe.

INDUSTRY PERSPECTIVE

In contrast to explaining media attraction from an audience perspective, we can examine explanations from an industry perspective. Both perspectives share a focus on satisfying users' needs. However, the industry perspective is also very concerned with the importance of conditioning users for future exposures that are more numerous and last longer. There is this dual focus (attraction and conditioning) under the industry perspective because it is so expensive to attract audience members that once they are attracted, media businesses have a strong motivation to train their users for repeat exposures so the businesses can amortize the huge attraction costs over many exposures.

Attraction

Media businesses go about attracting users by discovering the needs of those users and then designing messages and experiences that satisfy those needs. Because digital media are so vigilant at monitoring the interactions of their users, they have been very successful in recognizing audience needs as they first emerge.

Conditioning

While attracting audience members is an essential task for all media businesses, conditioning users is just as important. This conditioning takes two forms: training new users to become loyal users and training users to use word of mouth to attract their friends so the audience size grows.

Growing Loyalty   Media businesses need to train new users to become loyal so that they continually expose themselves to messages and experiences provided by that media business. They do this by convincing new users that the messages and experiences they provide are more efficient and effective ways of satisfying their needs compared to any alternative. Efficiency means low cost. It is important for media businesses to convince potential users that they can satisfy their needs at a lower cost (time and money) to them compared to alternatives. Thus many digital media businesses offer their messages and services to users at no financial cost. Effectiveness means that it is important for media businesses to convince potential users that they can satisfy their needs in a more fulfilling manner, that is, with a greater payoff in terms of reward or emotion.

Media businesses are constantly aware of the need to condition audiences for repeat exposures. Hindman (2018) says, "Building an online audience is like pumping air into a balloon with a slow leak. One has to keep pumping, to keep up a constant level of investment, or previous efforts will quickly be lost. These indirect costs of distribution are not optional. For a news site or a blog, maintaining an above-average level of stickiness is a matter of life and death" (p. 13). "**Stickiness**" refers to a digital media company's ability to get their site's users to stay longer during exposure sessions, and then to get those users to return to the site again and again for subsequent exposures. "Stickiness is like a constantly compounding internet interest rate, in which a small early edge in growth creates a huge long-term gap. Differences in stickiness do not add up, they multiply together" (Hindman, 2018, p. 2).

One thing that digital media companies do to build stickiness is to create "recommender systems," which are algorithms that attempt to make each user's exposure sessions more efficient. These recommender systems collect data on users' interests and the selections those users have made during past exposures. The algorithms then use all those data to predict what each user will be most interested in experiencing during his or her current exposure session. For example, digital sites like Netflix and Amazon present their users with an overwhelming number of choices, so in order to funnel their users' attention down to a few choices that are likely to interest them the most, those businesses use recommender systems. "Recommender systems make sites stickier, and users respond by clicking more and visiting more often. Over time sites and apps with recommender systems have grown in market share, while those without have shrunk" (Hindman, 2018, p. 60).

Growing Audience Size   Media businesses need to train new users to use word of mouth to attract their friends so the audience size grows. Mass media have a strong incentive to increase the size of their audiences; they try to create audience habits so they can depend on people repeatedly exposing themselves to their messages. This is especially the case with digital media. While digital media companies have a clear economic advantage and a strong motivation to attract audiences, they also experience significant challenges, because there is so much competition.

These companies experience major economic advantages when they increase the size of their audiences because of the concept of **first copy costs**. In all industries, the cost of producing the first product of something is always higher than the costs of producing subsequent copies of that product. While the production of each product requires additional expense for materials and labor, the costs for planning and designing the product to begin with are overhead costs that are typically substantial. If a company only makes one copy of a product, that first product must earn back a great deal of revenue to cover all costs. But if a company makes many copies of the same product, then those overhead costs can be spread out over those many copies. First copy costs must include all the development and planning of the product, whereas each subsequent copy includes just the cost of materials for producing that one copy. For example, the cost of producing the first copy of an automobile could be hundreds of millions of dollars, because you have to pay the designers, build a factory, hire factory workers, and train them before you can manufacture the first automobile. These huge costs for overhead can be amortized over two automobiles if you manufacture a second one, so there is a strong motivation to amortize the overhead costs of thousands of copies. Of course there are also variable costs of manufacturing, that is, the costs of raw materials (steel, glass, upholstery, electronics, etc.) increase with each additional copy manufactured. But when we consider both overhead costs and variable costs, the total cost of manufacturing each unit decreases with more units manufactured.

With mass media, the costs of planning and producing a message is fairly substantial, but the cost of adding each additional person to the audience is very small. With mass media, the difference between first copy and second copy costs is even greater. For example, the first copy cost of producing an issue of a magazine might be several million dollars because you have to pay all the writers, the photographers, and the editorial staff overhead. Producing the second copy would be just pennies for paper and ink. With digital media, the cost of the first copy can be very high (in the case of setting up a major social networking platform or developing an online game) or it can be very low (sending a tweet), but the cost of second copies is zero. For example, an online game with a million players encounters no additional cost when it adds another player. Once you create a blog, there is no cost to you when each new follower is added. Given this characteristic, producers of digital messages have a strong economic incentive to increase the size of their audiences because doing so increases the amount of revenue without increasing the costs. And digital messages do not get used up no matter how many times they are shared or copied (Brynjolfsson & McAfee, 2014).

Exposure Habits

The media have been very successful in attracting and conditioning people, as evidenced by the media exposure habits that have been developed over time across all kinds of people.

ANALOG MEDIA

Box 3.1 presents a sampling of research about analog media's ability to attract and condition audiences. Some of this research has focused on particular media, especially television. We know a lot more about attraction to the medium of television than the attraction to other media because most of the media effects research has been conducted since the 1960s, during which time television was the most dominant of all analog media. Many research studies have been conducted to determine why certain kinds of content (such as violence, news, etc.) exert a greater attraction than other types of content.

Box 3.1. Overview of Research Examining Attraction and Conditioning With Analog Media

EXPOSURE BY ANALOG CHANNEL

- Television (Eastman, Newton, & Pack, 1996; Hawkins, Tapper, Bruce, & Pingree, 1995; Kaye & Sapolsky, 1997; Krcmar, 1996; Krotz & Eastman, 1999; Lang et al., 2005; Mares & Woodard, 2006; Riggs, 1996; Rosenstein & Grant, 1997; Zubayr, 1999)

  o Viewing television is inertial (Hawkins et al., 1995).
  o Repeat viewing rates of television programs are relatively low (Zubayr, 1999).
  o People often expose themselves to more than one media message at the same time (Schmitt, Woolf, & Anderson, 2003).
  o Increased TV viewing beyond a certain point displaces other media use (Koolstra & Van der Voort, 1996).
  o Teens generally decline in TV use throughout adolescence except for an increase in late-night viewing (Eggermont, 2006).
  o Continual exposure to television can lead to addiction (Horvath, 2004; Jhally, 1987; Kaplan, 1972; Mander, 1978; McIlwraith, 1998; Winn, 1977)

- Books (Koolstra & Van der Voort, 1996)

EXPLAINING ATTRACTION BY MESSAGES

- Program promos trigger exposure to programs (Eastman et al., 1996).
- For attraction to news: People have a high need for cognition, that is, they like to listen to diverse points of view, like to deliberate about problems, and like to engage in thinking (Tsfati & Cappella, 2005).
- Attraction to reality television series is predicted by the following:

  o Need for companionship and voyeurism (Papacharissi & Mendelson, 2007)
  o External locus of control, low mobility, and low interpersonal interaction (Papacharissi & Mendelson, 2007)

- Violent content (Krcmar & Greene, 1999; Krcmar & Kean, 2005; Slater, 2003; Vandewater, Lee, & Shim, 2005)
- Health information (Rains, 2008)
- Sports (Gantz, Wang, Paul, & Potter, 2006; Knobloch-Westerwick et al., 2009)
- Sad films (Oliver, 2008)
- Pornography (Allen, D'Alessio, & Brezgel, 1995)
- PBS (Sherman, 1995)
- Coverage of the death of Princess Diana (Brown, Basil, & Bocarnea, 2003)

EXPLAINING ATTRACTION BY AUDIENCE CHARACTERISTICS

- Exposure habits (Ball-Rokeach & DeFleur, 1976; Freedman & Sears, 1966; Himmelweit, Oppenheim, & Vince, 1958; Himmelweit, Swift, & Jaeger, 1980; Jhally, 1987; Kaplan, 1972; LaRose & Eastin, 2002, 2004; LaRose, Lin, & Eastin, 2003; Lazarsfeld, Berelson,

& Gaudet, 1944; Levy, 2007; Maccoby, 1954; Mander, 1978; McIntosh, Schwegler, & Terry-Murray, 2000; McLeod, Ward, & Tancill, 1965; Rosenstein & Grant, 1997; Shah, McLeod, & Yoon, 2001; Sherry, 2004; Slater, 2003; Webster & Phalen, 1997; Winn, 1977; Yuan & Webster, 2006)

- Personality traits (Grimes, Bergen, Nicholes, Vernberg, & Fonagy, 2004)

  ○ Sensation seeking (Slater, Henry, Swaim, & Cardador, 2004)
  ○ Lower self-esteem: Girls with lower self-esteem are more likely to play video and computer games (Funk & Buchman, 1996)
  ○ Need for companionship seeking through parasocial interactions (Greenwood & Long, 2009; Papacharissi & Mendelson, 2007)
  ○ High need for cognition (Slater, Henry, Swaim, & Cardador, 2004)
  ○ Deficient self-regulation (LaRose & Eastin, 2004)

- Cognitive characteristics

  ○ Locus of control (Papacharissi & Mendelson, 2007)
  ○ Motives (Ball-Rokeach & DeFleur, 1976; Krotz & Eastman, 1999; Papacharissi & Mendelson, 2007; Reiss & Wiltz, 2004)
  ○ Expectations that media messages will give people information they can use to talk with others (Riggs, 1996)
  ○ Involvement with stories (Brown, Basil, & Bocarnea, 2003; Morgan, Movius, & Cody, 2009; Reagan, 1996)
  ○ Personal interest (Reagan, 1996)
  ○ Existing knowledge on topics (Moy, Torres, Tanaka, & McCluskey, 2005; Shah, Cho, Eveland, & Kwak, 2005)
  ○ Existing attitudes about elements in the messages (Cho, 2005; Lo & Wei, 2005)
  ○ Ability to identify with people in the messages (Basil, 1996; Knobloch-Westerwick & Hastall, 2006)
  ○ Low cognitive effort to process (Lang et al., 2005)

The most detailed part of the attraction literature has focused on testing factors about the audience as a way of explaining attraction, especially looking at how habits are developed and reinforced, personality traits, and cognitive characteristics.

Habit plays a significant role in television viewing behavior. Media companies must work hard to create and maintain exposure habits. When a television series presents a continuing dramatic story line, viewers are more likely to watch every episode and thereby have their viewing reinforced (Zubayr, 1999). Also, television programmers know that by scheduling a show at the same time every week, they can be more successful in reinforcing viewing habits (Sherman, 1995).

Researchers have also found that viewing television is inertial, which means that the longer a person looks at the screen, the greater likelihood that the looking will continue. This inertia is also related to whether people's exposure is motivated by a viewing strategy, which is a conscious plan that governs looking for particular things. When people do not have an exposure strategy, they are more likely to experience attentional inertia (Hawkins, Tapper, Bruce, & Pingree, 1995).

The way the media alter people's exposure patterns over time is a complicated procedure involving many factors. To illustrate, Cooper and Tang (2009) conducted a study to determine the factors that are most influential in habitual television exposure, and their findings suggested that there was no single factor that explained exposure to television; it takes many variables to explain people's media use habits. Their top seven factors (ritualistic motivations, use of the internet, audience availability, the cost of multichannel service, age, instrumental motivations, and gender) in combination explained only about 30% of viewing behaviors.

Even when people have a large number of television channels available, they typically have a relatively small viewing repertoire, which is the set of channels they typically watch. For example, Chinese viewers were found to have a viewing repertoire of about 13 channels, which is around one third of the channels available (Yuan & Webster, 2006). Americans typically have a larger choice of channels and a smaller repertoire (Webster & Phalen, 1997).

Finally, habitual viewing of television can reinforce behavioral patterns over time. For example, Eggermont (2006) conducted a study to look at the trajectories of television viewing throughout adolescence. Results indicated that changes in viewing habits are different when daytime, prime-time, and late-night television viewing are examined separately. Although daytime and prime-time viewing showed a decline, viewing during later waking hours increased. Teenagers who have access to a television set in their room watch more; male viewers tend to avoid the "family hour" and "female contents."

Sports fans become more ritualistic in their behavior over time. Compared to viewers of other types of TV programs, sports fans are highly ritualistic. Many sports fans engage in a variety of previewing activities as well as follow-up activities (Gantz, Wang, Paul, & Potter, 2006).

Lang et al. (2005) found that characteristics of news stories altered TV viewing behaviors. In their experiment, viewers used a remote control device to choose among four local news programs that varied systematically by story length and pacing. In general, pacing and length have greater effects on younger viewers. Fast pacing increased viewers' evaluations of the newscasts but, when combined with long stories, decreased younger viewers' time spent on channel. Viewers' cognitive effort, physiological arousal, and recognition all decreased before and increased after a channel change. Frequent channel changing was associated with lower cognitive effort and recognition.

The reinforcing of media exposure behaviors over time has been found to be related to audience factors. For example, people will become more dependent on media that meet more of their needs (Ball-Rokeach & DeFleur, 1976). People who already have a habit of media exposure will continue with that habit and the habit will get stronger over time (LaRose & Eastin, 2004; Rosenstein & Grant, 1997), especially people who are deficient in self-regulation (LaRose & Eastin, 2004). For example, Papacharissi and Mendelson (2007) reported that watching reality television series is predicted by a need for companionship and voyeurism. They also found that viewers who have an external locus of control, low mobility, and low interpersonal interaction were more likely to have behavioral habits of viewing reality series (Papacharissi & Mendelson, 2007). In another study, Reiss and Wiltz (2004) conducted a survey where adults rated themselves on 16 motives to watch reality TV. They found that people who watched reality TV had above-average trait motivation to feel self-important; they also scored high on need to feel vindicated, friendly, free of morality, secure, and romantic as compared with others. The authors concluded that people prefer TV shows that stimulate the feelings they intrinsically value the most, and these feelings are individually determined. Also, as personal interest in a topic increases, the number of media sources they use increases (Reagan, 1996).

DIGITAL MEDIA

Because the research examining the attractiveness of digital media is much newer than the research examining attractiveness of analog media, its literature is much smaller. However, it appears that the effects are of a legacy type, that is, more recent media research is finding that the factors about media messages and characteristics of users that have been found to explain attraction to analog media are the same as the factors that attract people to digital media. For example, the findings displayed in Box 3.1 that show the factors about media messages and characteristics of audience members that have been found in analog media to lead to effects are likely to be found with digital media as well.

Research studies conducted on digital media so far have been designed to examine effects that follow from factors of digital media that are different from analog media. For example, in a very early study examining attraction to digital media, Parks and Floyd (1996) found that people, especially females, use the internet to develop personal relationships and that the longer that people rely on the relationships they develop online, the more likely it is they will increase the amount of time they spend online. Another example of research into a special feature of digital media is attraction to digital games. Lucas and Sherry (2004) conducted a large-scale survey of young adults' reasons for video game use, their preferred game genres, and the amount of game play reported. Female respondents reported less frequent play, less motivation to play in social situations, and less orientation to game genres featuring competition than did males.

There are many more examples of research studies that have tested how special features of digital media trigger an attraction effect. These are reported in subsequent chapters. The way special features of news in digital media attract audiences is reported in Chapter 4; the features of digital advertising on attraction, in Chapter 5; digital entertainment features, in Chapter 6; social networking sites, in Chapter 7; features of living in digital worlds, in Chapter 8; and competing in digital games, in Chapter 9.

Addiction

The public and media researchers have been concerned about how the attraction features of digital media can be so powerful that they lead to an addiction effect. The research that has been conducted on this topic so far indicates that addiction is a cascade type of effect that begins with people being attracted to some form of digital media, and then over time can evolve into a **displacement effect**, then a dependency effect, and eventually into addiction. For more on this cascade-type effect, see Chapter 10. In this section, I will first present a definition of addiction and then show the process of the cascading effect that can lead to addiction.

ADDICTION DEFINED

There is a difference between heavy use of media and addiction to the media. Addiction in general requires that a person lose control over performing certain behavioral sequences, that is, the person does not just want to perform certain behaviors; the person has to perform them and cannot prevent himself or herself from performing them obsessively. The American Psychiatric Association (APA) says that merely depending on a substance or behavior isn't enough to warrant a diagnosis of addiction. "Many hospital patients depend on opiates, for example, but that doesn't make all hospital patients opium addicts. The missing ingredients are the sense of craving that comes from an addiction, and the fact that addicts know they're ultimately undermining their long-term well-being" (Alter, 2017, p. 80). "The truth about addiction challenges many of our intuitions. It isn't the body falling in unrequited love with a dangerous drug, but rather the mind learning to associate an substance or behavior with relief from psychological pain" (Alter, 2017, p. 89).

A 2011 extensive review of the literature on behavioral addiction found that 41% of the world's population has suffered from at least one behavioral addiction over the past year (Sussman, Lisha, & Griffiths, 2011). To arrive at this conclusion, the researchers examined 83 published studies of behavioral addictions (gambling, love, sex, shopping, internet, exercise, and work addictions) as well as substance abuse addictions (alcohol, nicotine, and narcotics) that included 1.5 million respondents across four continents. They found that these addictions are not trivial because they include the loss of ability to choose freely whether to stop or continue the behavior and the experience of behavioral-related adverse consequences. Alter (2017) adds, "The age of behavioral addiction is still young, but early signs point to a crisis. Addictions are damaging because they crowd out other essential pursuits, from work and play to basic hygiene and social interaction" (p. 10).

The APA recognizes internet addiction as a serious behavioral problem. The APA says that internet addiction has four essential components: (1) excessive internet use, often associated with a loss of sense of time or a neglect of basic drives; (2) withdrawal, including feelings of anger, tension, and/or depression when the computer is inaccessible; (3) increasing tolerance, including the need for better computer equipment, more software, or more hours of use; and (4) adverse consequences, including arguing, lying, poor school or vocational achievement, social isolation, and fatigue (Aiken, 2016, p. 70). While the APA statement focuses on internet addiction, its criteria apply to all forms of the media.

ADDICTION RESEARCH

The research on media addiction did not start with the rise of digital media. This line of research is almost as old as the field of media effects.

Analog Media

Early media researchers have found that people become addicted to analog media (Himmelweit, Oppenheim, & Vince, 1958; Horvath, 2004; Jhally, 1987; Kaplan, 1972; LaRose, Lin, & Eastin, 2003; Maccoby, 1954; Mander, 1978; McLeod, Ward, & Tancill, 1965; Winn, 1977). For example, Jhally (1987) argued that there is "significant evidence that this watching activity is less than free, that it is somehow out of our control. Further, it is not as if there were no recognition of the harmful effects of this watching—people know what is happening to them." He says that people overindulge, and this gives them a sense that their viewing is "beyond their control," and that it "affords them no real sense of satisfaction. The activity seems almost to stand in a hostile relationship to the individual's self-perceived preferences. The activity seems to be alienated from the watchers themselves" (p. 181).

Horvath (2004) used principles developed by psychiatrists to develop a measure of problem television viewing and found that many people do exhibit an addiction problem with the media. The measure contains four factors measuring distinct components of addictive behavior: heavy viewing, problem viewing, craving for viewing, and withdrawal. These factors were positively related to an alcoholism screening instrument adapted to television use.

People who are addicted to TV are more likely to be easily bored and to score high on the neurotic and introverted dimensions of the Eysenck Personality Test. Addicts are more likely to use TV to distract themselves from unpleasant thoughts, to regulate moods, and to fill time (McIlwraith, 1998).

Digital Media

Addiction to digital media is widespread. A study of American adults found that 10% to 12% exhibited internet addiction. They found that people spend an average of 50 minutes each day on Facebook, which is about the same amount of time that people spend daily eating and drinking. In another study 61% said they slept with their mobile phones either under their pillow or on their nightstand. In the same study, 98% of respondents said they knew that texting while driving was dangerous but 75% of respondents still admitted to doing so (Aiken, 2016). Also, a 2014 European study of more than 13,000 adolescents in seven European countries found that 13.9% of them showed signs of problematic internet use such as compulsive behavior that caused problems for them at home and school (Aiken, 2016).

A recent study found that 24% of teens reported using the internet "almost constantly" and that 50% of teens reported feeling addicted to their phones. Also, 59% of parents reported that they felt their teens were addicted to their phones (Brooks & Lasser, 2018).

In a *Newsweek* article, people described getting on Facebook and quickly becoming addicted to it (Levy, 2007). People would feel compelled to check the site many times a day to visit their friends' sites and see what was new with them; some people had hundreds of friends linked to their sites.

Conclusions

This chapter focused your attention on media attraction. It showed you that in general exposure to the media grows each year. Recently that growth has come mostly from exposure to digital media, but people still spend a lot of time with analog media, although time spent with analog media is starting to show reductions for the first time.

People are attracted to media when they believe it can satisfy their needs for information, entertainment, and other experiences—especially the needs for competition and for social contact. Media businesses work hard to attract their audiences and then condition them over time for repeated exposures. This continual conditioning sets up an effect cascade where users begin using media to displace real-world experiences, then grow dependent on media exposures, and finally become addicted to media, which is a very serious negative, long-term effect.

CHAPTER 4

Effects of Exposure to Digital News and Information

The news industry has undergone significant changes over time, especially over the past few decades with the rise of digital media and their various platforms for presenting news. These changes have stimulated criticism and led some scholars to question whether the news industry can continue to be viable. For example, Johnson (2012) explains,

> The overarching system of news is transitioning . . . from a small set of hierarchical organizations to a distributed network of smaller and more diverse entities. Because this transition involves the failure or downsizing of many of those older organizations, and because those organizations have, for the past few centuries at least, been our primary conduits of reported news and

commentary, many thoughtful observers have seen that transition as a crisis and a potential threat. (p. 79)

McCaffrey (2010) adds, "The news industry is in the midst of a period of profound transition. The advent of the Internet Age has rendered obsolete long-standing models of how to gather and communicate the news." Given "the breakneck pace at which change has occurred over the past two decades, it's likely that we are in for an era of perpetual transformation, one with few certainties and no fixed outcome" (p. 3). In his classic book *The Sociology of News*, Schudson (2003) argued that journalists have been trivializing the news in order to satisfy what the news industry perceives the public now wants, which led Schudson to ask, Can journalism continue to be publicly important?

Are the concerns expressed by critics of news valid? Are the trends of journalists trivializing news and the fragmentation of the audience forces that will destroy the news industry? To answer these questions, let's examine the way the news industry has evolved over time with the rise of **traditional media** and then the transition into digital media.

Evolution of News

The desire for news goes back to preliterate culture; humans have always expressed an interest in the events surrounding them (Harrison, 2006). In the beginning, news was very much personal and local, that is, people were most concerned about events that affected their daily lives (e.g., threats from invaders, impact of weather on their crops, and changes in local regulations) as well as the lives of their families and friends. News was transmitted almost exclusively through interpersonal conversations, so it was very local and immediate.

The idea of "news" changed when people began relying on the media to get information about current events—first from newspapers and magazines, later from radio, and then from television. People were strongly attracted to these analog media as sources of daily news but have shifted their attention more recently to digital media as sources.

The idea of "news" has been evolving as the media have been evolving over the last several centuries. When we look at what people regard as news today, it appears very different than what was regarded as news several decades ago, and that is very different than what appeared to be news several centuries ago. In order to understand these changes in the idea of "news," we need to examine how analog and then digital media have evolved to satisfy the public's continual need for current information about their worlds.

NEWS IN ANALOG MEDIA

Until the sixteenth century, the average person accessed information through interpersonal conversations. Then a group of men in Italy began collecting information about current events in their local area, printing that information in pamphlets, and selling those pamphlets to local citizens. This was the beginning of the newspaper industry. By the seventeenth century, these pamphlets evolved into daily newspapers first in Germany and then throughout Europe. These early newspapers presented a simple listing of facts, which made them hard to read because the facts were not presented as a story with any context or flow.

The audience for these early newspapers were elites, that is, people who could read and who could afford to pay for information. "Merchants, in particular, had a keen awareness of the value of information, and the dangers of acting on false rumour" (Pettegree, 2014, p. 3). Therefore, these journalists were most concerned with the accuracy of their information so they worked to corroborate their facts to give them greater credibility.

When the early settlers in America clustered into colonies, they had a strong need for daily information about what was going on in their colony as they formed governments, fought off threats from natives and nature, and adjusted to regulations imposed by European powers that were financing the colonies. Within each colony, people started several newspapers, each with its own political point of view.

Rise of "Big News"

Following the American Civil War and the rise of the industrial revolution in the mid-nineteenth century, the population was undergoing fundamental changes. One of the major changes was a growing sense of nationhood, so the population wanted information beyond their locale; people also wanted information about their nation as well as other countries so they could understand America's place in the world. Another change was the dramatic increase in literacy rates due to compulsory education. Most people were able to read, so they could get information from sources beyond interpersonal conversations. Some entrepreneurs (e.g., William Randolph Hearst and Joseph Pulitzer) regarded these changes as an opportunity to develop newspapers with very large circulations in the growing population centers of the United States. These entrepreneurs realized that in order to appeal to a large readership, they needed to move away from obvious political partisanship in their stories and make their reporting appear "objective" so as not to offend any group of readers. By avoiding political bias in reporting, they could broaden the appeal of their newspapers to a wider group of people and thus increase the revenue of their newspapers.

The growth of huge circulation newspapers ushered in an era of "big news." The central feature of "big news" was the rise of journalism as a profession. Newspapers needed to build and maintain their credibility so that the public would trust that they were providing coverage of the most important events each day and that their coverage was composed of facts rather than biased opinion. When radio became a mass medium in the 1920s, local stations affiliated with national radio networks, which each had a news department where professional journalists decided what was most important each day, wrote particular kinds of stories, and broadcast those stories every day to keep the population informed. When television became a mass medium in the 1950s, it followed the big news model in its effort to present news stories that expert journalists deemed to be most important each day.

Erosion of Exposure

This idea of big news reached a peak in the 1980s; then the audience began declining for the traditional media platforms that provided news to the general population. This erosion was slow at first but then increased with the rise of digital media that could better satisfy the population's need for news.

These declines were dramatic for newspapers. The number of daily newspapers decreased from 1,750 newspapers in 1970 to 1,350 newspapers in 2012 (Pew Research Center's Journalism Project, 2014). In 1984, the circulation for daily newspapers in the United States was 63.3 million, and that declined to 30.9 million by 2017 (Barthel, 2018). "U.S. newspaper ad revenue was $65 billion in 2000, but had plunged to just $18 billion by 2016" (Hindman, 2018, p. 132). During this time the number of journalists shrank. Employment at daily newspapers peaked at 74,410 employees in newsrooms in 2006, down to only 39,210 by 2017 (Barthel, 2018).

The decline in news seeking from analog media is especially stark among adolescents. The Kaiser Family Foundation (2010) conducted a survey of young Americans ages 8 to 18 and found that from 2005 to 2010, the average amount of time people spent reading magazines and newspapers each day dropped from 14 minutes to 9 minutes for magazines, and from 6 minutes to 3 minutes for newspapers. Also, the proportion of young people who read a newspaper in a typical day dropped from 42% in 1999 to 23% in 2009 (Pew Research Center, 2012).

As analog newspapers watched their audience erode, many established websites to hold on to their subscribers. In 2006 there were 8.2 million unique visitors each month to a daily newspaper website, and this had increased to 11.5 million by 2017 (Bialik & Matsa, 2017). While this strategy of providing both print and online versions of news reporting simultaneously helped traditional newspapers to survive, those traditional newspapers also faced strong competition from other online providers of news such as **digital-native news outlets**, which are online digital operations that originated on the internet and were not spin-offs from traditional news organizations. By 2018, there were hundreds of these digital-native news outlets with the largest 35 averaging at least 10 million unique visitors per month. Roughly 13,000 employees worked as reporters, editors, photographers, or videographers in the newsrooms of digital-native outlets in 2017, which was twice the number of employees they had in 2008 (Stocking, 2018).

The audience for TV news displays a different pattern depending on whether the TV news is local or national. While viewership for national TV news shows has remained relatively stable, there has been a steep drop in viewership for local news. In 2008, the combined viewership of evening network-produced news (ABC, CBS, and NBC) was 22.8 million, and it increased slightly to 23.8 million by 2016 (Matsa, 2017, June 16). However, exposure to local TV newscasts has been falling. Viewership for local newscasts in the morning have decreased from 12.3 million in 2007 to 10.8 million in 2016; early evening, from 25.7 million to 20.7 million; and late-night news, from 29.2 to 20.3 million (Matsa, 2017, July 13). Also, viewership declined for the three major cable news channels (CNN, Fox News, and MSNBC) in 2017.

Although analog media providers of news were experiencing declines in their audiences since the 1980s, they were still attracting a larger audience than digital media news providers until recently. In 2017, half of all Americans said that they got their news from television, while 43% said they got news from online sources (Gottfried & Shearer, 2017). Also, a recent secondary analysis of the data from the 2010–2014 World Values Survey ($N = 81,229$) across 56 countries was conducted to assess the relative frequency of exposure to television news versus the internet and mobile phone as information sources. In 105 of the 112 comparisons (93.8%), traditional television was still found to be used more frequently as a source of news than were either the internet or mobile phones (Robinson, Zeng, & Holbert, 2018).

NEWS IN DIGITAL MEDIA

The news audience for digital media continues to grow. When **social networking sites** began offering news, the shift away from analog sites accelerated.

Exposure Shift

In 2013, 30% of the general population said they got their news from Facebook, 10% said they got their news from YouTube, and 8% said they got their news from Twitter. Furthermore, this survey found that 26% of the population got their news from two social networking sites, and 9% said they used three or more social media sites for news (Holcomb, Gottfried, & Mitchell, 2013). Facebook founder and CEO Mark Zuckerberg bragged in 2007 that Facebook was the biggest source of news in the entire world. Zuckerberg said, "We're actually producing more news in a single day for our 19 million users than any other media outlet in its entire existence" (Pariser, 2011). By 2019, more than 2 billion people were regular users of Facebook and 52% of Americans were getting their news from Facebook (Newbury, 2019).

This shift away from analog to digital media can be seen across all age groups but is especially dramatic among younger people. Donsbach (2010) writes, "Younger people are increasingly using blogs, chatrooms or community networks such as Facebook and MySpace to receive what they think is 'news'" (p. 43). Also, the Pew Research Center's Journalism Project (2014) reported that 48% of 18- to 29-year-olds watched online news videos, while only 27% of 50- to 64-year-olds and 11% of those 65 and older did the same. By 2017, 43% of all adults were saying they got their news from online sources; furthermore, 67% of Americans were saying they get at least some of their news on social media sites, such as Twitter, YouTube, and Snapchat (Bialik & Matsa, 2017).

The shift toward digital media sources of news has been helped considerably by the widespread use of mobile devices. Hindman (2018) writes,

> The growth in tablet and mobile ownership is impressive. The iPhone and iPad, both category-defining products, date to just 2007 and 2010

respectively. By 2017, 77 percent of U.S. adults owned a smartphone, and 51 percent owned a tablet device. News is a popular activity for those who own both sets of devices; 45 percent of Americans say they often get news on a mobile device, while an additional 29 percent say that they sometimes do. (p. 142)

Changes in News Content

Digital media not only offer users greater convenience in seeking news; they have also developed a different model for the content of news that users find very attractive. While the content of digital news originally followed the model established for news by analog media, the digital content has evolved away from that model as it took advantage of the characteristics that distinguish digital media from analog media. Compared to news content from analog media, news content from digital media is more immediate, more local, and shorter, as well as offering multimedia features.

More Immediate   Digital media give people quicker access to news. People do not have to wait for an analog newspaper to be delivered or for a broadcast news site to present the news of the day at fixed times; instead, audiences can get continuous access at any time as well as anywhere by using their mobile devices. By 2014, 36% of all adults were watching online news videos, and 54% said they got news on a mobile device (Pew Research Center's Journalism Project, 2014). And by 2017, 85% of U.S. adults said they were getting their news on a mobile device (Bialik & Matsa, 2017).

A key factor that explains why digital media are more immediate with their news is that they allow for user-contributed content. There are now billions of people with smartphones all over the world, and whenever these people see something that might be newsworthy, they can take a picture or record the action in video on their phone and quickly upload it to the internet where everyone else has immediate access to it. For example, Twitter has become a trusted source of fast news. Tweets were found to be just as accurate as official reports when it came to tracking the spread of cholera after the 2010 earthquake in Haiti; they were also at least 2 weeks faster with reporting information to the public than were traditional media outlets (Brynjolfsson & McAfee, 2014).

Furthermore, journalists now rely on Twitter to provide them with valuable information about what is happening in the world. And it is now apparent that Twitter has a stronger influence on determining the news agenda than do traditional media. In a research study that compared the agenda-setting power of Twitter with that of analog media, Valenzuela, Puente, and Flores (2017) found a positive, reinforcing influence between the journalistic agendas of TV and Twitter. Furthermore, they found that the Twitter news agenda exercised more influence on the TV news agenda than the TV news agenda exercised on the Twitter news agenda.

While journalists often monitor content on Twitter to get leads for stories and sources of information, journalists have also used the internet in a more proactive way with **crowdsourcing**, which is a technique journalists use to generate leads and information. When using crowdsourcing, journalists begin by designing an internet platform where they put out a call for information and then manage the data that are uploaded to the site. A good example of the use of crowdsourcing by journalists occurred in 2012 when D. Brian Burghart, an editor at the *Reno News and Review*, started writing an article on police killings and found no comprehensive data on the topic (Gates, 2019). There were bits and pieces on internet sites where local police departments had reported data and where journalists had written stories about individuals killed by police, but there was no centralized agency (like the FBI) that collected and reported such data nationwide. Burghart designed a self-financed web-based platform that asked users to submit information on police killings. For two years he fact-checked the data that were submitted and then finally published an article in 2014 that focused on patterns of police killings that he could not have developed without the help of hundreds of contributors through crowdsourcing.

More Local   Chris Anderson, editor of *Wired* magazine, explains that a person's interest in a subject is inversely proportional to its distance from that person in terms of geography and emotions. The closer an event is to us, the more we find it interesting, that is, newsworthy (cited in Johnson, 2012). This explains why so many people have been abandoning traditional journalism as provided by analog media and instead have increased their reliance on specialized digital platforms that can satisfy their needs for news better. The focus of most traditional news organizations is on the aggregate level (where stories are selected that would seem to appeal to the greatest number of people) rather than at the individual level (where stories would have a special appeal to the particular needs of each individual). Because people vary so widely on their emotional attachment to any given topic, the news audience is fragmenting, and traditional news organizations cannot satisfy the range of needs for news across the diversity of people in any large group.

Digital media are able to present news that is **hyper-local**, which means they are able to personalize news stories to satisfy the particular needs of each niche audience. People want news about those things that interest them personally, that is, things that are most proximate to them, not just geographically but also psychologically. They care less about what professional journalists think is most newsworthy.

Shorter News Stories   "All else being equal, news organizations generate more traffic with lots of little stories, rather than fewer medium-sized ones. Data from Chartbeat shows that less than 10% of users scroll down to the end of a typical news article—most users, in fact, scroll only to the halfway point. This suggests that reporters often spend lots of time writing words that barely get read" (Hindman, 2018, p. 149). Hindman continues, "Increasingly, these findings are shaping newsroom policies. On May 6, 2014, both the Associate [*sic*] Press and Reuters . . . issued separate memos asking reporters to keep most news stories under five hundred words" (p. 149).

Related to the shortness of news stories is the degree to which stories report issues and events in depth. A recent study found that news organizations that emphasize the use of audience metric data publish fewer in-depth stories and that the use of metrics also influences the selection of events that get covered (Arenberg & Lowrey, 2019). This means that some news organizations are being guided in their selection of news much more by audience metrics than by journalistic expertise to determine what gets covered as news.

Multimedia News Stories   News stories on digital platforms can offer readers more than text; they often also include photographs as well as links to video and audio information.

> Multimedia content attracts more traffic than plain-vanilla text articles. This includes interactive elements and graphics, which have long been associated with high levels of reader engagement. But text stories that include videos or even simple slide shows typically outperform text alone. Some digital news sites already aggressively exploit this finding. Huffington Post and Buzzfeed, for example, have both invested heavily in slideshows (HuffPo) and scrollable image galleries (Buzzfeed). (Hindman, 2018, p. 151)

WHY THE SHIFT?

Why are many people abandoning analog media and instead seeking news from digital media? The simple answer to this question is that digital media are able to offer news that satisfies audience needs better than analog media do. Most people find that using digital sources to access news is easier and cheaper to use than analog sources. Furthermore, people are satisfied with their choice of different sources of information. When Purcell and Rainie (2014) asked people if they feel that digital technologies have made them feel better informed than five years ago, they found that 81% of respondents said they were better informed about products and services to buy; 75%, about national news; 72%, about popular culture; 68%, about hobbies and personal interests; 67%, about friends; 65%, about health and fitness; and 60%, about family. Notice how important "news" is about products, friends, family, and personal health.

Some researchers attribute the decline of time people spend seeking news on analog media to an increase in the number of people who are what they call "news avoiders." For example, a recent national survey of U.S. youth ages 12 to 17 found that half the respondents rarely if ever accessed what the researchers regarded as sources of traditional news, so the researchers labeled these adolescents as "news avoiders" (Edgerly, Vraga, Bode, Thorson, & Thorson, 2018). In another study, Toff and Nielsen (2018) conducted 43 in-depth interviews with infrequent users of conventional news and found three primary reasons for avoidance. One reason was that many avoiders feel the news will find them and they do not need to make any effort to expose themselves to news outlets. A second and related reason is the belief that the news is all around them and that they can simply absorb what is important. And a third reason for news avoidance is a belief that news outlets often present conflicting facts so people don't know what to believe and people therefore would prefer to avoid the dissonance they feel when exposing themselves to traditional news providers.

The problem with the studies that result in claims that there is a growing number of people who are "news avoiders" is that the designers of those studies use a narrow, traditional definition of what news is. So when these researchers notice that people are spending less time with traditional news sources, they conclude that news avoidance is growing. But an alternative conclusion seems more likely to explain the way the public has been shifting its attention with regard to seeking out sources of information. We should not ignore the fact that people are spending more time with the media and much of this time is motivated by a need to continually get updates on things people regard as most important to them. Thus people are not avoiding information; they are avoiding what experts regard as proper sources of news and instead are seeking information that is more important to them personally, such as the developments in specific groups to which they belong that represent their strongest attachments and the places of greatest meaning in their lives.

While most people have been moving away from typical news sources that are staffed by professional journalists who use their expertise to select what they regard as the most important events of each day, people are still using the media extensively to find information that satisfies their individual personal needs for information (Lee, Choi, Kim, & Kim, 2014; Moon & Hadley, 2014; Revers, 2014; Xu & Feng, 2014). Furthermore, people—especially younger people—are spending more time each year searching for meaningful information from the media. In a nationally representative survey from the United States, millennials were found to be more likely to rely on multiple platforms for news than were other age groups (Diehl, Barnidge, & Gil de Zúñiga, 2019). And not all of these platforms are what researchers would regard as legitimate sources of real news. But to the people who use those sources repeatedly, they are legitimate and valuable.

When we realize that what researchers regard as sources of news is very different than what the general public regards as sources of news, we are confronted with this question: Should news be defined by what experts (editors of major news organizations and researchers) think or what the public thinks? Clearly people continue to demonstrate a great curiosity about their world as evidenced by the increasing amount of time they spend with the media to seek out and communicate information.

Effects on Individuals

The research into the effects of digital news exposures on individuals generally follows a pattern of testing for legacy-type effects. That is, researchers have been designing digital studies that look a lot like studies that examined the effect of exposure to analog media. In general, the findings of the research indicate that exposure to digital media results in the same kinds of effects as does exposure to analog media. However, digital media's influence may be a little stronger than analog media's influence because digital media's influence is more pervasive (with so many more sources of information and access so constant with digital devices) and more involving for users (with its interactive capabilities).

BEHAVIOR

As you saw in previous sections of this chapter, people have been shifting their exposure behavior away from analog sources of news and into digital sources. This trend has stimulated researchers to ask two types of questions about this shift in behavior: Why is this shift occurring? And what are the effects of this shift on other behaviors?

Reasons for the Shift

Why have people been shifting their exposure behavior away from analog sources of news and into digital sources? Researchers have focused on four reasons: personal needs, selective exposure, recommendations from friends, and habit.

Personal Needs   When people decide which news source to use, they appear to be motivated less by seeking out sources that are most credible in presenting their vision of what is most important; instead, people seem to be motived more by personal goals for information. This motivation is most apparent when people seek out news about politics (i.e., positions on important issues, actions of political leaders, and platforms of candidates running for political offices). The selection of a news source has often been explained by political partisanship (Knobloch-Westerwick & Lavis, 2017). People who are politically conservative will gravitate to news sources that are likely to present news from a conservative point of view, while people who are politically liberal will search out news sources that are likely to present the news from a liberal point of view.

However, other researchers have found that political partisanship is too simple an explanation for why people choose certain sources of news. For example, Feldman, Wojcieszak, Stroud, and Bimber (2018) argue that when people search for political news and information, they are motivated by *more* than their simple partisan biases. These researchers found that the drivers of selectivity are more complex than general political attributes; rather, the motivations are contextual and reflect people's engagement with particular issues. The researchers conducted a study to test whether people typically select information content that is more interest based (i.e., choice of entertainment over politics) or partisan based (i.e., choice of pro-attitudinal over counter-attitudinal or balanced news). They found that issue-specific engagement variables (including perceived issue understanding, issue importance, and issue attitude strength) predicted both interest-based and partisan-based selectivity above and beyond the influence of general political knowledge, news interest, and strength of political leanings. A study of Norwegian users of Facebook found that people who were more active politically were more likely to get their news from Facebook than from traditional news outlets (Larsson, 2019).

Selective Exposure   The idea that people selectively expose themselves to news content has been around for a long time, but it is even more important today with the fragmentation of audiences and the proliferation of choices. **Selective exposure** is a psychological concept that says people seek out information that conforms to their existing belief systems and avoid information that challenges those beliefs. In the past when there were few sources of news, people could either expose themselves to mainstream news—where they would likely see beliefs expressed counter to their own—or they could avoid news altogether. Now with so many types of news constantly available to a full range of niche audiences, people can easily find a source of news that consistently confirms their own personal set of beliefs. This leads to the possibility of creating many different small groups of people with each strongly believing they are correct and everyone else is wrong about how the world works.

Recommendations from Friends   Researchers have known for a long time that people take recommendations from friends when selecting media content. With social network sites (SNSs) those recommendations are easy to track when friends tag certain news sites. Kümpel (2019) designed several experiments to test the idea that coming across news on SNSs largely depends on news-related activities in one's network. He found that when people search for news on Facebook, they look for stories that their friends have tagged. However, he also found that the tags had more influence on people who already had a high interest in news and that tags exerted little influence on people who were less interested in news.

Habit   Researchers have tested habit as an explanation for how people select their news sources. When people spend a great deal of time on SNSs to connect with their friends, it is easy to stay on those sites to get news rather than seek out other sources of news. Arendt, Northup, and Camaj (2019) argue that consumers of news often lack the motivation, time, or cognitive capacity to select news content in a conscious way where they deliberate the strengths and weaknesses of a range of news sources before carefully picking one for their own exposures. Instead, most of the time people use mental shortcuts that enable them to make quick exposure decisions. Then once they choose a particular news site, they automatically continue to expose themselves to that source.

A six-wave panel study was conducted in Sweden over a period of 5 years to see if there was a relationship between online media usage and political interest among adolescents (Moeller, Shehata, & Kruikemeier, 2018). The researchers found reinforcing spirals with only noninteractive political information usages of online media.

Other Behaviors

What are the effects of this shift on other behaviors? Researchers have focused on three areas: how users of digital news share that news with others, how they engage in public discourse, and how they use that information for cultural assimilation.

Sharing News   People can do more with news than simply consume it; they often share it with others, which involves curation. News curation is the reconstructing, reformulating, repurposing, reframing, and sharing of news through social media. Park and Kaye (2019) conducted a survey of 1,135 South Korean adults to examine how they engaged in news curation. They found that news curation was positively related to political knowledge.

Shin and Thorson (2017) examined large Twitter data sets collected during the 2012 U.S. presidential election to determine how partisanship shaped patterns of sharing and commenting on candidate fact-check rulings. Their results indicate that partisans were much more likely share fact-checking messages that supported their own candidate and/or denigrated the opposing party's candidate. This pattern shows that people are motivated less by correcting inaccuracies in news reporting than they are by sharing stories of any kind that support their own positions on issues.

Many people use Twitter to disseminate information quickly and widely. One reason for this is that many Twitter users have created ego networks where they personally identify with a particular kind of information or opinion. Liang and Fu (2017) conducted an analysis of more than 6,500 representative ego networks containing nearly 1 million following relationships from Twitter and arrived at three conclusions. First, they found that network redundancy was positively associated with the probability of being retweeted, even when competing variables are controlled for. Second, they found that network redundancy was positively associated with information redundancy, which in turn decreases the probability of being retweeted. And third, they found that the inclusion of both ego-alter similarity and tie strength can reduce the influence of network redundancy on the probability of being retweeted.

In another study of diffusion of information on Twitter, Liang (2018) found that people are more likely to share their opinions and information supporting those opinions with people who are likely to hold *other* opinions, and this practice is likely to increase political diversity on social media.

Engaging in Public Discourse   Digital sources of news give audiences a chance to respond to stories and thus contribute to public discourse on the issue covered in the news story. Chen and Lu (2017) conducted an experiment ($N = 272$) to test whether disagreement—either civil or uncivil—has a chilling effect on public discourse, which they argued was vital to a deliberative democracy. By analyzing the comments posted on a news story about abortion, the researchers found that both forms of disagreement caused negative emotions and aggressive intentions. However, only uncivil disagreement led people to respond back uncivilly.

Exposure to political sites online was found to trigger political conversation and online texting. Shah, Cho, Eveland, and Kwak (2005) conducted a study that examined the role of the internet as a sphere for public expression. They used a two-wave national panel survey data and found that online media complement traditional media to foster political discussion and civic messaging. These two forms of political expression, in turn, trigger participation behaviors in civic functions.

In many democracies, political discourse has polarized and become more confrontational. Post (2019) argues that this polarized discourse is shaped by a few highly visible activists who are also heavy news consumers. These antagonists watch mainstream news closely and perceive news coverage to be hostile to their particular positions on issues, and these hostile media perceptions encourage antagonists to intensify their discursive participation and to use polarizing communication styles, such as exaggerations, incivility, or lies.

Cultural Assimilation   News coverage can aid in cultural assimilation or hinder it. This is the finding from a three-wave longitudinal survey that was designed to examine how news coverage of Muslims helped or hindered them from successfully integrating within their countries (Saleem, Wojcieszak, Hawkins, Li, & Ramasubramanian, 2019). The researchers found that at Time 1 the negative news coverage of Muslims significantly reduced Muslims' strength of identification as an American at Time 2, which led to lower trust in the U.S. government at Time 3. These findings suggest that negative media portrayals can have adverse effects on the national identification of some minority groups, and that these effects may be stronger than those of personally experienced discrimination.

BELIEFS

Researchers have found that exposure to news in digital media can shape people's beliefs much like exposure to news in analog media.

Trust in News

Although people have been shifting away from analog media toward digital media to get their news, most people express beliefs that the news presented by digital media is less trustworthy than the news presented by analog media. For example, only 5% of web-using U.S. adults in 2017 exhibited a lot of trust in the information they get from social media, nearly identical to the 4% who said so in 2016. This level of trust is much lower than trust in national and local news organizations as well as information coming from friends and family (Bialik & Matsa, 2017). Also, McLeod (2019) found that 72% of Americans agree that traditional media consistently report stories they know to be false or purposefully misleading for political or financial gain. And about one third of U.S. adults said they often see made-up political news online (Bialik & Matsa, 2017).

A content analysis of how the term "fake news" was being used on Twitter found that it was a politicized term where emotional conversations overshadowed logical discussions of the term. Findings also revealed that social media users from opposing political parties communicate in homogeneous environments and use "fake news" to disparage the opposition and condemn real information disseminated by the opposition party members (Brummette, DiStaso, Vafeiadis, & Messner, 2018).

Citizens' levels of mistrust toward the media, as well as their beliefs that the media are biased, have increased in past years in most Western democracies. Ardèvol-Abreu and Gil de Zúñiga (2017) analyzed data from a two-wave panel in the United States to explore negative beliefs about journalism. They found that media trust and perceived bias relate to media consumption differently. When people believed social media were trustworthy, they demonstrated higher levels of use of social media for news. In contrast, when people believed the media were biased, their levels of news exposure in general were lower.

Beliefs about the credibility of news sources have been found to be related to the way sites brand their news. Arendt, Northup, and Camaj (2019) argue that consumers of news often lack the motivation, time, or cognitive capacity to select content in a deliberate way; instead, they opt for mental shortcuts. One of these mental shortcuts people often use is their perception of branding, which is a gut-level evaluation. That is, if they perceive that a news source is a particular brand (political orientation, or type of news), then they will automatically continue to expose themselves to that source.

Agenda Setting

The agenda-setting effect was first observed in the early 1970s when analog media were the exclusive providers of news. This effect shows up as the public believing the agenda of what is important based on the media agenda, that is, what the media report as being most important. In the 1970s, there was a clear media agenda because the news stories that were covered each day were the same across all news providers—newspapers, news magazines, radio, and television. But now with the proliferation of digital news providers, researchers have become concerned that there is no longer a recognizable news agenda across all news providers, and if this is the case, there can be no agenda-setting effect. However, research still shows support for the agenda-setting effect. For example, Chen, Su, and Chen (2019) tested for an agenda-setting effect in China and found there was a consistent media agenda and that it influenced the public agenda in that country.

Beliefs About Gender

Gender is often presented in a stereotypical manner in the news media, so constant exposure to these portrayals can lead to a polarization of beliefs. To test this idea, Han and Federico (2018) conducted two experimental studies using different samples—that is, college students (Study 1) and adult U.S. citizens (Study 2). They found that when news stories framed conflict along gender lines, people developed more polarized beliefs.

Cyberchondria

When people search out health information on the internet, they typically use short-cuts and superficial searches rather than engage in systematic processing of online information. This is the finding of a study conducted by Klawitter and Hargittai (2018) who interviewed a diverse group of American adults about how they seek health information online. This unsystematic searching out of health information is often blamed for a condition called **cyberchondria**, which is a belief by many people that they have a serious illness when in fact they do not. Because there are many digital sources of health news and information, people can easily access lists of symptoms, although they do not have the extensive medical training needed to make sense of all this information, so people often erroneously diagnose themselves as sick. Then they go to their doctors to tell them what is wrong and ask for specific treatments and drugs. Most times the self-diagnosis is wrong (Aiken, 2016).

COGNITIONS

Exposure to digital news creates cognitive effects, especially increases in general knowledge, political knowledge, and the way people process health-related information.

Knowledge

That people can acquire knowledge from their exposure to digital media is such an obvious conclusion that researchers rarely test for it; instead, researchers tend to focus more on identifying the factors that enhance—or detract—from this learning. One such study was designed to determine the effect of modality (embedded multimedia, traditional multimedia, and text-only format) on readers' knowledge gain (Pincus, Wojcieszak, & Boomgarden, 2017). They found that knowledge gain is slightly decreased by multimodality, that is, higher learning was associated with simpler message presentations using fewer media in a lesson.

It has often been argued that digital inequalities undermine the democratizing potential of the internet by increasing—rather than reducing—a knowledge gap. While many people engage in public discourse through participatory media, knowledge gaps limit engagement in the networked public sphere. Participatory web platforms have unique potential to facilitate a more equitable production of knowledge. Shaw and Hargittai (2018) conducted a study to examine online participation of contributing information in the context of Wikipedia editing, and found evidence for knowledge gaps, where some people who have more knowledge also tend to share it more, which tended to increase the knowledge gap.

Learning information has long been associated with attention, that is, the more attention people give to particular messages, the more they will learn from them. This has also been found with learning from websites (Nguyen et al., 2017). These researchers found that older adults (over 65) paid more attention to websites with illustrations and audiovisual elements and hence learned more from them. In contrast, younger adults (25 to 45) learned more from simpler messages that were all text.

Research has found that people are likely to learn erroneous information in news sites (Amazeen & Bucy, 2019). However, that learning can be avoided when people have a working knowledge of how the news media operate. This knowledge will help people identify instances of fabricated news and native advertising, thereby discounting the information presented in those types of sites.

Political Knowledge

It has long been known that people will acquire a greater amount of political knowledge when they expose themselves to more news. However, this simple relationship might be deceptive. A more complex relationship was found in a study that explored the relationships between measures of Facebook use and political knowledge levels using a pair of representative samples of U.S. adults (Park & Kaye, 2018). The findings indicate that although the mere use of Facebook was unrelated to political knowledge scores, *how* Facebook users report engaging with the SNS was strongly associated with knowledge levels. While greater exposure to news sites might be associated with greater acquisition of bits of learning, knowledge is not the same as a sum of the number of bits of information a person has, especially if those bits are erroneous, misleading, and lack credibility (Cacciatore et al., 2018; de Zúñiga & Chen Guest, 2019).

Health Information Processing

An online sample of American adults ($N = 767$) found that certain types of health behavior functions (i.e., health affirming versus health detection/treatment) prime individuals to process information with either defensive or accuracy motivation. Such information-processing motivations, in turn, influenced the contribution and consumption of user-generated health content. Individuals' information search for health-affirming behaviors instigated a defensive motivation. Moreover, while both information-processing motivations influenced user-generated content consumption, only defensive motivation had a significant effect on user-generated content contribution (Hong & Beaudoin, 2018).

Kreps (2017) argued that the growing use of digital health communication channels has produced dramatic changes in the way people process health information by combining mass and interpersonal communication in two different ways. He says that one way of processing health information is to use media and interpersonal sources of information sequentially as they work toward a decision; individuals obtain health information online that they discuss interpersonally with health providers. The second way of processing health information is to rely on discussions with others online. He argues that both of these methods can be used to improve health education, health promotion, and health behavior change.

ATTITUDES

Researchers have also found that exposure to digital news can lead to attitudinal effects, particularly in the way people make judgments of the credibility of news stories as well as their tolerance for errors in those stories.

Judgments of Credibility

When news stories are presented in a conflict framework, people are more likely to make judgments about the credibility of the experts quoted in the story. This is the major finding of an experiment on 333 participants who were exposed to news stories about media effects (Martins, Weaver, & Lynch, 2018). Researchers also found that when the participants judged the news story's credibility to be high, they were more likely to change their existing attitudes.

Tolerance for Errors in News

The accelerating news cycle means there is a risk that errors become more common. However, people generally hold a positive attitude that the news media publish correct information and that they have little tolerance for errors (Karlsson, Clerwall, & Nord, 2017).

PHYSIOLOGY: EYE TRACKING

An experiment that monitored participants' eye tracking of internet posts found that the posts that contained positive images elicited a higher level of visual attention than those with negative images or no images. Furthermore, high visual attention was associated with higher intentions to click and share posts with positive images (Keib et al., 2018). In the experiment, participants viewed a series of 29 social media posts of news stories, each of which was paired with no image, a positively valenced image, or a negatively valenced image. Participants' attention to the images was captured via eye tracking, and they answered dependent measures to gauge level of emotion and arousal, as well as intention to click and share.

AFFECT

News stories that trigger emotional responses are more likely to also trigger higher levels of attention to those stories. In one study, researchers measured levels of enthusiasm, anger/aversion, and anxiety in response to brief summaries of 50 news stories (Neuman, Marcus, & MacKuen, 2018). The researchers found a dramatic variation across news stories and emotional reactions. They also found an unexpected inverse correlation between education and level of emotional response to news, that is, those people with the lowest levels of education exhibited the strongest emotional responses to the news.

The way people process news was examined in a study by de los Santos and Nabi (2019). They designed an experiment to trigger emotional reactions (anger, fear, and hope) and then analyzed how those emotions influenced how their participants processed those news messages. They found that participants who read emotional stories depicting anger and especially hope spent more time on the story page than those who read stories that elicited the emotion of fear.

Conclusions

As you can now see, the idea of what is news has always been in a state of dynamic change. Until the rise of news pamphlets and newspapers in Europe in the sixteenth and seventeenth centuries, people's idea of news was limited to the current events taking place in their immediate vicinity in their everyday lives. Then the idea of news shifted to pamphlets presenting daily listings of facts. Later there was a shift to newspapers presenting stories from a particular political point of view to audiences that wanted up-to-date information to support their political orientations. The era of "big news" arose when newspapers shifted toward presenting facts objectively rather than editorializing particular political positions. Then there was a shift toward making news more entertaining rather than purely factual. Now we are experiencing a shift into having a wide variety of news platforms so that people with any kind of news perspective or any kind of need for current information can find at least one source of what they consider to be useful news.

The key to understanding the nature of news today is to recognize that news organizations are businesses that are trying to market products that will satisfy the needs of a particular audience segment. Because the population is so fragmented by needs, there are many different kinds of news providers. The positive effects of this situation are that people have more choice than ever and that everyone can find a provider of news that best satisfies her or his needs. The negative effects of this situation is that the sharing of a common set of information has seriously eroded, which makes it more difficult for individuals to understand the full picture of their world and to understand how other people can come to hold very different beliefs about the world than they do.

Further Reading

Hindman, M. (2018). *The internet trap: How the digital economy builds monopolies and undermines democracy.* Princeton, NJ: Princeton University Press. (240 pages with endnotes, bibliography, and index)

This book takes an economic approach to explain two negative trends in the development of the internet. One trend is the rise of monopolies as successful internet companies dominate their industries. The other trend is the undermining of democracy by destroying local news journalism and replacing it with stories that news organizations think people would find most interesting rather than information that would challenge them or educate them broadly about the important issues of the day.

O'Conner, C., & Weatherall, J. O. (2019). *The misinformation age: How false beliefs spread.* New Haven, CT: Yale University Press. (266 pages with endnotes and index)

The authors present lots of cases to illustrate that misinformation is frequently presented by media and believed by the public. Most of their examples are about how scientific findings are presented. While sometimes these findings are reported inaccurately through innocent means, many times their inaccuracies are motivated by organizations intent on presenting a particular point of view so they either hype or discredit the findings for political purposes.

CHAPTER 5

Effects of Exposure to Digital Advertising

Digital media have given advertisers many new opportunities to expose their potential customers to their persuasive messages. This chapter begins with an examination into how the rise of digital media has fundamentally changed the way advertisers think about potential customers, how they design their advertising campaigns, and the new tools of persuasion that digital media now offer advertisers. This examination provides you with the context to understand how advertising in digital media has been affecting individuals.

Table 5.1. Digital Revolution in Advertising

1976	First instance of spam when Digital Equipment Corporation (DEC) sends unsolicited messages promoting sales events for its latest models; generates criticism and sales
1979	Redifon Computers creates Compact Office System, which allows users to use the internet to place orders for goods
1982	France Telecom introduces Minitel, a nationwide online ordering system
1992	SMS messaging made available with the build-out of 2G mobile network
1993	Clickable web ads appear
1994	*HotWired*, first web magazine, launches; first site to provide advertisers with data about user traffic and metrics
1994	U.S. government promotes ecommerce by moving web hosting from NSFNET to a commercial network
1994	Search engines launched (Yahoo and AltaVista)
1994	Idea of search engine optimization (SEO) introduced as a way of measuring the marketing power of a brand
1995	Nokia introduces first smartphone
1998	Google and MSN search engines launched; Google develops PageRank, which measures quality and strength of inbound links to determine relative value of sites; GoTo.com launches bidding for higher placement in search results
2001	3G mobile connectivity debuts
2003	Site-targeted advertising debuts; Google AdWords allows ad placement via keyword, domain name, topic, and demographics; quickly becomes Google's main source of revenue
2005	Google offers personalized search results based on user's search histories
2007	Programmable ad buying debuts; ad exchanges sell ads across multiple ad networks with real-time bidding on a per-impression basis
2009	Ad.ly in-stream advertising service pays Kim Kardashian $10,000 per tweet
2010	Twitter introduces Promoted Trends and Promoted Tweets as a way to help advertisers target specific people
2011	U.S. internet ad revenue reaches $7.68 billion; ad-blocking software introduced
2014	Ad bots create fake traffic that allows sites to charge higher click rates to advertisers
2015	Real-time bidding takes off, enabling real-time buying and selling of ads on a per-impression basis
2015	Amazon.com accounts for more than half of all ecommerce by selling nearly 500 million products online
2015	Yahoo admits that it punishes users who employ ad blocking by holding back their personal email
2016	Ad spending on social media campaigns increases to $24 billion in United States
2017	Ad spending on social media campaigns increases to $36 billion in United States and $283 billion worldwide, which is about 37% of all media ad spending

Source: Adapted from Young (2017).

Contrasting Traditional and Digital Advertising

As analog media have grown over the past century, they have become more dependent on revenue from advertising. And as advertisers have been paying more and more money to analog media businesses in order to expose their prospective customers to their persuasive messages, they have developed a traditional model for the design, execution, and evaluation of their ad campaigns.

Now with the rise of digital media, advertisers have been given all kinds of new tools they can use to identify potential customers and persuade them to buy their products. These new digital tools have stimulated many advertisers to develop a very different way of designing their ad campaigns. It is becoming clear that digital advertising has evolved away from traditional advertising in at least three ways. First, digital advertising campaigns follow very different strategies. Second, they exhibit a different orientation toward audience exposure. And third, they work from a different perspective with the way they exercise persuasion.

STRATEGIES

A primary difference between digital and traditional advertising campaigns is the way they construct and execute their strategies. Traditional advertising campaigns are structured to progress through several discrete stages one at a time, while digital advertising campaigns are more dynamic as they respond to unplanned opportunities that may occur over the course of a digital advertising campaign.

Traditional Strategy

The traditional advertising strategy is composed of three separate stages: planning, execution, and evaluation. Advertisers begin the planning stage by conducting research to analyze the overall economy, their consumers, a history of their product development and its advertising, and a history of their competitors' products and their advertising. This information is then organized into a situational analysis that forms the basis for their recommendations about the coming year's marketing goals, techniques to reach those goals, and budgets. Traditional advertisers use the information in the situational analysis to create a **copy platform** for each ad.

Once the overall advertising plan is polished and finalized, it is implemented. Copy platforms are used as guides for the production of each ad by copywriters, musicians, photographers, and videographers. The ads are then placed in analog media (television, radio, newspapers, magazines, etc.) as media buyers select vehicles (particular newspapers, television shows, etc.) that have audiences with high concentrations of their potential customers.

The third and final stage is evaluation. Measures are taken to determine how successful the planned campaign was in achieving its advertising and marketing goals. For example, researchers conduct surveys to see if a high enough percentage of the target market was exposed to ads and if potential customers were exposed to the ads enough times to make them want to buy the products. Sales figures are analyzed to determine if that ad campaign generated enough revenue to meet its objectives.

Digital Strategy

In contrast to the traditional advertising **campaign strategy**, digital advertising campaigns begin with some general goals that are then altered and refined as digital tools are used to interact with potential customers. During these continual interactions, digital advertisers learn more and more about their potential customers' needs, and this continuous flow of information helps those advertisers create and test techniques that incrementally move potential customers through various stages of thinking about their products and toward product purchasing.

With digital advertising campaigns, the planning, execution, and evaluation are not separate stages; instead, digital advertisers are constantly collecting information that tells them (a) how well they are attracting and persuading potential customers and (b) how they can make changes to their strategy to increase its effectiveness at every decision-making point throughout the entire campaign. Thus digital advertisers are continually monitoring the emerging needs of their prospective customers, and then immediately presenting their products as the best way to satisfy those needs.

EXPOSURE ORIENTATION

A second way that digital advertising differs from traditional advertising is with its orientation concerning audience exposure to their ad messages. Advertisers who rely on traditional media typically exhibit a push orientation toward exposing audiences to their messages. This means advertisers are using analog media to push their messages onto their target audiences. That is, when people are seeking information in newspapers or magazines and when they are seeking entertainment from radio or TV, advertisers insert their ad messages into those exposures. Those ad messages are designed to push audiences from ignorance about a product to knowledge about the product, from no attitude about a product to a positive attitude about a product, and from no usage of the product to repeated usage of the product.

In contrast, advertisers who rely primarily on digital media typically exhibit a pull orientation to advertising. This means that advertisers monitor audiences' use of digital media and wait for people to express an interest in a product (or a need that their product could satisfy); then digital advertisers engage with those audience members to pull them to their company's website as well as into other experiences that would give those individuals more information about the advertisers' products and to stimulate them to interact with advertisers by inviting them to participate in contests, promotions, and interactions on digital platforms.

Digital advertisers continually monitor how people use search engines, social networking sites, and games in order to pull information from them about their evolving needs, rather than push their own predesigned messages onto those individuals.

Digital advertisers use the data they have mined from monitoring what people say on social media sites and through product ratings services and then use that information to pull people into an experience with their products. As advertisers make their observations, they notice patterns (about how people acquire information, how they form their attitudes and share them with others, and how those attitudes shape their buying behaviors) that meet and enhance their expectations.

PERSPECTIVE

When advertisers design a campaign that relies on traditional media, they are using an **outbound advertising perspective**. The outbound perspective on advertising takes a *prescriptive* approach that relies on experts to design an advertising campaign and then to execute it by buying access to targeted audiences in the traditional media. Advertising campaigns that rely on traditional media are typically organized hierarchically with control at the top by experts who make decisions about marketing campaigns, the use of advertising, the design of ad messages, and the placement of those messages in analog media. Once the plan is finalized, it is executed in full and then evaluated to determine how effective it was.

In contrast, when advertisers design a campaign that relies on digital media, they use an **inbound advertising perspective**. The inbound perspective takes a *responsive* approach where advertisers identify consumers who express an interest in their products and then use digital media to interact with those potential customers in a way that guides those potential customers toward product purchasing. Advertisers spend a lot of time observing people in their everyday lives as those people express their needs to friends and as they try to satisfy those needs through the shopping for products online. Advertising with digital media is much more process oriented where advertisers continually make adjustments to respond to challenges and opportunities as they arise.

Advertisers using an inbound perspective try to talk *with* audience members rather than talk *at* them. This means that advertisers try to engage their audiences through participation and sharing. Advertisers identify the social media platforms that their target audiences use most and then monitor activity on those platforms, that is, digital advertisers analyze the conversations people have about their needs and product usages. Advertisers try to engage people when they express a need by showing those people how their products can satisfy those needs. Young (2017) captures the essence of digital advertising succinctly: "In digital video you seek fans, you don't buy audiences" (p. 146).

Tools of Digital Advertising

By using many of the features offered by digital media, advertisers have been developing new approaches to identify potential customers and then persuading those potential customers to buy their products. This section describes the major tools digital advertisers use to accomplish these two types of tasks.

Box 5.1. Contrasting Outbound and Inbound Advertising Perspectives

OUTBOUND ADVERTISING

- Purpose is to reach out to potential customers by placing ads in media and in locations where those people normally spend their time
- Heavy use of traditional mass media to disseminate ads widely to target audiences
- Ads must be compelling enough to attract people to pay attention to those ads.
- Information flow is one-way, from advertiser to consumer.
- Success of the ad campaign is measured after all the ads have been run; success focuses on two criteria:

  ○ Reach: Percentage of target group that was exposed to at least one ad during the campaign
  ○ Frequency: The average number of times each person in the target group was exposed to ads in the campaign

INBOUND ADVERTISING

- Purpose is to guide potential customers through a buying funnel once those people have expressed an interest in the product by visiting a website
- Heavy use of social media: SNS, blogs, video and photo sharing, chat rooms, message boards, LISTSERVs, wikis, social bookmarking, and mobile applications
- Information flow is interactive across networks of consumers; companies interject themselves into those networks to befriend consumers, listen to their needs, and influence them in conversations.
- Advertising focuses on communicating with potential customers in an ongoing dialogue.
- Messages are personal and immediate; each message is delivered at the precise moment that an individual target person needs it.
- Success of this advertising procedure is measured continuously by monitoring how well this procedure moves potential customers through the buying funnel. When problems are identified, they can be corrected immediately.

Source: Adapted from Scott (2013).

TOOLS FOR IDENTIFYING AUDIENCES

Digital media offer advertisers tools for identifying audiences beyond what the analog media offer. These digital tools include the generation of metrics, monitoring searches, monitoring activity on social networking sites, and specialized forms of ratings services.

Metrics

Advertising is an information-based industry, so advertisers have always been generating data on their products, their customers, and how to reach those customers through advertising. With analog media, advertisers focus on television and radio ratings among their target audiences, newspaper and magazine subscriptions and pass-along rates, and exposures to billboards and other forms of outdoor advertising.

The rise of digital media has created some additional metrics that advertisers have found valuable. These metrics can be organized by advertising objectives. One advertising objective is exposure, that is, how often potential customers have been exposed to ads and information about a particular product. When measuring exposure of potential customers, the key digital metrics are the number of unique visitors to a website, the number of pages viewed on the site, the frequency of visits to the site, the average visit length, and **click-through rates** (number of times that visitors click on a hot button that takes them to a different site).

Another advertising objective is attitude management. When measuring attitudes, the key digital metrics are the number of likes, the number and kind (positive or negative) of comments posted, brand perception, and product reviews/ratings.

When measuring the advertising objective of audience involvement, digital advertisers use the metrics of completion rates (viewing entire video or other form of advertisement message), number of downloads, number of times users share information with their friends, number of recommendations in social word-of-mouth communication, and number of referrals.

Because these metrics are so important to advertisers, digital platforms have monetized their services to charge for them. For example, Anderson (2012) explains that digital technology has allowed for platforms to charge advertisers by actual performance. While traditional advertising charges clients by audience size, digital advertising charges clients by how often prospective customers perform some action of interest to the advertiser, such as clicking on a hot button in a digital ad.

While performance pricing is a great new tool for advertisers, it also has a downside. Anderson explains that pay-per-click advertising "generates the incentive for fraudulent clicking (sometimes through vast networks of 'zombie' computers taken over by viruses, and whose owners are unaware of their computers' actions) in order to generate revenues on false presences" (p. 364).

Monitoring Searches

People surf the web to get information on products they intend to buy. Therefore, this is a valuable source of information to advertisers who have an inbound perspective and a pull orientation. Digital advertisers monitor how people surf the web—especially their use of search engines—to identify those people who conduct searches for the products they are selling. Because these searchers are expressing an interest in their particular products, they are regarded as prime consumers.

Monitoring Social Networking Sites

Advertisers also monitor postings on social networking sites so they can identify emerging needs. They examine interactions among friends to look for things that people complain about and use this information to identify potential customers. Digital advertisers regard social media as an especially good place to monitor conversations and to mine for data on emerging needs as well as a way of creating brand-loyal customers. The Content Marketing Institute says that 89% of advertised brands are now using social media, with Facebook being the dominant platform (used by 85% of all brands) followed by blogs (75%) and emailed newsletters (75%; Tuten & Solomon, 2018).

Ratings Services

Websites where consumers can post comments expressing what they think about products are provided by **ratings services**. Some of these sites are run by the companies that manufacture particular products so they can monitor consumer reactions to their brands. There are also more general ratings services (such as Yelp, Foursquare, and Angie's List) that solicit product reactions on a wide range of brands that they do not manufacture or sell. Digital advertisers regard ratings services as a valuable source of information about what people like about their product and how their products can be improved to increase their value to consumers.

TOOLS FOR PERSUADING AUDIENCES

Digital media also provide advertisers with tools to persuade audiences that the analog media do not. Advertisers with a pull perspective regard these tools as being very helpful in persuading individuals to try and buy their products.

Search Engine Optimization

By monitoring how people use search engines to get information on products they intend to buy, digital advertisers learn about how people use keywords to guide their searches and how those people use hot buttons to visit sites. Digital advertisers then use this information to alter their keywords and thereby increase the probability that potential customers will quickly find listings for their specific products when those potential customers conduct their searches. This process is called **search engine optimization (SEO)**.

Some search engines allow advertisers to buy ads that run next to a search's hit list. For example, in 2000 Google began running small, textual advertisements alongside their search results. Also, search engines also allow advertisers to buy placement in searches, that is, the more money advertisers pay to a search engine, the higher ranked that advertiser's products will appear in a hit list when people engage in a search for that product. Carr (2010) explains that Google changed its original search algorithm, which was originally based only on keywords, to also include advertiser-bought placement.

Rather than selling advertising space for a set price, they (Google) decided to auction the space off. It wasn't an original idea—another search engine, GoTo, was already auctioning ads—but Google gave it a new spin. Whereas GoTo ranked its search as according to the size of the advertisers' bids—the higher the bid, the more prominent the ad—Google in 2002 added a second criterion. An ad's placement would be determined not only by the amount of the bid but by the frequency with which people actually clicked on the ad. That innovation ensured that Google's ads would remain, as the company put it, "relevant" to the topics of searches. Junk ads would automatically be screened from the system. If searchers didn't find an ad relevant, they wouldn't click on it, and it would eventually disappear from Google's site. The auction system, named AdWords, had another very important result: by tying ad placement to clicks, it increased click-through rates substantially. The more often people clicked on an ad, the more frequently and prominently the ad would appear on search result pages, bringing even more clicks. Since advertisers paid Google by the click, the company's revenues soared. (Carr, 2010, p. 155)

By the end of the decade, Google was generating more than $22 billion a year, almost all from advertising.

Buying Funnel

Digital advertisers continuously use what they learn from their observations to make continual adjustments as they interact with their prospective customers and guide them through a buying funnel. The **buying funnel** refers to the way digital advertisers attempt to pull prospective customers through a sales process step-by-step to give them information about their product, and then shape their attitudes and stimulate their behavior to buy the product. Tuten & Solomon (2018) say the buying funnel has five stages: increasing awareness of brands and products, influencing desire, encouraging trial, facilitating purchase, and reinforcing brand loyalty. In working through these stages, advertisers rely on several newly developed tools: online personalization, social media influencers, and electronic word of mouth. Notice that the buying funnel does not conclude with purchasing the product. Digital advertisers want more, that is, they also want to continue interacting with customers to get them to avoid buyer's remorse, continue to buy the product, and even tell their friends about how great the product is (Tuten & Solomon, 2018).

By monitoring how people conduct internet searches for products in a particular category, advertisers can examine how people change their keywords as they develop an interest in a product. Advertisers watch what keywords people use at the top of the funnel, that is, the keywords consumers use when they are not aware of a particular product. These keywords are very general and refer to typical needs. Advertisers then monitor how the keywords change as people move through the funnel so that those advertisers can incorporate those changes in keywords into their messages at various levels of the funnel to increase the chances that potential consumers will move further through the funnel from the top of the funnel with the wide mouth all the way to the narrow bottom where the product purchases are made.

Thus the buying funnel is a procedure that begins when advertisers interact with people as soon as they demonstrate any kind of interest in a product (e.g., searching for the product online, conversing about the product on an SNS, or visiting the company's website). Through continual interactions, advertisers try to move people step-by-step through this buying funnel by providing them with additional information, answering their questions, shaping their attitudes, and stimulating a desire to try the product. And finally, advertisers try to condition their buyers to act as advocates for the product when those buyers interact with their friends on social media sites and in real life. Thus the inbound perspective on advertising is much more oriented toward generating continual interactions with consumers and trying to get them not just to buy the product but also to like the product so much that those consumers in essence work for the company for free by sending their own messages that transform the advertising campaign into a viral movement.

Personalized Interactions

Personalization is a new advertising tool that takes advantage of digital media features that allow for **micro-targeting** (i.e., focusing on the particular needs of relatively small numbers of individuals and continually interacting with them in special ways). Because digital media make it possible for advertisers to assemble a huge amount of data on individuals by tracking their internet searches of all kinds as well as the concerns they express on social media sites and other digital platforms, they acquire a great many personal details about each individual. This puts advertisers in a position to craft a special appeal for each unique person.

U.S. advertisers, challenged to gain the attention of target consumers in an increasingly fragmented media environment, invested $40.1 billion in personalized digital advertising in the first half of 2017, the highest level of spending on record, and a 23% increase over the same time period in 2016 (Sruoginis, 2017). Likewise, the level of personalization possible in message targeting has also increased exponentially. An expanding clickstream of data based on thousands of website users' interactions (collected both overtly and covertly) has enhanced advertisers' efforts to tailor ads to individual consumers.

Influencers

Digital advertisers hire people to serve as **social media influencers**. These are typically ordinary people who frequently post their opinions online and who have attracted a large number of followers. These people generally present themselves as having expertise in a specific area, such as healthy living, travel, food, lifestyle, beauty, or fashion. This expertise is what is responsible for attracting a large number of followers.

Digital advertisers invest in selected influencers to create and/or promote their branded content to both the influencers' own followers and to the brands' target consumers. Influencer-produced branded content is considered to have more organic, authentic, and direct contact with potential consumers than brand-generated ads

(Talavera, 2015). A recent Twitter study suggested that consumers accord social media influencers a similar level of trust as they hold for their friends (Swant, 2016).

For example, Chen and Yuan (2019) conducted an online survey of social media users who followed at least one influencer. Their results showed that the informative value of influencer-generated content was keyed to the influencer's trustworthiness, attractiveness, and similarity to the followers. When customers trusted influencers' posts, they were more likely to learn more about the products and even to purchase them.

The popularity of influencer marketing has been growing exponentially. A recent report stated that, in 2018, 39% of marketers had plans to increase their budget for influencer marketing, and 19% of marketers intended to spend more than $100,000 per campaign (Bevilacqua & Del Giudice, 2018). These influencers are typically well paid with a range running from a low of about $200 to nano-influencers (someone with about 10,000 followers) up to about $500,000 for a celebrity Instagram post. However, digital advertisers are becoming more careful to check the accuracy of the number of followers that influencers claim to have. For example, it has been found that a person can buy 1,000 YouTube followers for about $49, and the cost of buying fake followers on Facebook and Instagram is even less (A bubble bursts, 2019, p. 32).

Electronic Word of Mouth

Electronic word of mouth (eWOM) refers to any positive or negative statement made by potential, actual, or former customers about a product or company, which is made available to a multitude of people and institutions over the internet. Social media websites, especially Facebook, Instagram, YouTube, and Twitter, have been found to be especially useful in getting ordinary people to spread information and attitudes about products.

Word of mouth has always been a valuable marketing tool. For centuries, people have been asking for the opinions of their peers and family members when shopping in brick-and-mortar stores. Now with digital media so widespread, word of mouth has gone electronic, where thousands and even millions of people can be exposed to particular postings about products. The emergence of SNS and microblogs has greatly increased the ability of consumers to come together in groups of friends or strangers to discuss brands, share updates, offer advice, and relive experiences. Digital technologies have revolutionized the way consumers search for products and services, seek reviews from current and past consumers, and eventually decide whether to purchase. As a result, eWOM is now considered as an essential component of the consumer decision-making journey (Moran, Muzellec, & Nolan, 2014).

Consumers are increasingly turning to the internet to search for and share product information, and these practices result in large volumes of consumer opinions being available online (Reichelt, Sievert, & Jacob, 2014). The majority of eWOM-supporting websites permit the identity of the sender to be concealed. However, SNSs identify message senders, so SNSs are open and transparent as the message appears on the user's own profile page as well on the news feeds of friends connected to that user.

Brands use eWOM to leverage their fan and follower connections in order to attract new customers (LaPointe, 2012). One way in which this leverage manifests itself is in terms of brand-initiated or fertilized eWOM (Trusov, Bucklin, & Pauwels, 2009). On SNS, this activity consists of brands incentivizing their fans to spread firm-created communications with their friend connections. For example, Tesco, a British multinational grocery and general merchandise retailer, ran a "Share & Earn scheme" where the retailer's Facebook fans earned loyalty card points for sharing products with their friends online.

Generally, eWOM is viewed as entertainment and builds the perception of user friendliness. Strong relationships between the eWOM sender and the receiving community lead to higher message credibility. Credibility is also guided by perceived competence or level of experience with the topic, as well as how relatable the information is with members of the receiving community (Moran & Muzellec, 2017).

Ratings Services

You saw in a previous section that ratings services are a valuable source of information about what consumers think about all kinds of products and services. Ratings services have also been used as a tool to create positive attitudes about products. That is, digital advertisers often pay people to post positive reviews of their products so that when other people read the reviews, those products have higher (more positive) ratings than they would have had without the paid postings.

Recommender Systems

Some digital platforms offer so many choices that users can become overwhelmed. For example, Amazon.com offers more than 600 million products for sale. To help their users navigate their way through all these choices, that platform uses recommender systems. These are algorithms that use information about a particular user to narrow the number of choices down to a manageable number. Jian and Mackie-Mason (2012) explain, "A recommender system recommends items to best suit an individual's tastes, while relying on a data set of opinions contributed by users. Typical recommendation systems employ some form of collaborative filtering: a technology that automatically predicts the preference of a user based on many others' tastes" (p. 401).

The two most used types of recommender systems are person-to-person and item-to-item recommendations. The person-to-person recommender type of system groups by people, that is, it uses information about a person to group him or her with other people who have expressed similar tastes. In contrast, the item-to-item recommender type of system groups by items, that is, items that shoppers typically buy together are grouped so that when a person expresses an interest in a particular item, the recommender system presents other similar items for the person to consider. Netflix—a movie rental and recommendation site—uses an algorithm of this type (Jian & Mackie-Mason, 2012).

Recommender systems increase a website's stickiness, which is the website's ability to keep users on the website and not leave. Hindman (2018) explains: "Sites live or die based upon their stickiness—their ability to attract readers, to make those readers stay longer when they visit, and to convince them to return again once they leave. Even slight differences in site stickiness compound quickly and rapidly create enormous differences in audience." He continues, "Recommendation systems are one of the most powerful tools available for sites to keep and grow their traffic, and those who cannot deploy them are at a profound competitive disadvantage" (p. 48).

Some recommender systems have gotten so sophisticated that marketers claim they can guess what you want before you even express it.

> Recently Amazon was awarded a patent for what it calls "anticipatory shipping." Essentially Amazon wants to start shipping you a package before you officially clicked "buy." The retailer would predict what you want before you actually buy it by relying on—what else?—digital data. Factors such as previous orders, product searches, historical purchasing behavior, demographics, and wish lists among any number of other categories of data, could help inform algorithms designed to predict your next purchase before you actually make that purchase. (DuBravac, 2015, pp. 111–112)

Gamification

Advertisers have been increasingly using games in digital media to make advertising more entertaining for their audiences (Terlutter & Capella, 2013). The use of digital games by advertisers can be organized into two categories: placing ads in existing digital games (in-game advertising) and creating new digital games for the purpose of advertising their products (advergames).

Advertisers have been placing paid messages about their products inside digital games in the form of display ads (Tuten & Solomon, 2018). These display ads include billboards, movie posters, and storefronts or simply ad space within the game screen. Some of these display ads are static, and some are dynamic. Static **in-game advertising (IGA)** is a fixed placement in the game when the game is launched, and it cannot be modified after release of the game. Static ads are hard-coded into the game and ensure that all players view the same advertising messages. The advantage is that static advertising does not need online access to broadcast the images into the game. The disadvantage is that no modifications can be made after the game has been launched. In contrast, dynamic ads are embedded into the game play of certain players whom the advertiser wants to reach and so the advertiser pays a premium for this opportunity to reach particular players. Although dynamic ads are costly, they are regarded as having higher value because they offer advertisers a higher degree of control in the targeting of special types of consumers.

From their very early stages, advertising has appeared in digital games. Arguably the first advertisement that appeared in a digital game was a self-promotional advertisement in the game Adventureland for its next game titled Pirate Adventure (1978). Since then, advertising in digital games has developed continually, and especially over the past decade advertising in digital games has evolved into an important way to communicate to the millions of people who play digital games (Terlutter & Capella, 2013). The global video game market generated more than $116 billion in revenues in

2017 and was expected to reach $125.4 billion by 2018 (Newzoo, 2017). The growing popularity of digital games has led advertisers to embrace this new opportunity to engage with potential consumers.

A particularly successful type of IGA has been in social networking sites, such as Facebook. The reasons participants engage in social network gaming include interactions with friends, relationship building, teamwork and/or competitive play, role-play identity, and escapism from reality. Due to the prevalence of social network sites, the number of users of social network games is often high. For instance, FarmVille 2 on Facebook—a digital game in which players grow and harvest crops and raise animals on a 3D farm—regularly has more than 10 million monthly active users, with more than 60 million monthly users reported in November 2012, making them obviously an interesting vehicle for advertising purposes. For instance, in FarmVille 2, players can plant blueberries by the brand Cascadian Farm (a real U.S. company that markets organic blueberry crops) on their virtual farms as opposed to the virtual blueberries. According to data presented by Zynga, the developer of FarmVille, more than 310 million Cascadian Farm organic blueberries had been planted by FarmVille players after a short time span and brand awareness for Cascadian Farm increased by 550% through product placement in this social network game (Terlutter & Capella, 2013).

Social network games typically try to incorporate friends in game play to intensify exchange within the network. In FarmVille 2, players' farming production greatly increases if they play together with their Facebook friends (for example, if they seed the organic Cascadian Farm blueberry crops together).

Advergames are distinct from IGAs, as they are games specifically designed and created to promote a brand, product, service, or idea. The main aims of advergames are to deliver a powerful message for the advertised brand and to achieve higher traffic on brand websites. Advergames are usually free of charge, downloadable from or playable on the brand's website, easy and fun to play, and offer quick rewards (Terlutter & Capella, 2013).

Advergames typically allow for short playing time as well as for longer play time and can be easily played during short breaks in the day on tablets or smartphones. Advergames have become fairly ubiquitous, and many advergames feature food products.

Native Advertising

Native advertising is the use of paid ads that emulate the look and feel of the nonadvertising content in which they are embedded. Unlike display ads or banner ads, native ads don't look like ads; instead, they typically look like news stories. Advertisers use native advertising to present their persuasive appeals without the risk of triggering defenses in audiences, that is, when audiences think that something is an advertisement message, they are more likely to ignore it or to discount its message.

The use of native advertising is older than digital media; advertisers in analog media have been using native advertising for decades. But with the recent rise in digital media, the amount of native advertising has increased greatly in popularity among advertisers (Harms, Bijmolt, & Hoekstra, 2017). In 2017, marketers spent $25.12

billion on native advertising, and were expected to spend $41.14 billion in 2019, accounting for 61.4% of total display ad spending (eMarketer, 2018).

The covert nature of native advertising has raised concerns among regulators and the public (Lee, Kim, & Ham, 2016; Wojdynski, 2016). The focus of the debate is that covert advertising could be deceptive and misleading because many consumers might not be able to identify the material as being an advertisement when it is masked as a news story. Although native advertising does require a disclosure, the use of unclear disclosure wording (e.g., "presented," "promoted," "sponsored," "suggested," and "recommended") often confuses consumers.

One form of native advertising is the **advertorial**. Advertorials are advertisements camouflaged as editorial material, such as legitimate news stories. The advantage of advertorials for advertisers is that they can fool audiences into thinking they are not ads and instead are objective presentations of accurate facts, so the audiences do not engage their defenses like they do when they recognize paid advertisements. Advertorials have been around for decades in the traditional media, but with the rise of digital media it has been even easier for advertisers to create advertorials to mislead consumers.

Effects

Even though the phenomenon of digital advertising is relatively new, there is already considerable research literature on the topic. The studies in this literature were designed to answer three questions. First, what factors can digital ads use to increase their probability of attracting audience attention? Second, what is the public reaction to digital advertising techniques? And third, among all the tools that digital media offer to advertisers, which ones have been found to be the most effective?

ATTRACTING AUDIENCE ATTENTION

Researchers have designed studies to answer this question: What factors can digital ads use to increase their probability of attracting audience attention? Almost all of these studies have found legacy effects, that is, researchers have selected factors of ads that have been effective with analog media and designed studies to see if those factors were also effective with digital ads. For example, a prevalent study with analog media has been to test whether the effectiveness of the ad varies with the size of the ad. As with tests using analog media, the findings of ad size are equivocal when tested with digital media. On one hand, larger ads have been found to enhance brand recognition and recall (e.g., Baron, Brouwer, & Garbayo, 2014). On the other hand, they are considered more intrusive and annoying, so they are more likely to be avoided (Goldstein, Suri, McAfee, Ekstrand-Abueg, & Diaz, 2014).

As consumers are often exposed repeatedly to a brand's ads, researchers have tested whether it is better to use the same ad consistently or to vary the ad. While repetition of the same ad can increase brand recall and users' intentions to click on those ads

(Yaveroglu & Donthu, 2008), frequent repetition can also increase perceived intrusiveness (Ying, Korneliussen, & Grønhaug, 2009). When advertisers vary the content of their ads so that users are not exposed to the exact same ad repeatedly, user avoidance is reduced (Kim, 2018). Also, ads have been found to be more effective when they appear in an uncluttered environment (Yaveroglu & Donthu, 2008).

Among engagement tactics, emotional appeals seem to play an important role. Research shows that effective emotional appeals tend to trigger more positive effects (Eckler & Bolls, 2011) and generate high arousal (Belanche, Flavián, & Pérez-Rueda, 2017), especially when they use humor (Campbell, Thompson, Grimm, & Robson, 2017). Furthermore, consumers are influenced by not only the level of emotions but also the dynamic variation of emotions in an ad (Teixeira, Wedel, & Pieters, 2012).

Moving away from testing legacy effects, some researchers have tested how interactivity, which is offered only by digital media, influences the effects of advertising. Siemens, Smith, and Fisher (2015) have found that digital advertising is more effective when advertisers give people more active control over their interactions on websites.

Also, unlike analog media, digital media platforms typically allow for users to post information that can be accessed by other users of those platforms. This **user-generated content (UGC)** is typically made public and is defined as "all publicly (or partially publicly) available online information initiated and/or created by end-users, as opposed to by media professionals" (Knoll, 2016, p. 284). The openness of these participatory technologies has the potential to enhance or to diminish the intended effects of advertisers' planned messages by allowing users to post their opinions that either indicate a like or dislike of the advertised products (Knoll, 2016; Liu, Burns, & Hou, 2017; Walther, DeAndrea, Kim, & Anthony, 2010). Although about 20% of social media users actively engage in creating UGC, many less active social media users are the receivers of UGC, and their brand attitudes and purchase intentions may be affected by being exposed to UGC (Jin & Phua, 2014; Knoll, 2016).

PUBLIC REACTIONS TO ADS

It is interesting to note that research has found people are less willing to tolerate advertising on digital platforms than they are in the traditional media (Logan, 2011, 2013). This leads to increased mental avoidance of online ads and a reluctance to engage with advertising messages (Baek & Morimoto, 2012). As people realize they are constantly inundated with advertising, there has been a growing awareness that personalized advertising has become increasingly intrusive and unwelcome, so many people have been installing ad-blocking software on their digital devices (Cortland, 2017; Scott, 2016). As of 2017, an estimated 615 million devices were using ad blockers, which represents more than one fifth of internet users in many countries (PageFair, 2017).

Researchers have found that the use of ad-blocking software has been motivated by several different reasons, including a desire to avoid constant interruptions (Cortland, 2017; Ghose, Singh, & Todri, 2017; Goldstein et al., 2014; Söllner & Dost, 2019), a need for people to protect themselves from invasions to their privacy (Brinson, Eastin, & Cicchirillo, 2019; Cortland, 2017; Goldfarb & Tucker, 2011), a fear that ads that may infect their devices with malware (Parra-Arnau, Achara, & Castelluccia, 2017), and a belief that blocking ads will improve performance and speed of browsing because messages without ads use less bandwidth (Parra-Arnau et al., 2017). Many digital media users experience an incentive to switch to the most effective ad blockers (Ray, Ghasemkhani, & Kannan, 2017).

The ad industry has been trying to discourage the use of ad blockers by trying to present less disruptive ads (Interactive Advertising Bureau, 2018). Many advertisers fear the proliferation of ad blockers threatens the revenue streams of many websites and raises concerns about the viability of digital advertising as a whole. Because ad blockers reduce the number of reachable consumers, they end up increasing the cost of effective ads (Dahlen & Rosengren, 2016; O'Neal, 2016). As a result, U.S. publishers and advertisers estimate that ad blockers cost them more than $28 billion in revenue in the first half of 2017, and this figure was forecast to exceed $35 billion by 2020 (Davies, 2016).

Researchers have been testing strategies to get people to avoid using ad blockers, but the findings of this research so far have not been very helpful. For example, a field experiment with 294,331 users was run to test whether banner appeals can reduce ad blocking. The results showed that these appeals reduced ad blocking among only 1% of the ad blocker users. Also, among frequent visitors who encountered repeated banner appeals, this percentage only increased to 2%. However, the repeated use of banners has led to users visiting those websites less often, which suggests a trade-off between reducing ad blocking among some users and further increasing avoidance behaviors among others.

EFFECTIVENESS

Several major reviews of the research literature on the effectiveness of digital advertising have been published. The first of these was conducted by Ha (2008), who reported that digital advertising was generally superior to analog advertising, particularly print. Then in 2019, Liu-Thompkins conducted a review of 303 articles on digital advertising published in major advertising and marketing journals since 2008 and concluded that analog advertising was a bit more effective than digital advertising, primarily because when people are online they typically pay less attention to the ads. He also concluded that there is a consensus that digital advertising produces positive returns, but the magnitude varies significantly by product category, customer segment, and ad format. Thus as the research on this topic grows, more complexity is revealed. The rest of this section will display what the research has found so far delineated by type of advertising effect, type of ad, and consumer behavior.

By Type of Advertising Effect

One key distinction among advertising effects is whether the effect is simple exposure or whether the ad triggers some form of user engagement with the ad or the product. This distinction is very important to digital advertisers because when they use an inbound advertising perspective, they need to motivate their potential customers to engage with the ads. High engagement has been shown to increase online ad effectiveness (e.g., Calder, Malthouse, & Schaedel, 2009; Teixeira et al., 2012).

Advertisers have known for years about a **mere exposure effect** (Zajonc, 1968), which is when people learn something from an ad or have their attitude about an advertised product changed even when they do not pay much—if any—attention to the ad. Just being exposed to an ad is enough to generate an effect. This legacy-type effect has been found with digital advertising where people can develop more favorable attitudes about products by simple exposure to ads even when they pay little attention to them (Goodrich, 2014; Yoo, 2009). Duff and Faber (2011) explored the boundary conditions of mere exposure effects and found this effect is less likely to occur when people are bothered by interruptions with ads and begin to actively avoid them.

Hedonic Adaptation   When we buy something new, we reset the standard we use for assessing our level of happiness. Typically, at first, we are happy when we purchase an advertised product, but this feeling of happiness erodes over time, so we experience a drive to make another purchase in order to get us back to that level of happiness. This is what psychologists call hedonic adaptation or putting people on a hedonic treadmill where we have to keep buying new things to recapture the feeling of happiness (Brooks & Lasser, 2018).

Hedonic adaptation is also explained by a social comparison mechanism. When we compare what we have with what others have, we typically feel deficient because there are others who have more than we have. This motivates us to "up our game" in order to acquire more possessions. As we acquire more and more possessions, we compare ourselves to even higher-status people who have even more possessions so that there is always a gap between what we have and what other people have; this continually perceived gap keeps us feeling unhappy (Brooks & Lasser, 2018).

Online Information Seeking   Advertisements have been found to stimulate people to go online to search for information about the products, services, and issues they see advertised. For example, Housholder, Watson, and LoRusso (2018) conducted a study of the role of political advertising in stimulating information search. They found that increased advertising volume was associated with increased online information seeking.

By Type of Ad

Researchers have tested the power of different kinds of advertising to lead to digital effects.

Online Reviews   When people go online to seek information about advertised products and services, they frequently go to sites that provide product reviews. Some of these sites display reviews of a wide variety of products from many different providers (such as Yelp and Amazon.com), while others are sites run by the companies that manufacture and/or sell the products. A problem that is slowly coming to light about these review sites is that they allow for fake reviews. There are companies that have been found to hire consumers to provide reviews of excellence for their products, even by people who are not users of those products. For example, one researcher identified more than 150 private Facebook groups where sellers openly solicited people to provide five-star reviews in exchange for receiving their product for free (Reviews, 2019, p. 33).

People are becoming aware of the potentially manipulative nature of online reviews. The more control people have over creating user-generated reviews of products online, the less credence people place in those reviews when forming impressions of the products (DeAndrea, Van Der Heide, Vendemia, & Vang, 2018). This study also found that the less people are confident that user-generated reviews are truly produced by third-party reviewers, the less people trust those reviews.

Online Searches as Advertising   As an advertising format, search advertising involves a unique combination of keyword, ranking, and bidding price considerations. On the keyword selection issue, research shows that clicks tend to be more frequent for less common and more specific keywords (Jerath, Ma, & Park, 2014; Rutz & Trusov, 2011) and for keywords containing the advertiser's name (Klapdor et al., 2015). Regarding ranking and bidding price, researchers argue that bidding a high price to gain a top position may not always be wise. Although a higher position can increase clicks, the increase in clicks may not be enough to cover the increase in cost incurred when paying for search rankings (e.g., Xu, Chen, & Whinston, 2011). Furthermore, findings are conflicted on whether a higher search result ranking increases (Rutz, Bucklin, & Sonnier, 2012) or decreases (Xu, Chen, & Whinston, 2011) the rate at which consumers end up visiting a company's website. The success of search engine optimization techniques depends in large part on what competitors are doing to optimize internet searches in their favor (e.g., Chiou & Tucker, 2012; Simonov, Nosko, & Rao, 2018).

Gaming   Advertisers weave their brands into the entertainment context of games, aiming to create a strong emotional and psychological connection with the consumer and to increase retention. Many game components can influence consumer response, such as game reward structure, visual design, and narrative story (Hofacker, Ruyter, Lurie, Manchanda, & Donaldson, 2016).

Research has generally pointed to a positive effect on attitude toward in-game advertising (IGA; Winkler & Buckner, 2006), attitude toward the brand (Glass, 2007), and purchase intention (Adis & Jun, 2013). When looking at cognitive outcomes, a meta-analysis found an overall positive association of IGA with recall that was sensitive to factors such as brand familiarity (Gross, 2010), brand prominence (Van Reijmersdal, Rozendaal, & Buijzen, 2012), difficulty level of the game (Dardis et al., 2015), and product–game congruence, with incongruent or less fitting advertising resulting in higher recall levels (Vermeir, Kazakova, Tessitore, Cauberghe, & Slabbinck, 2015). Recently, Vyvey, Castellar, and Van Looy (2018) conducted a between-subjects experiment (N = 561) and found that the more feedback (visual and auditory) that was provided to players, the more those players enjoyed the game and the more likely they were to recall the brand being advertised. Also, players experienced more enjoyment when the character's facial expression, vocal sounds, and a progress bar confirmed their achievements.

eWOM   Moran and Muzellec (2017) reviewed the empirical literature on electronic word of mouth (eWOM) and found that judgments of the degree of credibility of eWOM were related to how much respondents rated the credibility of both the source of the information and the message itself. They found that the credibility of the source was influenced by how closely the receiver was tied to the sender through a sense of shared community. They also found that users' judgments about how competent advertising sources were was related to their prior experience with the product.

Jorgensen and Ha (2019) conducted a study to investigate the inclusion of eWOM on SNSs and found that women relied more often on family members and eWOM on SNSs to gain product information and that women also had more positive attitudes toward products reviewed on SNSs.

Native Advertising   Jung and Heo (2019) conducted a study to investigate how ad disclosure and ad recognition predict the effectiveness of native advertising. Two experimental studies revealed that users' evaluation of a natively formatted ad was influenced by knowledge of social media advertising tactics and ad recognition, rather than the explicitness of ad disclosure.

Advertorials   Kim and Hancock (2017) found that advertorials were less likely to trigger advertising schema, especially consumer awareness of persuasive intent. And when people fail to use an advertising schema to process information from advertorials, they are more likely to be influenced to develop more positive attitudes toward advertorials than they did toward traditional advertisements due to decreased awareness of persuasive intent.

Personalization   Personalized advertising is widely believed to be an effective persuasion strategy. Personalization enhances advertising effectiveness by increasing personal relevance, reducing ad skepticism, and inducing more attentive processing (Baek & Morimoto, 2012; Maslowska, Smit, & van den Putte, 2016; Sahni, Wheeler, & Chintagunta, 2018).

Research has shown that a personalization strategy can have a significant positive impact on both advertiser revenue and consumer welfare (Song & Mela, 2011). But its effectiveness tends to decrease as consumers get closer to a purchase decision, suggesting a higher impact when information is the main goal (Bleier & Esenbeiss, 2015). The effectiveness of personalization is also contingent on other executional elements of an ad, such as its visibility (Goldfarb & Tucker, 2011) and content (Bruce, Murthi, & Rao, 2017). However, the rapid pace at which advertising personalization has grown in both volume and accuracy has not gone unnoticed by consumers, with most indicating disapproval of this practice (Aguirre, Mahr, Grewal, de Ruyter, & Wetzels, 2015; Turow, Hennessy, & Draper, 2015).

A typical personalized advertising process consists of two phases: The message sender first "learns" the message receiver's preferences and then "matches" the message to that person according to his or her preferences. While this sounds good, the research does not show that this technique is always successful, because the technique is built on assumptions that an individual's preferences are always stable (i.e., preferences remain the same over time) and that they are relatively extreme (i.e., preferences are highly polarized). For example, Li, Liu, and Hong (2019) tested these assumptions in a 2 (message type: personalized versus nonpersonalized) × 2 (preference stability: high versus low) × 2 (preference extremity: high versus low) between-participants experiment. They found little support for the assumptions.

Congruence   The effect of a digital ad depends on its context, that is, when an ad is placed in a message that presents information on the same topic as the product in the ad, the ad is generally more effective (Yaveroglu & Donthu, 2008; Yoo, 2009). However, more recent research shows that congruence effects are sensitive to other factors, such as how arousing an ad is (Belanche et al., 2017), the position of the ad on the screen (Li & Lo, 2015), and the relevance of the ad to consumers' goals (van't Riet et al., 2016; Zanjani, Diamond, & Chan, 2011). Furthermore, congruence interacts with creative elements such as ad complexity to determine their effects (Chun, Song, Hollenbeck, & Lee, 2014). Besides congruence, other contextual characteristics have also been examined, including contextual arousal (e.g., Duff & Sar, 2015), ad clutter (Yaveroglu & Donthu, 2008), and contextual valence (Yoo & Eastin, 2017).

By Consumer Behavior

In addition to variation of effect types and types of ads, the research examining the effectiveness of digital advertising has been found to be influenced by consumer behaviors.

Consumer Location   Research on location effects shows that mobile ads thematically relevant to the consumer's present location and goal lead to more purchases than those not congruent with the location (Grewal, Bart, Spann, & Zubcsek, 2016; van't Riet et al., 2016). This is even true for ads delivered to consumers near a competitor's location if a deep discount is offered (Fong, Zheng, & Luo, 2015). As further support for the importance of location, Zubcsek, Katona, and Sarvary (2017) have shown that consumers at the same location tend to respond to ads similarly, suggesting some underlying homogeneity attributable to location. Similar conclusions can be drawn from Goh, Chu, and Wu (2015), where consumer searches after receiving mobile ads about an event varied systematically based on their spatial distance to the event.

Multiscreening   Multiscreening is a form of media multitasking in which multiple screens are used at the same time. The key characteristics of multiscreening are that two visual tasks are combined with some temporal overlap and that visual attention must be divided between those two tasks/screens (Segijn, Voorveld, Pennekamp, & Smit, 2017). A recent Nielsen (2018) report indicated that 45% of U.S. respondents use a digital device very often or always while watching television.

Broadly speaking, studies of multiscreening and advertising effectiveness can be divided into those that examine cognitive advertising outcomes, such as brand and ad recall or recognition (e.g., Angell, Gorton, Sauer, Bottomley, & White, 2016; Duff & Sar, 2015), and those that consider affective advertising outcomes, such as brand attitude, purchase intention, or ad irritation (e.g., Beuckels, Cauberghe, & Hudders, 2017; Chinchanachokchai, Duff, & Sar, 2015; Segijn, Voorveld, & Smit, 2016).

Segijn and Eisend (2019) conducted a meta-analysis into multiscreening and advertising effectiveness. They found a negative direct effect of multiscreening on cognitive outcomes, but the results show no direct or total effect of multiscreening on affective advertising outcomes, but this again depends on various media-, advertising-, and research-related factors. Finally, the results show that attention, enjoyment, and resistance constitute the underlying mechanisms that explain the effect of multiscreening on memory and persuasion.

Conclusions

With the rise of digital media, much of advertising has changed from using an outbound perspective with a push orientation to using an inbound perspective with a pull orientation. This shift has enabled advertisers to become more effective in identifying potential customers and then guiding them through a buying funnel to convert them into users who will repeatedly use their products and services. It has also given them more efficiency by allowing them to focus their resources on people with the highest interest in and needs for their products.

This shift to digital media has opened up new opportunities for advertisers to get their messages to their prospective customers through the use of online searching, online personalization, social influencers, ratings services, recommender systems, electronic word of mouth, gaming, and native advertising. These new opportunities have stimulated researchers to examine which of these techniques are most effective as advertising tools.

Researchers who have tested for the effects of digital media have found that many of the test findings of advertising with analog media are the same, that is, there are many legacy effects. However, researchers have also found many unique effects of digital advertising due to the effectiveness of many tools that digital media offer advertisers. Because many of these tools give digital advertisers more ways of exerting their persuasive influence on people, the general population is noticing more ads and is expressing negative opinions about this intrusion of advertising messages as well as engaging in behaviors to avoid these messages. However, as more research is conducted, it is likely that digital advertising will be found to be more effective than analog advertising because it is more immediate, is more personalized, and allows people to interact with advertisers in a way that meets their needs more efficiently.

CHAPTER 6

Effects of Exposure to Digital Entertainment

The rise of digital media has had less impact on changing entertainment content—if we think of entertainment primarily as telling fictional stories—than it has had on the content types of news and advertising. While it has not fundamentally changed the way stories are told in the media, it has served to remove some of the constraints that entertainment has been subjected to in analog media.

This chapter begins with an exploration of the nature of entertainment storytelling in the media; then it shows how the rise of digital media has relaxed some of the constraints on storytelling that have been imposed by analog media. The chapter concludes with an overview of research on the current nature of media entertainment.

Entertainment Storytelling in the Media

Humans have been telling stories for more than 100,000 years. Haven (2007) points out that "every culture in the history of this planet has created stories: myths, fables, legends, folk tales" (p. 4). He says that not all cultures have created a written language, not all cultures have developed codified laws, and not all cultures have created logical argumentation, but all cultures have developed and used stories. What makes stories so useful for humans is that they are entertaining vehicles for communicating meaning. This communication of meaning depends on sharing a general story formula.

GENERAL STORYTELLING FORMULA

The general **story formula** serves as a guide for both storytellers and audiences. The formula helps storytellers navigate the process of making decisions as they select story elements and structure those selections into a meaningful sequence. Also, the formula helps audiences quickly process their perceptions about characters and efficiently follow the unfolding action.

The general storytelling formula presents guidelines about how to attract an audience, how to hold an audience's attention while the story unfolds so that the audience is pulled into the action and forms virtual relationships with the story's characters, and how to resolve the action with a satisfying conclusion. All entertainment stories are narratives that start with a generating circumstance where characters find themselves in some sort of a conflict situation. Characters can experience conflict with another character, with themselves, with an institution (such as the criminal justice system or religion), with society in general, or with ideas. As characters struggle to overcome obstacles along the path of achieving what they want, the conflict is heightened throughout the story to a point of climax where the conflict is resolved either by the character finally solving the problem that is causing the conflict or by the character adapting to the conflict in some way.

Thus the general storytelling formula exhibits three essential principles. First, all stories must generate conflict. This pulls audiences into the action, and people continue to follow the story to see how the conflict will be resolved. Second, all stories must be told through the point of view of a character. Producers of entertainment messages know that they must stimulate audiences to identify with a character so each audience member can experience the action through a particular character's point of view. Third, all stories need to trigger emotions in the audience; the more vivid the elements in the story, the more likely it is that strong emotions will be generated. The most successful storytellers are those who can trigger the strongest emotional reactions (fear, anger, lust, and laughter) repeatedly in their audiences. The emotional journey is the payoff for audiences that seek entertainment. The stronger the emotions, the more pleasurable the experience is for audiences and the more likely audience members will stay with the story to find out what happens.

Stories that conform to the formulas the closest usually have the largest audiences, because they are the easiest to follow. The more experience we have with entertainment messages, the more we learn about and rely on story formulas. We are conditioned to expect certain plot points, certain pacing, certain types of characters, and certain themes.

It is helpful to think of the general storytelling formula as the trunk of a tree. The tree has branches where additional storytelling guidelines are added to the general storytelling formula. Each branch is a different genre of story, such as mystery, action/adventure, romance, and comedy. Each of these major branches has its own sub-branches, and each of these has its own sub-sub-branches and twigs until we get out to the leaves, which are the different individual stories. Thus each individual story is a product of how a story producer has worked his or her way through all the design decisions from the trunk outward.

GENRES

To explain how the branches each add additional elements to the general storytelling formula, let's examine the genres of comedy, drama, and romance.

Comedy

With the comedy formula, minor conflict situations flare up and set the action in motion. The conflict is heightened verbally, usually through deceit or insults. Characters are developed by showing their idiosyncrasies and quick wit. The action is neatly resolved at the end of the show, and all the main characters end up happy, because the tension created by their problems has been eliminated, or at least significantly reduced.

One subgenre of comedy is the character comedy or comedy of manners. Here the humor arises out of character quirks that illuminate the craziness of everyday situations. Characters find themselves in difficult situations that we all encounter every day. As characters try to work their way through these situations, the absurdity of certain social conventions is illustrated, and this makes us laugh. Examples include *Seinfeld* and *The Big Bang Theory*. Another subgenre is the put-down comedy, where certain characters have power over other characters and exercise that power in humorous ways. Examples include *Two and a Half Men* and *The Office*.

Drama

Entertainment stories in the drama genre introduce a protagonist who is quickly put into a serious conflict situation. As the audience experiences the unfolding action through the eyes of the protagonist, the conflict grows progressively more serious until it reaches a climax where the protagonist resolves the action in some way.

The drama genre has three basic subgenres that illuminate three types of drama entertainment: tragedy, mystery, and action/horror (Sayre & King, 2003). Tragedy features a protagonist who is perceived by the audience as noble and good. However, bad things happen to protagonists either because they have a fatal flaw they cannot get around (as is the case in Shakespearean tragedies) or because fate has conspired to do them in, such as what happens in the movie *Titanic*). What audiences enjoy about tragedies is the opportunity to compare themselves with the tragic characters and feel better off than those unfortunate characters.

With the mystery formula, an important element of the plot is missing. For example, in a "whodunit" mystery, the *who* is missing. A serious crime usually triggers the story, and a focal character (usually a police detective or private investigator) must uncover information in order to figure out who committed the crime. Audiences are drawn into the story as they try to solve the mystery for themselves. In her book *Talking About Detective Fiction*, the best-selling novelist P. D. James (2009) says that "the formula for a successful detective story is 50 percent good detection, 25 percent character and 25 percent what the writer knows best" (p. 115).

The action/horror formula is primarily plot driven as good and evil fight it out in ever-deepening conflict. Characters are stereotypes or comic book types. Within a few seconds after being introduced to a character, we know whether that character is a hero or a villain. Characters are static and don't change. The plot relies on fast-paced action that maximizes arousal in the audience. The primary emotions evoked are fear, suspense, and vengeance. Violence is a staple in almost all of these stories. The formula of violence tells us that it is okay for criminals to behave violently throughout a program as long as they are caught at the end of the story. This restores a sense of peace, signaling the end of the story.

Romance

A romance story begins with a person experiencing either loneliness from a lack of a relationship or a relationship that is bad due to betrayal, jealousy, or fear. As audience members, we are led to identify with the main character and feel her pain. But she is full of hope for what seems like an unattainable goal. Through hard work and virtue, she gets closer and closer to her goal—even though she experiences frequent heartrending setbacks—until the story climaxes with the fulfillment of the goal, which transmits intensely pleasurable emotions to the audience.

Writers who have mastered this romance formula are very successful. For example, among all paperback fiction sold in the United States, about half is in the genre of the romance novel. One romance novelist who really understood the formula was Barbara Cartland. She published 723 romance novels, all following the same basic romance formula. Did she produce a body of great literature that will be read for centuries? No, of course not. Did she recognize a market for a particular kind of story and manufactured many products to meet that need? Her sales of almost 1 billion books indicates she did.

After years of watching stories on television and in the movies, we have become adept at following the formulas about characters, plots, and themes. We know these formulas so well that many of us think we can write and produce our own entertainment shows. Perhaps some of us can, but producing a successful entertainment message for mass media is very challenging. While the formulas are deceptively simple, making them work well is difficult.

MEDIA CONVENTIONS

The traditional media (especially broadcast TV and Hollywood films) have a strong motivation to attract large audiences to their entertainment messages. Thus they design messages to appeal to all kinds of people without offending anyone. The public has certain expectations about what it will and will not tolerate in entertainment. We can see where this line of acceptability is when the public gets offended and complains — particularly in the areas of bad language, sexual portrayals, and violence. Television programmers are essentially conservative and fearful of offending viewers, so they present content that they believe reflects mainstream American values.

This line of acceptability, however, changes over time as people get over their shock at a new kind of portrayal, and then eventually get used to it. For example, writing in the late 1980s, George Comstock (1989) pointed out that much of what was on commercial television at that time

> would not have been considered acceptable by broadcasters or the public 20 or even 10 years ago. Public tastes and social standards have changed, and television has made some contribution to these changes by probing the borders of convention accompanying each season. . . . These conventions of popular entertainment provide television, as they do other media, with rules that minimize the possibility of public offense. (p. 182)

Since Comstock wrote that, commercial television has continued to push the line of public acceptance, and what offended viewers in the 1980s (especially with language and sexual situations) hardly bothers them today.

Producers of entertainment messages realize they are taking on a huge risk, because using the media to tell entertainment stories typically consumes a great deal of resources, and the chance of earning back one's initial investment is very small. If they choose stories that are too standard and formulaic, they risk boring viewers who will not return to view subsequent episodes in a series. But on the other hand, if they break with the formulas too much, they risk confusing viewers or, worse, offending them.

When TV programmers guess right about breaking with entertainment formulas, they can attract fairly large audiences. The Fox television network rose to prominence in the 1990s by pushing the envelope of acceptability in TV storytelling with shows such as *When Good Pets Go Bad*, *World's Scariest Police Shootouts*, and *Who Wants to Marry a Multimillionaire?* While these shows drew a lot of criticism, they also attracted large audiences, and Fox grew to rival the big three dominant TV networks (ABC, CBS, and NBC) at the time.

MEDIUM CONVENTIONS

Telling an entertaining story presents a different challenge as you move from one analog medium to another. If you plan to tell a story in print, you have only one perceptual channel (eyes), and you need to use words to trigger vivid images in the minds of the readers. If you plan to tell a story in song, you again need to trigger vivid images and strong emotions, but you must do this through the audience's ears, not their eyes. With a song, you need to use words that sound good, not just look good. That is, the words must have a certain cadence that goes along with the rhythm of the music. Often the song has a rhyming pattern, which also presents a special challenge to songwriters. With popular music, words must tell their full story in about 3 minutes.

Commercial television is one of the most challenging media for telling stories. At first, it might seem the least challenging because it appears to have few perceptual constraints; that is, you can use audio as well as video elements. Also, you are not dependent on the reading abilities of audience members. However, it is very difficult to attract an audience on commercial television because there is so much competition for the audience's attention. Also, it is a huge challenge to hold onto an audience once it is initially attracted because commercial television interrupts stories frequently for commercials, and some of these breaks have a dozen or more ads and last for 4 or more minutes. Viewers can forget about the story or lose their motivation to stay tuned unless that story has really hooked them. Therefore, storytellers on television must do things to catch the audience's interest right from the beginning; they must build the action to a high point before each commercial break so that the audience will want to stay tuned throughout the commercial pod and find out what happens when the show returns, and they must keep the action interesting every minute so that people who are flipping through channels will want to stop and watch the show.

With television programs, not only must producers use the well-known formulas, but also they must be creative enough to break with the story formula to keep their stories fresh for viewers who have seen the same plot hundreds of times. These two tasks are extremely difficult to achieve at the same time, and this is why the percentage of television series that have lasted more than several dozen episodes is tiny.

TV programmers are usually very conservative with risk and typically force others to share the risk with them. For example, the major television networks have developed payment conventions that force producers to attract large audiences if they want to make money by paying only about 80% of production costs for new shows. To illustrate, let's say you have developed a new television show and the audience loved the pilot. The network contracts with you to produce a full season of 22 episodes. At this point you would be feeling extremely successful, because few producers are offered such an opportunity compared to the thousands of producers who are constantly pitching story ideas to network programmers. However, you are still facing a huge challenge. It will cost you about $40 million to produce those 22 episodes. Because the network pays a fee of only about 80%, you will lose about $8 million by the end of that season. If your show is cancelled after one season, you have a huge loss. So you feel a high degree of pressure to attract a large enough audience so that your contract will be renewed for a second season. If you are able to do this, you have the power to negotiate a much more favorable contract and you will start to make money. And the more times you get your show renewed for an additional season, the more you are demonstrating your ability to attract a large audience, and the more money you make.

Hollywood films are another very challenging medium because they cost so much to produce, and the risk of failure is so great with more than 90% of all Hollywood films failing to earn back their basic production costs at the box office. Producers continually analyze the most successful movies to try to find the magic formulas that made them so successful. For example, screenwriter Sue Clayton analyzed successful and unsuccessful Hollywood films to try to figure out which elements are most associated with success. From this analysis, she discovered a formula, which she calls the genetic blueprint for a successful movie. This blueprint calls for 30% action, 17% comedy, 13% good versus evil, 12% love/sex/romance, 10% special effects, 10% plot, and 8% music. This formula shows that *Titanic* and *Toy Story 2* were perfect movies (Baker, 2003). It is doubtful that we could ever reduce the formula for a successful movie or story to a precise mathematical formula, although there are many people who continue to try to do just that. It is important for you to realize that while there are many story formulas, they are not strict rules that always lead to success. Instead, they are guidelines that require creative interpretation to apply in order for producers to be successful in using them to attract large audiences.

Digital Media Relax Constraints

While entertainment storytellers who use digital media need to work from the traditional storytelling formulas, they also have some opportunities that storytellers using analog media do not have. That is, digital media have relaxed some of the constraints that analog media impose.

TIME

One of these constraints is time. Analog media have standard time limits for stories. For example, the convention for the medium of movies is about a 2-hour limit, and the convention for television is set by half hour and hour limits. And most songs broadcast on radio or sold as recordings have about a 3-minute limit. While many digital storytellers conform to these limits out of respect for audience expectations and habits, they are free to choose any time span they feel would best suit the effectiveness of their storytelling.

QUALITY

A second constraint that is relaxed with digital media is quality as evaluated by gatekeepers. Because digital media offer a wide variety of platforms for storytellers to upload their stories and share them directly with audiences, there is much less monitoring of quality and filtering out those offerings that do not meet a standard maintained by gatekeepers.

AVOIDING OFFENSE

A third constraint that is relaxed with digital media is the need to avoid offending potential audience members. The digitization of media messages has been altering the nature of entertainment in several important ways. Recall from the discussion above that two essential characteristics of entertainment in the traditional media were the importance of story and the need to attract large audiences. With digital media, story is still important, but the way media businesses attract large audiences has changed. With traditional media, producers of entertainment messages had to design their offerings to attract a large audience with a single message, so they were careful to build in message elements to appeal to many different kinds of audience members and avoid including any element that would offend any audience member. Each message had to be designed to appeal to broad audiences.

Digital media platforms, in contrast, offer many different entertainment messages, each designed to appeal to a different kind of audience. So while each digital message might attract a relatively small niche audience, the sum of all those niche audiences adds up to a very large number. Digital media attract very large audiences in total by providing many different kinds of entertainment messages, each specially designed to satisfy a different audience need for entertainment. Thus the variety and diversity across the range of entertainment messages are broader than they have ever been.

Entertainment With Digital Media

This diversity of entertainment messages is enhanced by the interactive feature of digital media. Digitization of media messages has made it easy for anyone to create their own videos and then upload them to an entertainment platform where large numbers of people can stream their videos. This has led to the creation of two types of entertainment platforms for digital media: producer created and interactive.

PRODUCER CREATED

Digital platforms with producer-created content (Netflix, Hulu, Amazon Prime, and others) arose in the late 1990s to give people more control over their entertainment exposures. These platforms give people the ability to watch what they want when they want and at their own pace. No longer do people have to arrange their schedules to begin their exposure to a particular entertainment program at the same time as everyone else. In contrast, digital platforms give each person the opportunity to select a different show and begin watching that show at a different time and at a different rate (pausing the stream whenever they want to take a break). Now we have entertainment services that offer thousands of programs to subscribers for streaming at our convenience.

Entertainment messages on the web (such as videos on Netflix, Hulu, and Amazon Prime) do not have the constraints of timing (they can be any length and accessed at any time) that videos on analog television channels have. However, digital messages face a great deal more competition.

Netflix

Founded in 1997, Netflix began as a mail-order provider of entertainment DVDs for rental or sale. Since then it has evolved to be a provider of video on demand by streaming from its huge library of television shows and movies. In 2012, it began producing its own original entertainment programming, and by 2016 it was producing more than 125 original series and films per year. It has grown to be the world's largest provider of entertainment with more than 148 million paid subscribers across 190 countries as of 2019. Netflix changes its set of offerings each month with about 7,300 television shows and about 5,500 movies being offered for streaming.

The huge scale of their business presents Netflix with two challenges. One challenge is to figure out what entertainment to provide to millions of subscribers worldwide, and the other challenge is to help their subscribers navigate through the overwhelming number of choices that Netflix offers.

Providing entertainment choices has always been a major challenge for entertainment providers. DuBravac (2015) explains that companies that produced entertainment content used to conduct focus groups to pilot test ideas for entertainment messages in order to find out what would appeal to the average person. The problems with focus groups are that they are expensive and that respondents' comments may be influenced by what they perceive as the demands of the research. That is, when focus groups are assembled, the participants are in a room with a group of strangers and a researcher who asks about what they like about a particular entertainment message; participants find this setting artificial, which could influence how they respond.

Now entertainment message providers monitor social networking sites to determine continuously what people like about particular entertainment messages and what they expect to see next. DuBravac (2015) says,

> Creators are going to want to be as close to their viewers' thoughts as possible—not just to determine if what they've done is working but also, as we have seen, to determine the future direction of the show. . . . The wall separating creators from viewers is getting thinner and more transparent every year. There will come a day when the wall disappears entirely and viewers will be taking an active role in the direction of their favorite shows. (p. 200)

Another challenge for these digital platforms is to help users navigate the choices. When subscribers sign in to Netflix, they have thousands of choices of entertainment messages to stream. This amount of choice is overwhelming, so Netflix has tried to help individuals make their choices more efficiently by showing them a small set of recommendations. Each individual subscriber is shown a different set of recommendations based on their personal preferences as computed by a recommendation algorithm. This algorithm takes into consideration a wide variety of information about each individual. DuBravac (2015) explains that today Netflix offers recommendations of movies you might like based upon some basic demographic details it has about you combined with your viewing habits and the viewing habits of its millions of other users. . . . But this is just the beginning. As we increasingly digitize our physical space, the number of inputs into these recommendation and discovery engines increases exponentially. . . . Now imagine that the Netflix home screen taps into other data sources in addition to your viewing habits. Perhaps it can also see the viewing habits of your friends by identifying them through their phones (which have the Netflix app). It can pull data from the camera built into the bezel of your television and know how many people are in the room. It can see if you are lying down or standing up. It can pull weather-related data from your home's thermostat. It might pull very personal information about you and your friends using your fitness trackers, such as how active you've been today. It might use heart rate and blood pressure to determine if you are excited or depressed. Then pulling in all of these diverse digital streams of data, it might be able to make movie recommendations that fit the people in the room and conform to your environment. (pp. 200–201)

Amazon Prime

Amazon.com launched a service called Amazon Unbox in 2006, which was rebranded several times until it is now a video-on-demand streaming service available to Prime subscribers to its retailing website. Initially it bought its content from major entertainment providers, but since 2013, it has also been producing original content. By 2019, it had grown to more than 100 million subscribers.

Hulu

Hulu was launched in 2010 as a joint venture by two huge media companies—News Corp. and NBC Universal—but is now owned primarily by the Walt Disney Company. Hulu currently has about 28 million subscribers in the United States and an additional 70 million in other countries.

INTERACTIVE PLATFORMS

There are many websites where users can upload their own videos and download the videos of others. These videos exhibit a huge range in length (from a few seconds to a few hours), topics, and quality. The range is so enormous that it is impossible to detect any dominant patterns in terms of settings, characters, or plots. In short, there are many stories now available for any entertainment need.

Sharing Videos

The most popular interactive video site is YouTube, which was created in February 2005; the first YouTube video was uploaded in April, and the site was opened to the public in November of that year. By July 2006, the company announced that more than 65,000 new videos were being uploaded every day, and that the site was receiving 100 million video views per day. By 2007, YouTube consumed as much bandwidth as the entire internet consumed in 2000. And by 2018, YouTube was reporting more than 1.6 billion unique visitors per month; users were viewing more than 5 billion videos every day; and users were uploading more than 100 hours of new video every minute (Aslam, 2018).

Kevin Allocca, who is YouTube's head of culture and trends, says,

> YouTube is a kind of experiment in human expression, and none of it by design, really. YouTube's founders, and the many employees who have since followed in their footsteps, did not adhere to a carefully plotted plan, but rather worked to magnify the behaviors and interests of those who used the service. In other words, the experience you have on YouTube has been shaped directly by our individual and collective activity. . . . When you upload a video file, YouTube's servers process the video by breaking it up into pieces and transcoding it into an array of different formats optimized for different screen sizes and connection speeds. Watching a video on a 4K television, a laptop with a high-speed connection, or a phone in a rural area could all require different types of video files. These files then get replicated and stored on servers all over the world so that someone watching "Double Rainbow" in Johannesburg does not need to access the same video file as a person watching "Double Rainbow" in Los Angeles. The more popular the video is, the more times it gets copied to all these different locations, meaning that for any popular video there might be a thousand instances of it out there in the world. So in that sense, YouTube videos are, quite literally, all around us. (Allocca, 2018, pp. 6, 10)

When you get onto YouTube, the home screen shows you a bunch of videos that you can watch. Out of the hundreds of millions of videos that have been uploaded to YouTube, how does the company decide which videos to present on the home screen? The answer is that it uses algorithms to tell it which videos are trending and lists those. Allocca (2018) says, "On YouTube, it's the audience's curiosities that drive the programming. It's the audience's needs that determine the most valuable moments" (Allocca, 2018, p. 168). Allocca (2018) explains that YouTube uses machine learning that allows computers "to draw conclusions based on historical patterns and statistics without needing to be explicitly programmed. Machine learning allows Google to take large, complex sets of data and make predictions or decisions that improve our experience, from the relevance of search results to the automatic organization of our photos. At YouTube, machine learning works to serve" the philosophy of giving people what they want (Allocca, 2018, p. 11). "Traditional media conditioned us to believe that the majority of people would be perfectly happy watching exactly the same things as one another, but YouTube has largely taught us otherwise" (Allocca, 2018, p. 11).

What makes a YouTube video successful? Allocca (2018) explains,

> When you give people something capable of suiting a multitude of unique purposes, it can be hard to predict how they'll use it. From the start, You-

> Tube's founders decided to let the people who used the platform define it.
> YouTube has been designed to adapt to how we use it in the moment, rather
> than how we have used it in the past or how we might be expected to use it.
> An infrastructure that lets anyone anywhere post and watch videos capital-
> izes on an unparalleled diversity of interests and perspectives, upending our
> traditional assumptions of how media works. (p. 14)

Allocca continues,

> There are many examples on YouTube where a piece of media derives its value
> from its plasticity. The answer to why this video or that meme is popular
> might have much less to do with any artistic quality and more to do with
> how flexible it can be as a vehicle for our participation. These are the clips
> and images that gain popularity not because they necessarily resonate with the
> audience artistically but because they turn the audience into artists too. It's
> actually not until the crowd becomes involved and participates that the work
> gains any real value at all. . . . To me "viral" means, quite simply, the quality
> of being primarily distributed through interaction. What that means is that
> whether something is viral is not a function of the number of views it receives,
> but rather of how people are coming across it. (Allocca, 2018, pp. 61, 227)

He lists the elements of virality as participation, unexpectedness, accelerators (the
presence of people, mechanisms, or organizations that rapidly accelerate the spread of
something), and transfer of power.

Sharing Music

People have been acquiring music through sharing networks since the software Napster
became available in 1999. A computer hacker named Shawn Fanning created Napster
as a file-sharing software program while he was a student at Northeastern University in
Boston. Napster was released in June 1999, and within a year, the software had been
downloaded by 70 million people who used it primarily to share their owned music
with other people. Napster used centralized file directories on the internet to connect
users to music files on thousands of individual computers, thus enabling any user to
download virtually any recorded music in existence for free.

In December 1999, the Recording Industry Association of America (RIAA) sued
Napster on the grounds that this music-sharing service allowed piracy of copyrighted
music. The RIAA eventually succeeded in shutting Napster down in July 2001. While
sharing music for free on internet sites has changed quite a bit since Napster was
closed, there are still many sites available for this service. Some of these sites are FMA,
Noisetrade, Musopen, Jamendo, and SoundCloud. The music industry has over time
adapted its perspective on sharing music without payment from privacy to a marketing
perspective. That is, when consumers have free access to some music, this can prime
the pump for greater sales.

Also, there has been a shift away from consumers purchasing physical recordings
(i.e., CDs) to downloading and streaming services. Sales of music on physical media
declined from 800 million units in 2004 to fewer than 400 million units in 2008, but

over that same period the total units of music purchased still grew—due to downloading and streaming from iTunes, Spotify, and Pandora. Now anyone has access to more than 20 million songs on services like Spotify and Rhapsody (Brynjolfsson & McAfee, 2014). Revenues generated by legal downloads and streaming of media content including music, video, and books were $24.9 billion in 2018 and are expected to increase to more than $40 billion by 2023 (Marketline.com, 2019).

Research on Media Entertainment

The research into media entertainment has typically been focused on two topics. One of these topics is documenting patterns of content in entertainment. The other topic is the effects from exposure to these patterns of content.

CONTENT RESEARCH

Until the 1990s, traditional media dominated with entertainment content. And up until that time, researchers believed that entertainment content followed standard formulas, so they could analyze a sample of entertainment messages and be able to document patterns that they could generalize to all entertainment messages. For example, researchers who were interested in documenting gender patterns in entertainment media would sample some shows in prime-time commercial television to determine what proportion of characters were males and what proportion were females and then generalize those proportions to all entertainment TV. Researchers would use a methodology called "content analysis," which is a scientific technique of counting occurrences of various things (e.g., characters' gender, age, ethnicity, and occupations). The ability of content analysts to generalize the patterns they find in their samples to the larger population of all TV shows relies on those samples of shows being representative of the shows in the larger populations of all shows. Until around the end of the twentieth century, the population of videos in the media was relatively finite, so researchers could identify the full population of videos and draw a random sample from that population. For example, in the early days of TV broadcasting, content analysts knew that more than 95% of all TV viewing was on shows offered by the three broadcast networks (ABC, CBS, and NBC). So if they sampled from the shows broadcast by those three networks, they could construct a sample that was representative of the total set of all video stories that Americans were watching. But over time, the number of outlets that Americans could use to access videos expanded as the number of cable channels increased into the hundreds. In the mid-1990s when researchers wanted to examine patterns of violence across all videos that Americans were being exposed to, they needed to select programs from 23 TV channels in order to create a sample that was reasonably representative of all the videos being presented to Americans (National Television Violence Study, 1999). Since then the number of videos available for entertainment viewing has increased to an amount that makes it almost impossible to construct a manageable sample of videos that could adequately represent all videos that are now available. Now the four TV broadcast networks (CBS, NBC, Fox, and ABC) each attract an average of only 1% of the viewing audience for their entertainment shows. If researchers wanted to conduct a content analysis now that could document patterns across the entire video landscape, they would have to include more than a hundred TV channels in their sample, which no one has attempted to do. Furthermore, they would have to sample videos from video-on-demand providers (e.g., Netflix and Hulu) and platforms that allow anyone to upload videos (e.g., YouTube). Now more than two decades into the new millennium, researchers can no longer construct samples of videos that would reflect the entire video entertainment landscape; instead, researchers are limited to examining only tiny slivers of the video universe. Content analyses now have a much narrower scope, such as examining body image themes in rap music videos (Zhang, Dixon, & Conrad, 2010), indirect aggression in animated Disney films (Coyne & Whitehead, 2008), or how characters on two TV series talk about gender (Van Damme, 2010).

It is still useful, however, for you to understand the dominant patterns that content analysts found in the past. This will sensitize you to issues about gender and ethnic equality or representation, about the prevalence of antisocial behaviors, and about the underlying values that may still be influencing media content. Most of these content analyses were conducted on network prime-time television entertainment programming from the 1960s to the 1990s, where researchers consistently found patterns of demographic imbalance as well as high rates of sexual portrayals and violence.

As for demographics, males were consistently found to be featured in entertainment stories much more than females and that when females were featured, they were shown as either mother figures or sex objects. As for ethnicity, 80% of all characters were White Americans. African Americans comprised only 2% of television characters until the late 1960s, when they portrayed about 10% of all characters. By the 1990s, African Americans had accounted for about 16% of the main and minor roles, which was higher than their percentage (12%) in the real-world population of the United States. Hispanics, however, did not fare as well. Although Hispanics made up about 9% of the U.S. population at the time, only about 2% of all television characters were Hispanic.

With the demographic of age, three quarters of all television characters were between the ages of 20 and 50, but in the real world, only one third of the population is between these ages. Young children and the elderly were continually underrepresented in television entertainment. Fictional characters younger than age 19 typically made up only 10% of the total television population, even though they made up one third of the U.S. population. Also, characters older than age 50 accounted for about 15% of all television characters.

The marital status was obvious with about 80% of the women but only about 45% of the men. Of those for whom you could tell their marital status, more than 50% of the women were married, whereas less than one-third of the men were married. This indicated that in television entertainment, women were identified through their personal lives and family roles, while men were more likely to be identified through their work lives (e.g., as police officers, doctors, or lawyers).

Sexual activity on television was found to be prevalent since the 1970s (Buerkel-Rothfuss, 1993; Cassata & Skill, 1983). If we limit our definition of sex to visual depictions of intercourse, the rate fluctuated around one (Greenberg et al., 1993) or two (Fernandez-Collado, Greenberg, Korzenny, & Atkin, 1978) acts per hour of prime time. In soap operas, the rate was even higher. If we expand the definition to include all visual depictions of sexual activity, such as kissing, petting, homosexuality, prostitution, and rape, the hourly rates went up to about 3 acts on prime time and 3.7 acts per hour on soap operas (Greenberg et al., 1993). And when the definition is further expanded to include talk about sex as well as sexual imagery, the rate climbed to 16 instances per hour on prime time (Sapolsky & Tabarlet, 1990). Most of this talk about sex was on situation comedies in the early evening, when it was presented in a humorous context.

The most recent major set of studies that examined sexual activity across the television landscape was conducted from 1997 to 2002. These studies analyzed 2,817 programs across 10 TV channels and found that about two thirds of all shows (64%) contained some sexual content and that 14% alluded to at least one act of sexual intercourse, although none of the videos in the sample showed this activity on screen. Among the 20 top-rated shows watched by teens, 83% contained sexual portrayals. The overall rate was about three scenes per hour. Two thirds (67%) of all network prime-time shows contained either talk about sex or sexual behavior, averaging more than five scenes per hour. And the rates of sexual portrayal continued to increase. Over that five-year time span, the percentage of shows portraying sexual intercourse doubled from 7% to 14% (Kaiser Family Foundation, 2003; Kunkel, Eyal, & Donnerstein, 2007).

Violence was the most studied form of content in all mass media from the advent of television as a mass medium around 1950 to the turn of the century. Scholars continually monitored the amount of violence on television, producing at least 60 major content analyses (see Potter, 1999), and then interest waned. Depending on the definition used, violence has been found in 57% to 80% of all entertainment programs (Columbia Broadcasting System, 1980; Gerbner, Gross, Morgan, & Signorielli, 1980; Greenberg, Edison, Korzenny, Fernandez-Collado, & Atkin, 1980; Lichter & Lichter, 1983; "NCTV Says," 1983; National Television Violence Study, 1999; Potter & Ware, 1987; Schramm, Lyle, & Parker, 1961; Signorielli, 1990; Smythe, 1954; Williams, Zabrack, & Joy, 1982).

In summary, content patterns found in television entertainment from the early 1960s to the late 1990s consistently found that the world depicted in entertainment videos differed from the real world in many significant ways. Of course, storytellers are under no obligation to capture real-world patterns accurately; their purpose is to delight and entertain. However, media scholars have pointed out that constant exposure to skewed patterns can lead to people forming skewed beliefs about the real world. (For more on these content patterns and their effects, see Potter, 2012, 2019.)

EFFECTS RESEARCH

There is much scholarly literature that examines how entertainment stories in the traditional media attract the attention of audiences, how people process those stories, and how they are affected by them. Researchers who are interested in determining the effects of exposure to entertainment stories in digital media have focused primarily on legacy effects. That is, much of the recent research that has examined how exposure to entertainment in the media affects people has been conducted to see if the same effects that were found from exposure to analog media occur when people are exposed to entertainment in digital media. Story producers can find a lot of useful information in this research literature, even though the findings are more suggestive than definitive because the results of many of those empirical studies present complex or equivocal results. For example, the research shows that violence is typically a story element that attracts and holds audience interest, but this does not hold for everyone, and it appears that it is not the violence per se but the arousing nature of violent portrayals that has been found to account for the attraction (Zillmann, 1991). Also, the research shows that humor is a desirable element to put into media stories. However, there are many different types of humor, and because humor is personal, not all audience members "get" all types of humor (Boxman-Shabtai & Shifman, 2014). Suspense has been found to be a useful characteristic of entertainment stories, but not all audience members enjoy suspense the same way (Shafer, 2014). While disgust repels and offends us, it has functionally evolved over time to attract our attention by presenting physical characteristics that disgust us (i.e., blood, guts, and body products) and by presenting socio-moral violations (i.e., injustices, brutality, and racism) that can trigger disgust. Thus many storytellers try to trigger the emotion of disgust in audiences in order to keep them engrossed and engaged; however, not all people like to feel disgusted when being entertained (Rubenking & Lang, 2014). Research has shown that in general people enjoy stories more that have a higher degree of realism, but realism can be assessed along at least six different dimensions (Cho, Shen, & Wilson, 2014). Because audience members differ in the kinds of emotions they want to experience when they seek entertainment, producers of entertainment stories need to understand their audience needs in order to know which kinds of emotions their audiences will tolerate and enjoy the most.

The effects of exposure to entertainment content in digital media generally follow the same patterns found by research that has examined the effects of exposure to various forms of entertainment-type content in the traditional media. Researchers who are concerned with the effects of digital media have focused their designs in several areas where digital media differ from analog media. One of these areas is exposure, because digital media offer unique exposure opportunities, given their interactive nature and the ability of people to access entertainment content constantly on mobile devices. A second popular area of digital effects research focuses on entertainment-type content that is especially prevalent on digital media —pornography and music videos.

Exposure

As you saw in previous parts of this book, there are continual increases in the amount of time people devote to digital media. A large portion of this exposure is with entertainment messages. For example, teens (13–18) expose themselves to an average of 9 hours of entertainment media use per day; this is in addition to the screen time for school or homework (Brooks & Lasser, 2018).

When seeking exposure to entertainment messages, more and more people are switching from appointment viewing options to streaming options that offer them greater freedom in managing their exposures. For example, Tefertiller (2018) conducted a nationwide survey and found that people who switched (or planned to switch) from cable television to video-streaming services as their primary source of video entertainment did so primarily because they were frustrated with using older television technology and preferred the advantages of streaming, especially the ability to watch what they want when they want. Interestingly, these findings held up across all groups of people with different entertainment needs. This means that people do not regard either cable offerings or streaming offerings as superior to other services in terms of entertainment choice or value; instead, people are motivated to switch for the technological advantages offered by streaming.

Streaming services give people more opportunity for **binge watching**, where people can expose themselves to a video entertainment series by watching multiple episodes in a continuous sequence lasting hours and sometimes days rather than watching one episode per week as each episode is released by analog video providers. Motivations for binge watching differ according to how often people binge watch (Sung, Kang, & Lee, 2018). People who binge watch a lot are typically motivated by a need to be entertained when simply passing time. In contrast, people who rarely binge watch are motivated by a need to be entertained by particular shows.

When selecting entertainment programs for exposure, people are influenced by recommendations from friends and other people. Waddell and Sundar (2017) conducted an experiment to determine the influence of social comments on people's liking of entertainment programs. They found a strong bandwagon effect where people were more willing to like a program when that program was rated high by other viewers. The researchers also found that when a video generated negative comments, potential viewers either avoided that video or, if they watched it, did not enjoy it much.

A series of experiments were conducted to examine why viewers like characters who perform negative behaviors (Tamborini et al., 2018). The researchers found that people use narrative cues in entertainment stories to trigger either internal or external attributions for a protagonist's harmful behavior. Internal attributions (where people believe that characters performed their bad behaviors because of character flaws) triggered people not to like those characters, whereas external attributions (where people believe that characters performed their bad behaviors because they were forced to do so against their will) triggered liking of those characters. These findings suggest that writers—when they want viewers to like their characters—should show viewers that external factors caused the character's harmful acts.

Sexual Content

Digital platforms offer a wide range of sexually explicit internet material, which is often referred to as **SEIM**. Research has typically found that exposure to this type of content is associated with sexual behavior. For example, van Oosten, Peter, and Vandenbosch (2017) conducted a longitudinal three-wave panel study among 1,467 adolescents (aged 13–17, 50% female) and found that exposure to SEIM directly predicted adolescents' willingness to engage in casual sex. This relationship was found across many types of sexual content, including sexually oriented reality TV, sexy self-presentations on social network sites, and pornography.

The strongest form of sexual content is **pornography**, which is typically defined as printed or visual material containing the explicit description or display of sexual organs or activity, intended to stimulate erotic rather than aesthetic or emotional feelings. Pornography continues to attract all kinds of audiences. Research has found that 75% of men and 40% of women download and regularly view pornography (Albright, 2008). In 2015, the cellphone pornography business was estimated to have reached $2.8 billion (Aiken, 2016, p. 81).

Even children are frequently exposed to pornography. "A common estimate is that boys, especially, are looking at sexually explicit images beginning at an average age of nine or ten" (Kamenetz, 2018, p. 74). More than 90% of all boys in the United States report that they have viewed pornography online before age 18 (Brooks & Lasser, 2018). Larchet (2019) says that "65% of Internet searches conducted by young Americans between 10 and 16 years old are for pornographic sites. An average American school student has looked at 1,400 explicit sexual references per year before leaving school" (p. 57).

Reactions to pornography vary, but in general, most reactions are positive. For example, one survey of adolescents reported that only one in five respondents said they had seen pornographic images that had shocked or upset them (Aiken, 2016, p. 148). Most people who are exposed to pornography say they found it enjoyable, which stimulated them to continue seeking exposure to it. In a three-wave panel study among adolescents ($N = 1,022$), Vandenbosch, van Oosten, and Peter (2018) found that watching sexually explicit portrayals predicted greater enjoyment and higher utility of such material during later exposures.

Exposure to pornography has also been found to influence people's sexual beliefs over time. For example, Wright and Tokunaga (2018) conducted two three-wave surveys in the United States and found that pornography consumption at Wave 1 predicted a more liberal set of sexual beliefs at Wave 2, which in turn predicted more support for abortion at Wave 3. They also found that support for abortion was a predictor of greater sexual liberalism, which in turn was a predictor of the consumption of pornography.

Exposure to pornography has been found to be related to sexual behavior. Vogels and O'Sullivan (2018) conducted a survey of young adults by asking them to complete an anonymous online survey about the frequency that they observed various sexual behaviors in online pornography, the frequency that they engaged in these behaviors, and their perceptions of the frequency that their peers engaged in these behaviors. Their findings showed that the frequency of viewing cunnilingus (men) or fellatio (women) in pornography predicted how often they engaged in oral sex.

As for the effects of exposure to pornography, the research shows equivocal patterns. Some studies show that such exposure leads to negative effects, while other research indicates that effects can be positive.

Negative Influence   The influence of pornography on sexual beliefs and behaviors bothers some scholars. For example, Larchet (2019) writes,

> Far from educating the young, as some suggest, such visits to sexual sites degrade the idea of sexual relations by showing them in their most perverted forms, rather than their normal expression, which is foreign to pornography.

> Youth is taught to see the person as a body, and the body as an object, by depicting sexual relations as a purely physical activity for selfish individual pleasure. Completely divorced from respect and love. (p. 57)

A 2015 survey conducted at a child helpline in the U.K. found that "10% of children 12 to 13 were 'worried they might be addicted to porn' and that 12% said they had taken part in, or had made, a sexually explicit video" (Aiken, 2016, p. 148).

Some scholars have designed research studies to examine ways to reduce the influence of pornography on viewers. Vandenbosch and van Oosten (2017) conducted a longitudinal study among 1,947 participants (13- to 25-year-olds) in order to examine the potential of porn literacy education at schools to attenuate the longitudinal relationship between exposure to sexually explicit internet material and views of women as sex objects. These researchers found that the relationship between SEIM and sexist views became weaker the more users had learned from porn literacy education.

In a meta-analysis of effects of exposure to pornography that leads to subsequent aggressive behavior, the type of pornography was found to be a key factor. Exposure to pictorial nudity reduces subsequent aggressive behavior, exposure of material depicting nonviolent sexual activity increases aggressive behavior, and media depictions of violent sexual activity generate more aggression than those of nonviolent sexual activity (Allen, D'Alessio, & Brezgel, 1995).

Mixed Influence   The consumption of pornography was found to be associated with an impersonal approach to sex among both men and women; among both adolescents and adults; and across countries, time, and methods. This was the finding of a major meta-analysis of the literature that included 70 reports spanning 40 years of research collected from more than 60,000 participants from 13 countries (Tokunaga, Wright, & Roskos, 2019). They found that viewing pornography leads to more positive sexual attitudes, which in turn increases the likelihood of engaging in impersonal sexual behavior. In another meta-analysis of this literature, the consumption of pornography was found to be related to lower interpersonal satisfaction with sex among men (Wright, Tokunaga, Kraus, & Klann, 2017).

Music Videos

Exposure to music videos has been found to influence people's beliefs and behaviors. As for beliefs, an experiment conducted on 153 college student participants found that watching music videos influenced their beliefs about whether interpersonal violence was abusive in relationships (Rhodes, Potocki, & Masterson, 2018). Participants watched one of two videos. One video portrayed overt interpersonal violence in a narrative form, and the other contained overt interpersonal violence but no identifiable narrative. Lyrics for both included violent content, but the music was distinctly different: one song was rap interspersed with somber singing and the other had an upbeat pop sound. The researchers found that the more their participants enjoyed the music videos and were transported into those videos, the less likely they were to perceive the psychologically controlling and demeaning behaviors as abusive.

As for influencing behavior, researchers have found that exposure to music videos can prime people's subsequent gazing behavior. In an experiment designed to investigate the effects of exposure to sexually objectifying music videos on viewers' subsequent gazing behavior, participants were exposed to music videos that were either high in sexual objectification or low in sexual objectification. Then participants' eye movements were recorded as they viewed photographs of 36 women models with various body shapes (i.e., ideal-size model or plus-size model) and degree of dress (i.e., fully dressed, scantily dressed, or partially clad). The researchers found that sexually objectifying music videos influenced participants' objectifying gaze upon photographs of women with an ideal size, but not plus size, body shape. Participants who were primed with sexually objectifying imagery looked at women's sexual body parts more than they looked at women's faces. This effect was found for women as well as men (Karsay, Matthes, Platzer, & Plinke, 2018).

Conclusions

The nature of entertainment has changed with the rise of digital media. There is now a much wider range of entertainment content available. Producers of entertainment content are using digital platforms to allow for streaming, which gives users much more control over what they watch and when they watch it. Also, digital media give everyone the means to record and edit their own videos and then upload them to video-sharing sites where those videos can be viewed by anyone in the world.

The effects of exposure to entertainment content in digital media generally follow the same patterns found by research that has examined the effects of exposure to various forms of entertainment-type content in analog media. Thus far, there is no pattern of research findings showing that the effects that arise from exposure to entertainment in digital media are different from the effects that arise from exposure to entertainment in analog media. The differences in effects arise from the type of entertainment content, not from the provider of that content. Of course, the literature on media effects from exposure to entertainment from digital media is still relatively new, so this conclusion may change as more researchers focus on the way the unique characteristics of digital media might heighten (or lessen) the power of entertainment messages to influence our ways of thinking, our beliefs, and our behaviors.

Further Reading

Allocca, K. (2018). *Videocracy: How YouTube is changing the world with double rainbows, singing foxes, and other trends we can't stop watching.* New York: Bloomsbury. (335 pages including endnotes and index)

Written by YouTube's head of culture and trends, this book presents a great many examples of videos that have been uploaded to YouTube. The author explores the question of why certain videos get no attention while others suddenly get viewed by millions of people.

CHAPTER 7

Effects of Using Social Media Sites

- Types of Social Media Sites
  - Friendship
  - Dating
  - Opinion Sharing
- Effects of Friendship Sites on Individuals
  - Behavior
    - Using Friendship Sites
    - Dependency
    - Cyber Bullying
    - Exercise
  - Affect
    - Managing Mood
    - Feelings of Burnout
    - Depression
    - Parasocial Relationships
  - Physiology: Brain Capacity
  - Beliefs
    - Social Norms
    - Narcissism
  - Attitudes
    - Attributions
    - Body Image
- Behavioral Effects of Dating Sites on Individuals
  - Exposure
  - Lying
  - Sexting
- Effects of Opinion-Sharing Sites on Individuals
  - Behavior
    - Expressing Opinions
    - Engaging in Collective Activities
    - Sharing News Content
    - Social Support
    - Offline Political Behavior
  - Attitudes
    - Reinforcing Attitudes
    - Altering Attitudes
  - Affect
    - Enjoyment of Sports
    - Envy
    - Anger
- Conclusions

Types of Social Media Sites

Social networking sites (SNSs) are platforms where people can meet and converse with others online. Tuten and Solomon (2018) define SNSs as

> online hosts that enable site members to construct and maintain profiles, identify other members with whom they are connected, and participate by

101

consuming, producing, and/or interacting with content provided by their connections. Profiles enhance the ability of members to develop a social identity when they add a profile picture or avatar, basic information about themselves, and other customizable options. Members maintain a social presence in the community that may indicate their availability, mood, friend list, and status. (p. 13)

There are hundreds of SNSs. The most visible and well known are Facebook, Instagram, Snapchat, LinkedIn, and Pinterest. By 2008, 24% of the U.S. population were regular users of social networking sites and this percentage increased to 79% by 2019 (Statistica, 2019).

There are basically three types of social networking sites. These types differ in terms of how the platforms offer users opportunities to satisfy their different types of needs. One type of SNS platform offers opportunities for social interaction where users are looking to meet others in order to create and maintain friendship-type relationships. A second type of SNS platform offers dating opportunities for people who want to screen for particular kinds of people whom they want to meet in real life either to have rewarding dating experiences in the short term or to use those dating experiences to achieve a long-term romantic attachment. The third type of SNS platform offers users the opportunity to share their beliefs and opinions with others. Of course, there are SNS platforms that offer opportunities for users to satisfy more than one of these needs; however, in this chapter, I will deal with each type separately in order to highlight the unique features of each type.

FRIENDSHIP

SNS platforms that are designed to offer users opportunities to develop and maintain friendships provide users with two kinds of tools. One kind includes tools that help users easily construct their own webpages by uploading text, photos, and videos. The second type includes tools that help users communicate with other users by allowing them to leave messages and reactions on each others' webpages.

The early adopters of SNSs were teenage girls who used them to keep in touch with their friends around the clock by posting photos and actively blogging. The major activity was **friending**, which is when people add you to their friends list and agree to be on your friends list. Friending typically gives users special privileges on the SNS. For example, on Facebook, a person's friends are granted the privilege of viewing and posting to one's timeline.

Many users felt it was a competition to have the largest friends list and therefore granted friend status to everyone who asked, thereby accumulating hundreds and even thousands of friends (Angwin, 2009). This led many users to consider different levels of friendship (such as close friends, acquaintances, and strangers who have friended them) and thereby set up different ways of communicating with them. For example, some users of Instagram created a second account known as a Finsta, which is short for "Fake Instagram," where the owner of the account limits access to only close friends.

The earliest SNS was SixDegrees.com, which was launched in 1997. Then Myspace started in the summer of 2003 by offering users a profile page with pictures and interests along with the ability to link to friends. Myspace allowed users to customize their profiles, and this had strong appeal for the early users. It also provided games, blogging (called journals early on), and even horoscopes. Myspace also allowed **fakesters** by permitting users to be whoever they wanted to be—themselves, a celebrity, a pet animal, or a wholly made up person with a created identity. Until April 2004, only Myspace members could view the profiles of other Myspace members, but because of the shifting focus to advertising support, Myspace was opened up to the outside world, and by 2008 Myspace was by far the most used social networking site. But then it went into decline as its chief competitor Facebook provided people with superior technology that served users' needs better, thus taking away most of Myspace's users and advertisers.

When Facebook was launched in 2004, it limited its membership to students at Harvard University, where it was initially developed. It then expanded to other colleges in the Boston area, the Ivy League, and Stanford University. During its first year, Facebook was much smaller than Myspace with just 10 million monthly visitors compared with 24 million for Myspace, but Facebook grew quickly as it expanded to include any university student, then high school students, and finally anyone at least 13 years of age. Facebook also introduced several new features such as "News Feed," which provided members with updates about their friends' activities. By the summer of 2011, Facebook had 600 million users worldwide and virtually eliminated Myspace (The new tech bubble, 2011). By 2018, Facebook had accumulated well over 2.2 billion active users worldwide and was still growing the number of users by double-digit increases each year. Of all American females, 76% were users of Facebook, and 66% of males were regular users (Zephoria, 2018).

DATING

While people frequently use a general friendship networking platform such as Facebook to move beyond friendships and into dating, there are SNSs specifically designed for partner seeking, such as Match.com, eHarmony, Tinder, OkCupid, Coffee Meets Bagel, Hinge, and Tastebuds, to name a few. There are now almost 8,000 dating websites worldwide, and almost 50 million Americans have tried at least one of these sites. Users of these dating websites were found to spend an average of $243 annually for memberships (Matthews, 2018).

These dating sites require users to set up an account where they fill out a questionnaire about themselves and the kind of potential dating partners they would like to meet. These sites use the information provided on member questionnaires to show each member potential matches. Some sites send users suggested matches, while others use GPS to help members find dates in their vicinity and then send them instant messages. For example, the dating app Tinder focuses on proximity and attractiveness. Tinder uses the GPS feature on mobile devices to show members photos of other members who are near them at any given time; users then swipe right on their mobile screens if they like a picture and want more information on that person. Thus Tinder places a premium on first-impression attractiveness as conveyed by each member's photo. Tinder was launched in 2013, and within three years it was in 196 countries where users were swiping 1.4 billion times and making 26 million matches every day. Tinder claimed to have generated 9 billion matches, which is more than the entire population of the globe (Aiken, 2016).

Some of these "dating" sites are designed to match users with virtual partners rather than real people. For example, LovePlus is a Japanese app video game that offers avatar love. This is a dating simulator designed to help people learn how to be in a romantic relationship. Guys get to choose Rinko, Manaka, or Nene and then date them online without having the hassles of actual real-world dating (Aiken, 2016).

OPINION SHARING

A popular type of interactive platform that allows people to share their opinions is the blog, which is a truncation of the words "web log." Blogs are websites where an individual posts personal opinions and invites responses from readers. Structurally, blogs consist of textual elements (diary notations, hobbies, quotes, lists of favorite sites, etc.), visual graphic elements (photographs, icons, web links), and interactive elements (online discussion, emails, etc.). Some blogs are focused on the authors themselves, while others are focused on issues or topics of shared interest. Blogs offer the potential for an unlimited size audience and unlimited freedom to talk about anything. Blogs are dialogic, that is, they elicit responses, so bloggers post their thoughts with the expectation of receiving reactions from their followers. The word "followers" is used to refer to people who read a person's blog, not necessarily people who agree with what the blogger says. Oftentimes, followers disagree with what the blogger writes, and this creates dialogues that sometimes grow very heated.

The first blog went online in 1994, and by 2012 there were more than 200 million blogs worldwide. Now it is impossible to tell accurately how many blogs there are, but by 2018, there were more than 440 million blogs on just the three most popular blogging platforms of Tumblr, Squarespace, and WordPress (Mediakix, 2017).

While most blogs feature the personal ramblings of opinionated individuals and receive only a few hundred visitors at most, there are other blogs that qualify as examples of mass media. These are highly organized blogs that are designed to attract large numbers of a particular kind of audience so that creators of those blogs can attract financial support from advertisers. For example, *Drudge Report* with 1.6 million unique monthly visitors and *Huffington Post* with 773,000 visitors are blogs that each generate a good deal of revenue through advertising. Although these are primarily political blogs, they also have added postings on entertainment, business, media, lifestyle, and other topics as a way to attract more followers, which makes them appear much like traditional newspapers in terms of the range of their content and appeal.

Included in this blogosphere is Twitter, which began in 2006 by allowing users to post tweets of up to a limit of 140 characters. Tweets are typically impulse messages containing mundane information about users' everyday lives (such as what they ate for breakfast) and their opinions about whatever they care about. By 2012, Twitter had increased to more than 555 million active registered users who sent an average of 58 million tweets each day (NumberOf.net, 2015). Since that time, Twitter has shrunk in terms of users but has grown enormously in number of tweets. By 2020, Twitter had 330 million active users who sent a total of 500 million tweets per day (Ahlgren, 2020).

Effects of Friendship Sites on Individuals

Although SNSs are relatively new, there is already fascinating research that shows how certain kinds of people are using SNSs to fulfill their special needs and to overcome their particular challenges. These groups include juvenile delinquents (Lim et al., 2012), homosexuals (Vivienne & Burgess, 2012), and people suffering with grief (Marwick & Ellison, 2012). Social media sites have been found to lead to many different kinds of effects—behavioral, affective, physiological, belief, attitudinal, and cognitive. By far the most researched of these are the behavioral and affect effects.

BEHAVIOR

The research that examines behavioral effects of using friendship sites breaks down into the categories of antecedents and consequences. Antecedent-focused research is guided by questions about why and how people use SNSs for friendship, while consequence-focused research is guided by questions about how exposures influence subsequent behaviors. The antecedent-focused research thus far has examined why people use friendship SNSs and why they develop a dependency on them. The consequence-focused research has examined how usage of SNSs has led to users experiencing cyber bullying and engaging in exercise.

Using Friendship Sites

The use of SNSs has continued to grow from about 1 billion people worldwide in 2010 to more than 2.6 billion in 2018 and is projected to continue to grow to more than 3 billion people by 2021, with Facebook having the greatest number of users (2.3 billion) of all SNSs (Clement, 2018). Facebook is so pervasive that it appeals to people all over the world and of all ages. For example, a nationally representative sample of U.S. adults (N = 2,003) compared the usage of Facebook by older adults (aged 65 or older) and younger adults (aged 18–65 years) and found that the two groups did not differ in the amount of time they spent on Facebook, the frequency of their visits, or their engagement in relationships (Yu, Ellison, & Lampe, 2018).

Why do SNSs attract so many users? To answer this question, scholars have gone back to some foundational ideas about human socialization originally articulated by George Herbert Mead and Erving Goffman. The influential sociologist Mead pointed out that people continually define themselves by trying on different roles (Mead, 1934). As people continually watch how others behave and think, they identify certain people as role models. We then closely observe these role models to figure out which behaviors to try out in our own lives.

Another prominent sociologist, Goffman (1959), built on this idea by pointing out that as we try these different roles, we are performing, that is, putting on a show if even just for ourselves. We act in ways that we believe our role models would act. This is how we evolve our personalities. We have an idea of who we want to be, and in order to realize that idea, we try out different behaviors to test how those behaviors impress other people. When we find those behaviors that trigger others to treat us the way we want to be treated, we continue to perform those behaviors, and eventually those behaviors become who we are.

SNSs give us an opportunity to experience far more social interactions online than we can experience in our unmediated lives. With the media, we can observe a much greater variety of personality characteristics than we can in real life. And with digital media, especially SNSs, we can try out a greater range of behaviors with a greater variety of people, to test which of those behaviors are the most successful in attracting the kinds of friends we want. SNSs allow us to present ourselves through text, photos, and videos. SNSs also allow us to develop special ways of communicating through abbreviations and symbols that serve to create special in-groups of friends. Examples of these symbols are **emoticons** (text-depicted pictures of emotional states such as smiles, frowns, and winks) and **emojis** (small icons and graphics of all kinds).

People can now post and archive their entire lives down to the smallest minutia. This has been labeled **lifelogging** (Raine & Wellman, 2012). Continually recording the details of one's life can be very useful, revelatory, and even life changing in the way it leads users to reflect more deeply about things like solidarity and autonomy (Bell & Gemmell, 2009). But there is also a downside to such lifelogging: When you digitize information and post it online, you open yourself up to other people hacking your data, transforming it in ways you did not intend, and sharing it without your permission. This can lead to embarrassment and even harassment.

Sherry Turkle in *Alone Together* (2011) writes about **Goldilocks syndrome**, where people use SNSs to make a special kind of friend—one who is neither too close nor too far in terms of psychological distance. Turkle explains that SNSs are a useful tool for users to maintain a kind of middle-level form of friendship where they can avoid interpersonal contact that is too close and intimate like phone conversations or too far and formal like writing letters. Turkle explains, "Texting puts people not too close, not too far, but at just the right distance. The world is now full of modern Goldilockses, people who take comfort in being in touch with a lot of people whom they also keep at bay" (p. 15).

The use of SNSs has also been found to be related to self-esteem, but in a curvilinear manner. A Dutch study of adolescents' use of Facebook found that the heaviest users exhibited a medium level of self-esteem (Cingel & Olsen, 2018). Adolescents low on self-esteem as well as high on self-esteem spent relatively less time on Facebook.

The use of SNSs has been found to vary by culture. For example, Xu and Armstrong (2019) conducted a study to examine how U.S. and Chinese athletes present themselves on SNSs. They found cultural differences, with the Chinese athletes' self-disclosure exhibiting much more gender stereotyping than did the self-disclosing of the U.S. athletes.

Dependency

Recent research has shown that many users of SNSs have developed a dependency on them in an effort to satisfy their need to belong. Ferris and Hollenbaugh (2018) found that dependency on Facebook was most strongly associated with motives of being part of a virtual community and meeting new people online. In addition, dependency on SNSs was found to be related to how much users wanted to engage with their local communities in real life. Also, an online survey of 890 SNS users between the ages of 19 and 59 who lived in 25 districts in Seoul found that dependency on SNSs was related to neighborhood belonging, efficacy of informal social control, efficacy of social cohesion, and community activity participation (Kim, Shin, Cho, Jung, Shon, & Shim, 2019).

Cyber Bullying

There are people who send digital messages to others with the purpose of causing harm by embarrassing, belittling, and/or harassing them; this is known as **cyber bullying**. In a recent survey, 23% of youth (10–23 years of age) said they have witnessed cruelty online, and 13% reported being a victim of it (Brooks & Lasser, 2018). It appears, however, that bullying online is not as prevalent as bullying in person. Kamenetz (2018) found that 7% of teens in their survey reported experiencing cyber bullying compared to 21% who reported being bullied in person.

Exercise

Using some features of SNSs can influence how people behave in the real world. One example of this is with exercise. Carpenter and Amaravadi (2019) collected data from an exercise-focused social media website as well as a mobile app that measured exercise. Their sample consisted of 31,200 users reporting 67,699 exercise events over 87 weeks. The researchers found that the amount of exercise reported by the user's social network as well as the size of the user's on-site social network affected the user's exercise behavior over time.

AFFECT

Exposure to social networking sites has been found to exert an influence on a person's feelings. These effects include managing mood, feelings of burnout, depression, and experiencing parasocial relationships.

Managing Mood

Research has found that the use of SNSs can trigger a positive as well as a negative mood. As for creating a positive mood, Johnson and Knobloch-Westerwick (2017) found that when people were in a negative mood, they tended to expose themselves to the photographs and status updates posted by friends as a way of improving their mood. This was especially the case with people who were high group identifiers, that is, people who felt the strongest attachments to their friendship groups.

The use of SNSs can trigger a negative mood, especially when users engage in social comparison. An experiment had participants read positive comments about strangers posted on SNSs. The researchers found that when participants felt they did not exhibit characteristics in their own lives that would trigger their friends to post such positive comments about them, their mood became negative. In contrast, when users relied on an emotional contagion perspective to interpret strangers' positive posts, their mood was positively affected. That is, individuals who tend to avoid engaging in social comparison reported higher positive mood after viewing positive posts than after viewing neutral or no posts (de Vries, Möller, Wieringa, Eigenraam, & Hamelink, 2018). These findings indicate that it is not the messages themselves as much as how users of SNSs interpret the messages that determines how SNS messages will affect their mood.

Feelings of Burnout

A survey of Australian youth found high rates of burnout "from constant connectivity to social media use" (Australian Psychological Society, 2015, p. 34). The authors argued that this burnout "lays the grounds for serious anxieties associated with social media use" (p. 37).

Depression

The amount of social media use has been found to be positively correlated with depression where levels of depression are highest among the heaviest users of social media (Kamenetz, 2018). Reasons for this finding are that people who are feeling depressed are more likely to use SNSs to ruminate about their social problems so that over time, they experience an increase in anxiety that is triggered by a fear that they may be missing something. To illustrate, a two-wave panel study ($N = 1,840$) of boys' and girls' use of Facebook found that depression was related to the amount of rumination they demonstrated online (Frison, Bastin, Bijttebier, & Eggermont, 2019). In addition, the researchers found that private Facebook interactions were predictive of relative increases in boys' and girls' perceptions of online social support over time (i.e., 6 months later). Thus, when Facebook users felt they were getting adequate social support from their online friends, they were more likely to exhibit fewer depressive symptoms over time.

A recent psychological survey has investigated the **FOMO factor**, or the fear of missing out, as a contributor to anxiety and depression among young users of social media (Australian Psychological Society, 2015). The authors report that 45% of Australian teens felt that their peers were having more rewarding experiences than they were.

Parasocial Relationships

Users of SNSs frequently develop parasocial relationships with other people who post on their sites. This is especially the case with users developing parasocial relationships with public figures and celebrities. Research on this topic has shown that a person's mood can be altered by how they interact with public figures on SNSs. When people interact with a public figure and receive confirming replies, they feel a greater sense of intimacy with that public figure than if the public figure ignores them or sends them a disconfirming reply (Dai & Walther, 2018).

Many media personalities have established parasocial relationships with their fans, and those fans experience all sorts of emotions in those parasocial relationships. Gregg (2018) conducted a study to examine what happens to fans during a "parasocial breakup." In a case study, the researcher found that when a large-market radio DJ was taken off the air, the fans with the strongest parasocial relationship with the DJ developed the strongest feelings of loss and the most negative feelings about the radio station.

PHYSIOLOGICAL: BRAIN CAPACITY

Researchers often refer to something known as **Dunbar's number** as a way of establishing a natural limit for the number of friendships a human can adequately maintain. Dunbar's number says that 150 friends is the upper limit. Aiken (2016) attributes this limit to a physiological basis when she says, "Given the size of the human brain, the number of social contacts or 'casual friends' with whom an average individual can handle and maintain stable social relationships is around 150. This number is consistent throughout human history—and is the size of the modern hunter-gatherer societies, the size of most military companies, most industrial divisions, most Christmas card lists" (Aiken, 2016, p. 128).

BELIEFS

People's experiences with social networking sites can influence their beliefs about social norms and narcissism.

Social Norms

Online social norms are frequently different than the social norms people learn in real life. For example, Sabra (2017) found that the social norms for grieving on Facebook among Danish users were different than the social norms for grieving in real life. She found that when people violated the internet norms, other users expressed negative attitudes toward those who used the internet to grieve and display their emotions.

Narcissism

There has also been a rise in self-reports of narcissism along with a decline in empathy among American college students since the 1970s, with the steepest drop in concern for others and perspective-taking since 2000 (Kamenetz, 2018). This rise in narcissism is likely to be a result of a complex interaction of factors that become active when people use SNSs. To illustrate, Jin and Ryu (2018) conducted a cross-sectional survey of 398 Instagram users (236 males and 162 females) and found a dynamic relationship of users' narcissism with their self-confidence, intra-sexual competition for mates, need to belong, need for popularity, loneliness, number of selfie/groupie posts on Instagram, and number of Instagram followers/followings.

ATTITUDES

Researchers have found that the way people make attributions about others and their attitudes about body image are influenced by their experiences with social media.

Attributions

Users of SNSs frequently make attributions about their friends from what they see posted on their friends' sites. A recent experiment found that fewer status updates on a profile led to evaluative judgments of the profile owner as being more depressed and less socially skilled than owners who post status updates more frequently (Tokunaga & Quick, 2018). The researchers also found that these attitudes about owners' level of depression and social skills deficits were used as a basis for making judgments about how attractive the owners of those profiles were.

Sometimes people have a great deal of information to use in making attributions, while at other times, people have little information and must make many inferences from their limited information. For example, compared to face-to-face communication, emails lack information that is conveyed through gesture, tone of voice, manner of expression, and context. Riordan & Trichtinger (2017) conducted three experiments to examine how people make attributions about writers of emails. The researchers found that people often make inaccurate evaluations about the meaning conveyed in emails as well as the people sending those emails, although most people think they are making highly accurate attributions.

One key factor about how people make attributions of other people and whether those people warrant their support has been traced to whether people believe the others are responsible for their distress. For example, an experiment was designed to examine the effects of identity cues concerning a support seeker's responsibility for his or her distress. Researchers found that their participants evaluated the support seeker more negatively, produced support messages containing lower levels of person-centeredness, and used fewer politeness strategies when participants attributed the support seeker as being more responsible for his or her distress than when the seeker was less responsible (Rains, Tsetsi, Akers, Pavlich, & Appelbaum, 2019).

Body Image

A good deal of research has shown that when people are exposed repeatedly to images of models with ideal bodies in analog media (especially fashion magazines and music videos on cable TV), people compare their own bodies to those ideal types, and this continual comparison fosters an evaluation that they are not attractive. This research has recently been expanded to digital media. For example, Kleemans, Daalmans, Carbaat, and Anschütz (2018) conducted an experiment in which 144 girls (14–18 years old) were randomly exposed to either original or manipulated (retouched and reshaped) Instagram selfies. Results showed that the manipulated photos were rated more positively than the original photos and that exposure to manipulated Instagram photos directly led to a more dissatisfied belief about their own bodies. Researchers also found that girls with higher tendencies to make social comparisons were especially affected negatively by exposure to the manipulated photos.

Behavioral Effects of Dating Sites on Individuals

Scholars who have published research on the effects of dating sites on individuals have focused on behavioral effects. Some of this behavioral research has examined anteced-ents, such as reasons for exposure, while some has examined the consequences of those exposures, such as lying and sexting.

EXPOSURE

Dating sites are popular with people of partner-seeking age. Research has found that 49 million people in the United States have tried a dating site and that 19% of adult singles are registered on at least one site, with the average person being on 2.4 dating sites (Dating Sites Reviews, 2018). People use these dating sites to increase the number of people they can consider for dating beyond the limited number of opportunities they feel they have in their real lives. They use the sites to share their profile as a way of attracting prospective dating partners and to read the profiles of other people so they can make their selections about whom they would like to meet.

LYING

More than half (53%) of all users of dating websites say they have lied about themselves. Typically the lies are about minor things like height, weight, and age, but sometimes it is more major such as not revealing they are already in a relationship. Surveys have found that 62% of online daters are already in a relationship or married (Matthews, 2018). Markowitz and Hancock (2018) conducted several studies of people who used mobile dating apps. They found that about 7% of messages were deceptive and that nearly two thirds of lies were driven by impression management, particularly self-presentation and availability management goals. A participant's lying rate was found to be correlated with the perceived lying rate of the partner, that is, participants who thought that others lied on their dating profiles were more likely to lie on their own profile.

One form of lying is **catfishing**, which is when someone pretends to be some-one they're not on a dating site, social network, or chat site. Sometimes they do this to scam people out of money, but FreeDating.co.uk found that their users were more likely to catfish because they were seeking revenge or simply because they were lonely or bored.

Business Insider reports that 10% of accounts on dating sites are fake. In fact, one dating site, SeekingArragement.com, has been deleting more than 600 fake accounts every day. Many of these fake accounts were set up by spammers who are trying to collect email addresses to send users unsolicited advertisements (Matthews, 2018).

SEXTING

Sexting is taking and/or sending sexually explicit or suggestive photos or messages via texting or other forms of digital media. In one large survey, 7% of teens reported that they had created sexually explicit images of themselves and shared them over social media. A survey of college students found that about one in four respondents recalled incidents of sexting during their teen years (Kamenetz, 2018).

Effects of Opinion-Sharing Sites on Individuals

The internet has 1.6 billion websites, and 500,000 are blogs where people can share information as well as express their opinions on any topic. The authors of these blogs generate more than 2 million blog posts every day (Galov, 2019).

Because digital media allow for sharing opinions in a way that analog media do not, the effects of this sharing represent a new category of media effects. The research conducted on this topic thus far has focused on effects on behaviors, attitudes, and affect.

BEHAVIOR

Exposure patterns, as well as lying and sexting, are behaviors that have been shown to be influenced by people's use of digital dating sites.

Expressing Opinions

As for expressing political opinions, an analysis of panel survey data from the 2016 U.S. election found that political expression on digital platforms increases users' desire to present themselves as politically active. Political self-presentation motivations were, in turn, positively associated with strengthened dimensions of political self-concepts (i.e., political interest, political self-efficacy, and perceived participation; Lane et al., 2019).

Twitter, the most widely used digital platform for political discussions, doubled the limit of characters in a tweet in November 2017. This provided researchers with the opportunity to examine whether this change would result in a change in the quality of comments. Jaidka, Zhou, and Lelkes (2019) analyzed 358,242 tweet replies to U.S.

politicians from January 2017 to March 2018 and found that doubling the permissible length of a tweet led to more civil, polite, and constructive discussions online.

Some people are reluctant to post their opinions on blogs and SNSs because they fear being attacked online and/or being socially isolated. Neubaum and Krämer (2018) conducted an experiment to test the expectation that being personally attacked can explain why people are more willing to voice a deviant opinion in offline rather than online environments. They found that when people face a personally relevant audience, they are prone to hold back their opinion because they fear losing control over the reactions of their audience. In another study, Neubaum and Krämer (2017) found that people's fear of isolation sharpened their attention toward user-generated comments on Facebook, which, in turn, affected their willingness to contribute to online discussions.

Engaging in Collective Activities

SNSs give people the opportunity to engage in collective activities such as building and maintaining a network of people with similar beliefs and values. An online experiment designed to examine why people used SNSs to engage in collective activity identified four reasons (Nekmat, Gower, Zhou, & Metzger, 2019). One reason was that people were more likely to engage in collective activity when they had stronger beliefs about the events and issues they were posting. Second, people were more likely to engage in collective activities when the posted information was from personal (friends and family) rather than impersonal (organizations) sources. Third, people engaged in more activity when the posted information was perceived as credible. And fourth, when people had stronger perceptions of their self and technological efficacy, they were more likely to engage in collective activity.

Sharing News Content

People who share posts in social media sites like Twitter are more likely to share news that supports positions with which they agree. As users select or discard content, they strategically highlight facets of events or issues so they can promote a particular interpretation (Aruguete & Calvo, 2018).

Social Support

Blogs are a means of sharing information among people who have particular problems. People use these blogs to connect with others in order to learn about how to deal with these problems and to provide comfort to others in the same situation. In a four-year longitudinal study, Yang and colleagues analyzed 90,965 messages posted on a health forum by 9,369 people who had a particular problem (irritable bowel syndrome; Yang, Zhong, Kumar, Chow, & Ouyang, 2018). They found that people engaged in considerable social support with each other and that both receiving and offering support significantly encouraged continuous social support exchange. The researchers also found that when patients self-disclosed their emotions when they were seeking support, they received significantly more support in return.

Offline Political Behavior

A survey conducted during the 2016 U.S. presidential election found that perceptions of social media were related to offline political participation (Kwak et al., 2018). The researchers said that when users of blogs had positive perceptions of political messages posted on social media, they were more likely to participate in real-life political activities. However, the researchers qualified their findings by saying that they did not hold for younger people.

ATTITUDES

When people use digital platforms to share their opinions, their attitudes are frequently reinforced or altered.

Reinforcing Attitudes

Many people use blogs to reinforce their existing attitudes (Cho, Ahmed, Keum, Choi, & Lee, 2018). That is, people will seek out blogs where their existing attitudes are expressed by contributors while avoiding those blogs where contributors express opinions contrary to their own. Thus blogs typically exert an **echo chamber** effect by serving to reinforce users' existing attitudes rather than challenging them by exposing users to a wider range of opinions.

Altering Attitudes

People are influenced by what others say on digital media platforms, particularly on Twitter. Winter and colleagues conducted an experiment where participants watched a talent show and read comments from Twitter about the contestants on that show (Winter, Krämer, Benninghoff, & Gallus, 2018). Results showed that participants' own comments and their private attitudes about the judges varied in line with the valence of those posted comments, that is, when the Twitter comments were positive, participants' attitudes were positive, but when the Twitter comments were negative, participants' attitudes were negative. These findings clearly show that people are influenced by the evaluative judgments others post on Twitter.

On October 15, 2017, actress Alyssa Milano popularized the #MeToo campaign, which sought to expose the prevalence of sexual harassment and assault in public domains by encouraging victims to share their experiences on social media using the hashtag *MeToo*. The online campaign rapidly grew into a global phenomenon, which was generally well supported. However, some criticized the campaign online as a *battle of the sexes*, which pitted men against women. To analyze this criticism, Kunst, Bailey,

Prendergast, and Gundersen (2019) conducted a cross-cultural survey to determine whether gender differences in attitudes and feelings toward #MeToo were due to underlying differences in ideologies and experiences that only partly overlap with gender. They surveyed respondents in the United States, where the campaign began, and in Norway, a highly gender-egalitarian country. In both countries, men expressed less positivity toward #MeToo than women and perceived it as substantially more harmful and less beneficial. These gender differences were largely accounted for by men being higher than women in hostile sexism, higher in rape myth acceptance, and lower in feminist identification. The results, hence, suggested that gender differences in attitudes to social media campaigns such as #MeToo might be best characterized as ideological differences rather than fundamental group differences.

In another test of how Twitter could influence public attitudes about a social issue, Lane, Coles, and Saleem (2019) conducted two experiments that manipulated the identity (White, Black, or anonymous) of a speaker in a message supporting the #BlackLivesMatter movement in order to examine its effects on White Americans' perceptions of the speaker and their ultimate support for the movement. Results indicated that identity cues affected evaluations of the speaker. Among White participants, White speakers were evaluated more favorably in general than anonymous speakers. Also, White speakers were evaluated as being less racist than both Black and anonymous speakers. Such evaluations were ultimately associated with increased support for #BlackLivesMatter.

Political opinions can be influenced not just by words in Twitter posts but also by images that are memes. Nee and De Maio (2019) analyzed doctored images (memes) posted on Twitter about Hillary Clinton during the 2016 U.S. presidential race. Through qualitative content analysis, researchers sought to identify whether negative memes reflected socially constructed gender stereotypes. Results indicated that gendered frames used in memes against Clinton were based on female biological/physical traits (weak, ill, unattractive), anti-feminine traits (dishonest, untrustworthy), and negative female politician traits (dictatorial, unqualified) that were incongruent with the perceived role of the presidency.

AFFECT

Researchers have found that people's feelings of enjoyment, envy, and anger can be shaped by the way they share their opinions on digital platforms.

Enjoyment of Sports

The use of digital platforms to express feelings can help users increase their enjoyment of sports. Smith, Pegoraro, and Cruikshank (2019) conducted a survey of sports fans to measure how reading comments on Twitter influenced their enjoyment of viewing live as well as mediated sporting events. They found that the heaviest users of Twitter reported the highest levels of enjoyment of those sporting events.

Envy

Online celebrities who exhibit their personal lives to many followers via digital platforms are called social media influencers. Typically these people appear to live glamorous lives, which could trigger envy in their followers. Chae (2018) conducted a study to examine the psychological process through which social media use and personality traits affect females' envy toward these social media influencers. Her study found that the way people use social media (exposure to influencers' social media and interest in specific content on influencers' social media) as well as users' personality traits (public self-consciousness and self-esteem) were associated with the frequency of comparison of one's life with that of influencers, which, in turn, predicted envy toward them. That is, the followers felt more envy toward the social media influencer the more they followed the influencer, the more the influencer talked about topics of interest to the followers, and the more the followers had low self-esteem and high self-consciousness.

Anger

Following politicians on social media has been found to be associated with anger directed toward presidential candidates whom individuals oppose and enthusiasm for their supported candidate. Weeks, Kim, Hahn, Diehl, and Kwak (2019) conducted a two-wave panel survey in the United States during the 2016 presidential election and found that politicians' social media feeds evoked emotional responses. People felt anger when experiencing posts that opposed their candidate and enthusiasm when experiencing posts that favored their candidate.

Conclusions

The phenomenon of social networking sites is rather new, but already research has documented a wide variety of effects. The most prevalent effect found so far is the way SNSs have attracted exposure and triggered other behaviors while people were using those many sites to satisfy their needs for establishing and maintaining friendships, for finding dating opportunities and meeting potential romantic partners, and for sharing information across a wide range of topics and interests. Research is also finding that people use SNSs to trigger emotions, to shape and especially reinforce attitudes, and to strengthen existing beliefs.

CHAPTER 8

Effects of Living in Virtual Worlds

- Virtual Worlds
- Social Interaction Virtual Worlds
  - Second Life
  - FarmVille
  - The Sims
- Instructional Virtual Worlds
  - Advantages
  - Types
- Effects of Virtual Worlds
  - Behavior
    - Try Out Behaviors
    - Social Interaction
    - Conditioning
  - Affect
    - Immersion
    - Feelings of Intimacy
    - Feelings of Attachment
  - Beliefs
    - About Self
    - About Norms
  - Cognitions
    - Constructing Meaning
    - Sense of Self
- Conclusions
- Further Reading

Virtual Worlds

Virtual worlds are digitally created environments that run on servers connected to the internet. They provide users with the means to immerse themselves in experiences that are alternatives to what they can or are willing to experience in their real lives. These worlds provide what are called "persistent ecologies," which means they continue to exist in stable forms even when a person is not in those worlds. The worlds continue to exist and do not reset each time people enter those worlds. However, virtual worlds are not static and unchanging, that is, visitors can influence the actions within those worlds, and they can even "build a life."

Each virtual world has a "distinctive aesthetic design and thematic orientation" to create its look and feel (Ryan, 2009, p. 25). These designs are defined by their rules, sense of play, and culture. Rules structure the organization of the designed system. Play is the human experience of that system. And culture is the set of larger contexts that users experience as they inhabit the system.

These virtual worlds are social, that is, they allow people to define themselves to others by the way they construct their avatars, which represent their digital identity in those virtual worlds. People interact socially by guiding their avatars to intermingle with other avatars. Thus people can form temporary alliances, ongoing friendships, and even romantic/sexual attachments.

These worlds are also economic, that is, they provide resources that can be acquired and exchanged. Avatars can work at tasks that can earn them rewards (possessions and even currency), engage in economic exchanges, and interact with other people through their avatars.

According to Castronova (2001) all virtual worlds exhibit three characteristics: interactivity, physicality, and persistence. "First a virtual world must allow simultaneous interactivity with and between multiple users in remote locations, with the users' actions impacting the environment and each other" (p. 6). For example, a console-based video game made to be played alone or with a friend in the same room does not constitute a virtual world. But an online platform where players, who are widely dispersed geographically, can inhabit that platform in order to compete or cooperate simultaneously with each other does qualify as a virtual world. Second, a virtual world's interface must represent an on-screen environment that is "generally ruled by the natural laws of each and is characterized by scarcity of resources." Therefore, an online world without a graphical interface, or one that represents a player avatar's physical movement in the game's space inconsistently, or one where multiple players can possess the same item from an environment simultaneously, would not constitute a virtual world. Third, "a virtual world must maintain its conditions persistently regardless of whether a player is connected or not. An online world that resets its environment to a consistent set of opening conditions whenever a player stars a new session is not a virtual world" (Ivory, 2009, p. 11).

The first virtual world to meet all three of Castronova's criteria was Meridian 59, which was a fantasy game released in 1996 by the 3DO Company. However, it did not have much commercial success, as indicated by its peak subscriber base of only about 12,000 people (Ivory, 2009). Since then, many other virtual worlds have been developed. There is even relatively easy-to-use software that allows people to create their own virtual worlds online. The best known of these software programs is Minecraft, which now has more than 120 million registered users. It has been called "an infinite sandbox" where users can build their own worlds, fix things when they break, and make up the rules as they go along. Minecraft has spawned a vast interpretive literature in the form of blogs, YouTube videos, video auteurs, and more (Kamenetz, 2018). Newer programs like Dreams are even easier to use than Minecraft, so there is reason to expect the number of people who are able to build their own virtual worlds to increase substantially over the next few years (Thompson, 2019).

There are basically three types of virtual worlds. One is the competitive game. The best known of this type of world are, for example, massively multiplayer online (MMO) games and **massively multiplayer online role-playing games (MMORPGs)** such as World of Warcraft and EverQuest. A second type of virtual world is one where there are no game rules or game-like objectives. These worlds are primarily designed to facilitate social interaction (Reinhard & Dervin, 2014). Examples of these virtual worlds include Habbo, which was launched in 2000 and aimed at teenagers; Second Life, launched in 2003; Twinity, launched in 2008 to allow Twinizens to navigate around virtual replicas of large cities in the real world; FarmVille, launched in 2009 as an agricultural simulation social network; and The Sims, which is an assortment of life simulation platforms. A third type is a virtual world that is constructed primarily for instructional purposes rather than entertainment purposes.

In the next chapter, we will explore the gaming virtual worlds; in this chapter, we examine the virtual worlds that are not considered games, that is, they are worlds created to allow people to engage in all kinds of social interactions that are largely noncompetitive. First we will examine the social interaction virtual worlds; then we will look at the instructional virtual worlds.

Social Interaction Virtual Worlds

The purpose of social interaction virtual worlds is to provide users with an experience where they can interact with other people through their avatars in a relatively cooperative manner. While these platforms provide experiences that are not designed to be competitive, there are users who exhibit competitive behaviors by trying to make as many friendships as they can and/or acquire as many virtual possessions as they can. However, these worlds are not constructed with rules that *require* users to compete; instead, these worlds leave it up to the users to decide how many people they want to meet or how many possessions they want to acquire—as in a person's everyday real life.

Also, these worlds are not constructed with the intention of teaching anything to users. However, the users can still learn valuable lessons about how to interact with others and how to engage in economic exchanges. The purpose of these worlds is not primarily to teach these lessons but to give people a place to play and to experience an existence that is an alternative to their everyday real lives. Let's take a close look at three of these virtual worlds: Second Life, FarmVille, and The Sims.

SECOND LIFE

The best known of these social interaction virtual worlds is Second Life. In 2003, Linden Labs launched Second Life as an open internet platform that provided a set of tools and three-dimensional spaces in which users could develop their own avatars, objects, and surroundings. Linden Labs emphasizes that Second Life is not a game. In Second Life, there is no winning, only living.

People who join the site are called residents. Anyone 13 years of age and older can join. Membership is free, although many residents pay a monthly $10 membership fee that enables them to purchase land parcels.

New users begin by constructing an avatar that is a virtual representation of themselves. Avatars may take any shape or form (human-like, animal, or object). Using a menu with a vast array of choices, residents can design how their avatar looks (body shape, hair, and clothes) and acts (personality traits and physical abilities). If residents feel the menu choices are not sufficient, they can design a customized avatar from scratch. Creating one's avatar as well as other objects in Second Life is done through purchasing features from other residents or through using a three-dimensional modeling tool that allows a resident to build virtual objects. This can be combined with a Linden Scripting Language to add functionality to objects (Strand, 2014).

Second Life avatars can explore the world, known as the grid, which features 3D user-generated content. As residents use their avatars to interact with other avatars, places, and objects, their primary concern is to build a social life by meeting other residents and participating in group activities, such as engaging in conversations; hanging out in virtual bars, restaurants, and cafés; building friendships of all kinds; dating, including engaging in sexual activity; designing and delivering artistic performances; engaging in political practices; pursuing commercial interests; and participating with others in religious rituals.

Due to the range of possible activities that Second Life allows, residents have created a variety of micro communities. Residents' activity within Second Life often spills out beyond the borders of that virtual world. For example, there is an abundance of blogs connected to specific Second Life communities, topics, and commercial activities. Also, movies filmed in Second Life proliferate on YouTube (Strand, 2014).

While Second Life is primarily a social world, it also has developed an elaborate economy. Residents make a virtual life by earning money and then buying goods and services. Residents can buy land, build and furnish a home, and launch a business. In Second Life, the currency is the Linden Dollar, which is convertible into U.S. currency. Ryan (2009) explains that by 2007, over 12 million economic transactions were being conducted each month as virtual goods were bought and sold, which totaled over $6.8 million in monthly economic transactions. In November 2003, Linden Labs changed the terms of service for Second Life to allow residents to retain intellectual property rights to their creations that would be honored in the real world as well as under U.S. law (Ryan, 2009). Ryan continues,

> This critical shift in ownership, which distinguishes Second Life from other competitors, has contributed to an explosion of creativity and innovation among entrepreneurial members. For example, some residents design clothing for avatars and have their designs protected so they can sell their line of clothing and benefit from the income those sales generate. This has made it possible for many residents to develop successful commercial businesses in Second Life. (p. 37)

Ryan (2009) says, "In any given week, 75 percent of Second Life residents create a new object from simple primitives, and 25 percent of those residents create content for use by other residents" (p. 38).

"This is play, certainly, but it is serious play," explains Sherry Turkle in her book *Alone Together: Why We Expect More From Technology and Less From Each Other* (2011, pp. 158–159). Turkle talks about a Second Life resident she interviewed named Pete who is married with two children in real life but was a very different person when he was on Second Life, where his avatar was in a serious dating relationship with an avatar named Jade.

On most days, Pete logs onto Second Life before leaving for work. Pete and Jade talk (by typing) and then erotically engage their avatars, something that Second Life software makes possible with special animations. Boundaries between life and game are not easy to maintain. Online, Pete and Jade talk about sex and Second Life gossip, but they also talk about money, the recession, work, and matters of health. Pete is on a cholesterol-lowering medication that is only partially successful. Pete says that it is hard to talk to his "real" wife Alison about his anxieties. (Turkle, 2011, p. 159)

In his book *Online a Lot of the Time: Ritual, Fetish, Sign*, Ken Hillis (2009) refers to Second Life not as a virtual world but as a "graphical chat," explaining that the platform lacked the explicit game elements of other massively multiplayer online worlds, such as a combat engine; required puzzle solving and teamwork; and a linear narrative. Hillis argues that Second Life is more like a social institution. He says the avatar in Second Life is an index of the human behind it; it is a re-embodiment of the human, a physical body translated and transported into a digital medium. The avatars are experienced as material but also abstract. They are not simply the pixels on the screen, but they become the person behind the avatar as well as the person in Second Life.

In 2007, Second Life reached a peak of 7.2 million residents, with about 1 million residents actively using the platform on a regular basis. Almost 60% of users ranged in age from 25 to 44, and the population was 43% female (as a percentage of time spent in-world; Ryan, 2009). By 2013, users had created 36 million accounts, but the number of active users had declined to about 600,000 and has stayed at that level (Jamison, 2018).

FARMVILLE

FarmVille is a popular online experience where players become virtual farmers who raise crops and livestock. It was developed by Zynga and launched in Facebook in 2009. It became the most popular game on Facebook from 2009 to 2011, when it had about 60 million active users.

FarmVille is an agriculture simulation social networking game that involves various aspects of farmland management, such as plowing land, planting crops, harvesting, and raising livestock. Players begin with an empty farm and a fixed starting number of Farm Coins, the primary currency in the game. Players custom design an avatar, which they can change at any time. While people participate in FarmVille activities, their level rises as they earn credits for performing certain actions in the game, such as plowing land or buying items. As players obtain more items, they progress through levels where more things become available for purchase using either Farm Coins or Farm Cash. Farm Cash is earned by leveling up or completing offers, or is purchased for real money.

FarmVille incorporates the social networking aspect of Facebook into many areas of gameplay. Contacting other players allows users to improve their farms more quickly, by using other players as farmhands or by gaining rewards from helping them.

Often the aid of other players is a substitute for Farm Cash, thus giving players an effective choice between spamming their friends with FarmVille messages and requests, or paying real-world cash.

THE SIMS

The Sims Online "is kind of like a very junior version of Second Life, where you can create an avatar that expresses aspects of yourself, build a house, and furnish it to your taste. Thus provisioned, you can set about reworking in the virtual aspects of life that may not have gone so well in the real world" (Turkle, 2011, p. 179).

Instructional Virtual Worlds

Instructional virtual worlds are designed primarily by educators who want to give users a more immersive, intensive learning experience than merely presenting them with information through a lecture or a webpage. They design a virtual world to allow users to interact with the phenomenon that those educators are trying to teach. Some of these worlds have game-like elements such as levels and goals to motivate users to continue their immersion. However, the purpose of these worlds is less to motivate users to compete or to interact in social situations; instead, the primary purpose is to teach users what the designers regard as important information about a particular phenomenon. Ryan (2009) observes, "More recently, virtual worlds are becoming arenas for formal and informal education" (p. 23).

> The emergence of the synthetic world or Multi User Virtual Environment (MUVE) offers educators, and those engaged in the tasks of teaching and training, not only an exciting new tool with which to interact with their students but moreover a tool which could be part of a much wider challenge to the established pedagogic practice of existing formal education. (Hollins & Robbins, 2009, p. 257)

These virtual worlds have generally been found to be successful in meeting their educational objectives. Rossi (2017) says, "It has been demonstrated that anyone from the highest achiever to the 'total academic failure' can benefit from the way virtual worlds impart educational content. The playing of games for hours shows that people can easily concentrate for that length of time and that during that time they are learning—even though the lessons may seem meaningless outside the game itself."

Students of any age can be fascinated by virtual worlds, so it can be deployed from preschool through to tertiary education and then continuously applied to in-work training. Transferring the lessons of gaming to educational applications produces the immediate benefit that the students can fully engage in the virtual world and learn their lessons there. These lessons are typically absorbed without users even being aware that formal learning is taking place.

ADVANTAGES

There are significant advantages to using virtual worlds for instructional purposes.

One advantage is that virtual worlds allow students to learn at their own pace. They are given instant feedback on their performance at every step in the learning process, and when students make mistakes, they can repeat steps at a speed that enhances their own learning. Also, students can experience this learning in their own locations. They do not need to spend time commuting to a classroom and can use that time instead to learn the tasks and material being taught in the instructional virtual world.

Another significant advantage of immersing people in virtual worlds for purposes of instruction is the opportunity to teach them how to perform dangerous tasks without harming themselves or other people. For example, educators have designed simulations to teach things like flying experimental aircraft, setting up a nuclear power station, engaging in armed combat, conducting surgeries, digging a deep mine, and making repairs to an oil refinery. Engaging in a simulation in a virtual world gives people the risk-free opportunity to learn critical processes and to practice them safely as many times as they need to while gaining the confidence and experience required to perform those tasks successfully before they have to perform them in the real world.

TYPES

There appear to be three types of virtual worlds for instructional purposes. One type is a virtual world that is set up to help users learn the skills and experiences they will need to function as professionals in the real world. For example, educators have created a virtual hospital for training health-care workers and a virtual battlefield for military missions (Wheelock, 2015).

A second type of virtual experience designed for instructional purposes is a world that allows users to immerse themselves in an historical time period or a different culture. In such worlds, users can create or reimagine works of art. And they can reproduce historic architecture, such as medieval castles, the Roman Coliseum, or colonial villages. Almost all virtual environments also have customizable avatars that allow users to extend their self-expression into the digital realm. One stand-alone virtual world, for example, that has been created purely for educational purposes is Arden: The World of William Shakespeare. This virtual world was conceived as an experience that could inform as well as entertain. "Arden's teaching function is served by immersing its users in the language, plots, and historical contexts of Shakespeare's plays" (Castronova et al., 2009, p. 166).

A third type of instructional virtual world is where educators use an existing virtual world platform rather than create a new one from scratch. Inside this existing virtual world, they construct an instructional experience and try to attract existing users to their new experience. Educators have used existing virtual world platforms, such as Second Life, Minecraft, OpenSim, and Unity, to create educational experiences within them (Wheelock, 2015). For example, Minecraft has grabbed teachers' and parents' attention vicariously as they witness their children engaging, collaborating, and problem solving. Unity is a game engine, which is a computer program that can be used by nonexperts to create avatar-based environments. The U.S. military is using Unity in very large-scale ways to create simulations that pretrain soldiers for dealing with dangerous or problematic situations without putting them in physical danger.

Effects of Virtual Worlds

Because virtual worlds are limited to digital media, researchers have expected to find very different kinds of effects arising from them compared to the effects they have documented from people using analog media. While the experience of being in a virtual world is very different than the experience of exposure to analog media, those digital experiences sometimes lead to effects that have already been well documented with analog media (e.g., behavioral conditioning, constructing beliefs, and constructing meaning).

BEHAVIOR

People use virtual worlds to try out behaviors and to engage in social interaction. These behaviors tend to condition further behavior of people when they use virtual worlds.

Try Out Behaviors

Turkle (2011) explains people use virtual worlds like Second Life to try out various behaviors as a testing ground for real life. When they find behaviors that work, they practice them to increase their social skills before trying them out in their real lives. She cautions though that "people don't forge online identities with the idea that they are embarking on a potentially 'therapeutic' exercise." She continues,

> Yet, in these performances . . . something else breaks through. When we perform a life through our avatars, we express our hopes, strengths, and vulnerabilities. They are a kind of natural **Rorschach**. We have an opportunity to see what we wish for and what we might be missing. But more than this, we may work through blocks and address insecurities. People can use an avatar as "practice for real life." (p. 212)

Social Interaction

Residents in Second Life spend a significant amount of time in social interactions with other residents. Although some residents are loners or keep to a small circle of friends, most residents spend their time in Second Life interacting with other avatars in informal and formal groups. For example, Boellstorff (2008) conducted an ethnography of Second Life residents where he became a resident himself so he could interact with others and observe the Second Life culture in detail over several years. One of his observations was that most residents are strategic in their social interactions. He said that when many residents begin a session in Second Life, they typically access a map of the Second Life grid that displays a green dot for each avatar in residence. They notice where the greatest concentration of dots are and use this as an indication of where the most interesting social gatherings are taking place. They then gravitate toward those social gatherings so they can connect with large numbers of people and share their social experiences.

Zheng (2009) conducted a study of Second Life residents and found that residents engaged in all sorts of social interactions, where many of those interactions were of an economic nature. That is, residents spent a good deal of time in marketplaces where they exchanged virtual goods and services. This finding led Zheng to speculate that "the convergence of public and market place may suggest a trend in the commercialization of virtual community" (p. 107).

Conditioning

Because participating in various activities in virtual worlds is pleasurable for many people, this experience conditions people for repeated exposures over time. The feeling of immersion is reinforcing to users of virtual worlds to make them feel comfortable and at home there, which leads to a desire to return to those worlds frequently (Turkle, 2011).

AFFECT

Researchers have found that when people use virtual worlds, they tend to experience feelings of immersion, intimacy, and attachment.

Immersion

Successful virtual worlds make users feel totally immersed in the fantasy experience. Turkle (2011) explains that simulation not only demands immersion but also creates a self that prefers immersion through the simulations in the virtual world. A desire to feel this sense of immersion is what drives users for repeated exposures to virtual worlds.

Feelings of Intimacy

Boellstorff (2008) has pointed out that one of the most "consistent findings of cybersociality research has been that virtual worlds can not only transform actual-world intimacy but create real forms of online intimacy. While many residents seek feelings of physical intimacy through sex, almost all residents seek it at a more basic social level of friendship, where they can share their most fundamental feelings, desires, and fears with a significant other." Observers of virtual worlds have long noted that persons engaging in forms of computer-mediated communication often "come to feel that the very best and closest friends are members of their electronic group, whom they seldom or never see" (Boellstorff, 2008, p. 156). And "friendships are the foundation of cybersociality" because "for most residents . . . friendships were a primary reason for their participation. Residents spoke of making life-long friends in Second Life" (p. 157).

Feelings of Attachment

Boellstorff (2008) found that many residents of Second Life were searching for feelings of attachment that could be created by a close social bonding. He found in his research that there were two primary models for social relations in virtual worlds: the friend and the partner. He said that while the drive for friendships was primary among all residents, for many residents, "romance was extremely important," which went beyond physical sexual activity to achieve a close bond of attachment (p. 166).

BELIEFS

Beliefs about self and social norms are influenced through experiences in virtual worlds.

About Self

People who spend a lot of time on Second Life and in role-playing games often say that their online identities make them feel more like themselves than they do in their real lives (Jamison, 2018). This belief is triggered each time a person enters the virtual world. Then over time as people spend more time feeling at home and like themselves in these worlds, this belief gets reinforced more and more.

About Norms

New residents in Second Life have to spend a considerable amount of time learning the social norms of that virtual world, just like people learn the social norms as children in the real world (Boellstorff, 2008). An example of a social norm in Second Life is how close avatars should stand to each other when talking. Another common norm is that a relatively high degree of altruism is expected. Residents are typically expected to offer free advice, support, and objects to other residents, especially new residents.

COGNITIONS

Experiences in virtual worlds influence how people construct meaning and their sense of self.

Constructing Meaning

Zheng (2009) found that Second Life residents construct social meanings for virtual places similar to the way that people construct meaning for places in the real world. Second Life has a geography of islands, neighborhoods, transportation systems, communities, and shared social spaces, which are the physical parameters of the virtual world. Through their interactions with others in those spaces, people come to construct meaning for those places. While Linden Labs created the virtual geography of Second Life, it is the residents who construct meanings for those places. Therefore, cyberspace becomes much more than physical geography of spatial territories; it also has a social geography consisting of a topography of relationships.

Sense of Self

One way to observe how people construct a sense of themselves in virtual worlds is to look at how they have designed their avatars. Mills (2018) conducted a content analysis of 360 female avatars in Second Life to examine how beauty was socially constructed. She found that most female avatars had the ideal body size and light-colored skin. She also found that most female avatars were designed to be sexually alluring to attract attention from other avatars.

Other researchers have found that when people construct their social identity in a virtual world, they do not radically alter who they are from real life. For example, Heider (2009) conducted a study of residents in Second Life and found that although Second Life gives people the opportunity to redefine themselves in radical ways, most residents do not radically redefine themselves. A likely explanation for this is that people enter a virtual world like Second Life not to become someone very different from their real selves (e.g., having superpowers or very different personality characteristics). Instead, people are seeking a way to explore who they really are in ways that real life does not allow them to do. That is, in virtual worlds the social limitations that constrain them in real life are gone, and people are free to be themselves more fully.

In his ethnography of Second Life, Boellstorff (2008) observed,

> In comparison to online games that coexisted with Second Life during the period of my fieldwork, Second Life was not predominantly a role-playing environment. Most of those with whom I interacted felt that role-playing, in the words of one resident, "quickly loses its appeal; then you concentrate on being yourself, since that's what most people are good at." For most residents, their primary mode of engagement with Second Life was as, in some sense "themselves." (p. 119)

He continues, "Their online lives could make their actual-world self more 'real,' in that it could become closer to what they understood to be their true selfhood, unencumbered by social constraints or the particularities of physical embodiment. Common in this regard was the view that virtual-world experiences could lead to greater self-confidence" (p. 121).

Conclusions

Cooperative virtual worlds are digital platforms that allow users to play and explore, much like they would do in their real lives if those lives had fewer social, physical, and economic constraints. These virtual worlds are not places where people typically redefine themselves in major ways and act in a wildly different manner than they do in their real lives. People enter these worlds seeking the pleasure of immersion in a more freeing experience than they are provided with in their real world. They use the experience to grow from where they are and achieve a greater sense of their true essence and of who they can be. Over time, they can build a substantial life—economically and socially—as they acquire more goods and develop more relationships. This long-term process continually conditions them for repeated exposures.

Further Reading

Boellstorff, T. (2008). *Coming of age in Second Life: An anthropologist explores the virtually human.* Princeton, NJ: Princeton University Press. (316 pages with endnotes and index)
    The author is an anthropology professor who spent two years in the virtual world of Second Life as a participant observer. In the book he explains how people act in that world and why they do what they do.

Gibson, M., & Carden, C. (2018). *Living and dying in a virtual world: Digital kinships, nostalgia, and mourning in Second Life.* Cham, Switzerland: Palgrave Macmillan. (154 pages with index)
    This is an ethnographic study of residents in Second Life. This study shows that there are many different reasons that people reside in Second Life as well as ways of living in that virtual world. Also, the line between the virtual world and the real world for residents is often blurred in interesting ways. The study focuses more on the rituals of dying and mourning than on the activities of the living.

CHAPTER 9

Effects of Competing in Digital Games

Box 9.1. Major Digital Games
- Digital Games
  - Who Are the Players?
  - MMORPGs
  - Digital Games as Sport
- Effects on Individuals
  - Behavior
    - Attraction
    - Displacement
    - Aggressive Behavior
    - Addictive Behavior
    - Real-Life Behavior
  - Affect
    - Emotional Arousal
    - Feelings of Well-Being
    - Enjoyment
    - Emotional Desensitization
  - Cognitions
    - Learning Game Rules
    - Immersion
    - Perception of Control
    - Perception of Competency
    - Type of Intelligence
    - Self-Objectification
  - Physiology: Brain Activity
- Conclusions

The desire to compete is a fundamental part of being human. Humans have played games for as long as civilization has existed, as pointed out by the Dutch historian and cultural theorist Johan Huizinga in his classic book *Homo Ludens*. For millennia, humans competed against themselves by trying to solve puzzles and solve mysteries. Humans invented card games and board games (e.g., checkers, chess, Monopoly) to compete against one person or several other people. Huizinga argues that games and play are what make our culture and civilization possible.

With the invention of computers, the competitive platform was greatly expanded. By playing a game against a computer, players can start the game anytime they want and pause the game for as long as they want, they can take as much time as they want to decide their next move, and they can receive immediate feedback on their performance. With the rise of the internet, they can now play against opponents anywhere in the world, so geography is no longer a limitation. Also, they can compete with very large numbers of players, such as in massively multiplayer online role-playing games (MMORPGs). And with the proliferation of mobile devices, they can take their game-playing experiences everywhere they go.

Box 9.1.   Major Digital Games

1970s

Pong (1972). Introduced by Atari as an arcade game; simple single-player game based on ping-pong, where a player uses two dials to manipulate a virtual paddle that hits and redirects a moving ball (blip of light) in order to prevent it from leaving the screen.

Maze War (1973). First game with first-person shooters.

Space Invaders (1978). A shooter arcade game where players use a laser to defeat wave after wave of descending aliens.

MUD (Multi-User Dungeon, 1978). A text-based role-playing game where players read descriptions of rooms, objects, and other players and then decide what actions to take to gain skills and powers that help them complete quests.

Flight Simulator (1979). Players are shown a screen of a control panel in a cockpit of an airplane, and they must make readings of the dials and manipulate the controls to take off, fly, and land the airplane.

1980s

Pac-Man (1980). An arcade game where players navigate Pac-Man through a maze while he eats dots and avoids four multicolored ghosts that become more aggressive the longer the play continues.

Pole Position (1982). An arcade game where players race a car around a track using a steering wheel and gearshift.

Tetris (1984). Players try to arrange blocks into various shapes to solve puzzles.

Super Mario Brothers (1985). Played on a console attached to a TV; players use a controller to navigate Mario and Luigi through the levels of the game.

SimCity (1989). An open-ended city-building game where players develop a city from a patch of undeveloped land by making decisions about infrastructure (roads, sewer lines, utilities, etc.) and public services (schools, parks, hospitals, transportation, etc.).

John Madden Football (1989). Players manage a football team and also control players on the field during a game.

1990s

Street Fighters (1991). An arcade game where players manipulate on-screen characters in a fight.

Myst (1993). A graphic adventure puzzle game played on a personal computer.

Pokemon (1995). Players catch fictional creatures called "Pokemon" and train them to battle each other for sport.

Tomb Raider (1996). Players use the fictional British archaeologist Lara Croft to solve puzzles as she travels around the world searching for lost artifacts and investigating dangerous tombs and ruins.

Grand Theft Auto (1997). An action–adventure video game series where players undertake missions that typically involve high action and violence.

Dance Dance Revolution (1998). An arcade game where players dance on a platform as squares light up signaling where dancers should place their feet.

2000s

Call of Duty (2003). A first-person shooter video game where players experience combat.

World of Warcraft (2004). The most well known MMORPG; action takes place in Azeroth where players control an avatar that goes on missions to earn advancements to higher levels of game play.

Angry Birds (2009). A best-selling app for mobile devices where players use touch screens to control birds as they try to save their eggs from green-colored pigs.

Minecraft (2013). A 3D sandbox (players have the ability to create, modify, or destroy their environment) video game.

Source: Adapted from Barton (2017).

In *Vintage Games 2.0: An Insider Look at the Most Influential Games of All Time*, Barton (2017) observes that digital games range from "Triple-A" major studio productions with budgets in the hundreds of millions to quickie "indie" projects designed by lone hobbyists using cheap or even free development tools.

There are now digital games that cater to every conceivable style and taste. Online distribution services like Apple's App Store, Microsoft's Xbox Games Store, or Steam make an overwhelming variety of digital games easily available to the public. For example, Steam alone has more than 3,700 games, far more than one person could play to any depth in a lifetime. There are games designed for all ages, genders, and even for cats and dogs!

Digital Games

Digital games offer competitive experiences to users in a wide variety of ways. In some of these digital games, players compete against a computer, some games offer players the opportunity to compete against each other in pairs, and some offer players the opportunity to play the game *with* many partners and *against* many other foes scattered all over the world. These games are typically either stand-alone platforms (e.g., an arcade installation, a console that is attached to a television receiver, or a handheld device that is dedicated to games) where players compete against a computer program, or they connect to servers on the internet where users compete against (and with) other players in real time.

What all of these games have in common are visual and audio features that attract users into the game, digital game codes that govern game appearance and play, and input devices that players use to communicate with the digital code in playing the game (Kerr, 2006). Also, digital games are like all of the other forms of mass media in the sense that digital games are commercial products that have been created in a manner to be highly attractive to particular niche audiences, and the games themselves are constructed to condition players for habitual use (Giddings & Kennedy, 2006). However, games are also different than other types of media messages in the sense that they do not take players through a story in the conventional narrative sense (Friedman, 1995). Instead, games offer the potential for players to construct their own stories as they move through the game. These games require the player to move beyond simply absorbing the meanings as presented and pay a heightened level of attention to the game's stream of stimuli that stimulates players to continually make quick decisions. As the consequences of their decisions unfold, players are drawn more deeply into the experience of writing their own stories. This participation gives players a sense of power and a sense of wonder as they explore how far they can progress in the game.

WHO ARE THE PLAYERS?

Many people think of digital game players as being pubescent male nerds who are solitary, reclusive, and socially inept geeks. However, surveys of digital game players have shown this stereotype to be highly inaccurate. People of all ages play digital games. The average digital game player is 30 years old, and 68% of all digital game players are at least 18 years old (Entertainment Software Association, 2013). Also, 47% of all gamers are women, with women over 18 being the fastest-growing market for digital games (Alter, 2017).

Among players of digital games, there is a gender difference, but that difference is not with how much time males and females play digital games; instead, the difference is in the type of games they play. Kowert, Breuer, and Quandt (2017) report that females exhibit "a strong preference for digital versions of traditional games (e.g., games that do not require a special set of skills or a large time commitment to complete), whilst males prefer more 'core' genres (i.e., not casual), such as physical enactment (e.g., fantasy/role playing, action/adventure, strategy, simulation) games" (p. 137). One reason for this difference is that "young men are socially reinforced to engage in video game play whilst young women are discouraged from engaging in the same, cross-sex stereotyped activity. As such, video games provide opportunities for young boys to meet social needs for inclusion and affection but do not serve the same functions for young girls" (p. 138).

Because there is such a wide variety of people who play digital games, marketers have moved beyond using demographics of age and gender to describe the game-playing market; instead, marketers now use psychographics to describe the types of digital game players. Over time, four clearly recognizable types of digital game players have emerged. Those types are explorers, controllers, achievers, and socializers. Explorers are players who are primarily motivated by curiosity; they want to wander around inside the game world to discover all its territories and experiences. Controllers are players who want to dominate others; they desire games with a high degree of competition so they can figure out ways to defeat and dominate worthy opponents. Achievers are players who are attracted to the games in order to build something, such as a city, an empire, or great personal wealth. Finally, socializers are players who like to interact with other players. They want the game to present challenges that require forming groups so that players have an opportunity to work together in accomplishing shared objectives. They are looking for social interaction in the games, so they seek out opportunities to join clubs and engage in cultural activities with others, such as weddings, parties, and other social rituals.

The video game industry is very healthy, with revenue increasing each year, and it employs 220,000 people in the United States alone. In 2017 it generated a record high of $36 billion in revenue, which included sales of hardware, software, and peripherals (Entertainment Software Association, 2018). But it is also a very risky industry. Only about 3% of electronic games earn a profit because the costs of development are so high. For example, designing a prototype for a modest digital game typically costs about $1.5 million. The minimum cost of developing a console game is typically about $7.5 million (Havens & Lotz, 2012), and that cost can escalate quickly. For example, the cost of developing Star Wars: The Old Republic was $200 million, and the cost of developing Grand Theft Auto V was $265 million (Valente, 2019).

MMORPGs

A popular form of digital games is the massively multiplayer online role-playing game (MMORPG). The earliest example of this type of game was MUD (Multi-User Dungeon), which was a digital translation of the popular Dungeons & Dragons board game. It "allowed multiple users to interact with the world and each other simultaneously via the Internet—and pit their avatars against each other in battle using a server-based incarnation of D&D's die-rolling system" (Ivory, 2009, p. 15).

One of the most popular and elaborate MMORPGs is World of Warcraft (WoW), which was released in 2004 and quickly grew to attract millions of players all over the world. In order to play WoW, players are required to purchase the computer software for $19.99, then pay a monthly fee of $14.99 to play online. By 2009, WoW had 11.5 million players worldwide, making it the most successful online video game in the world (Fritz, 2009). In its first decade, the game generated over $10 billion in gross income as it attracted more than 100 million subscribers. If WoW subscribers were a country, its population would be the 12th largest in the world (Alter, 2017).

Players of WoW inhabit a medieval-type world called Azeroth where their avatars roam across landscapes, fight monsters, complete quests, and interact with other players.

> Azeroth is a complex virtual world composed of two primary landmasses: the western regions of Kalimdor and the Eastern Kingdoms. Both of the areas are subdivided into distinct regions, with each having its own unique geography, ecology, culture, and inhabitants. Players move their characters through these "zones" in search of adventure, treasure, fortune, reputation, and conquest. The ostensive goal of WoW is to explore the world of Azeroth while "leveling up" a character, defeating a whole host of monsters, acquir-

ing equipment and rewards, and interacting with other players from around the world. (Boyns, Forghani, & Sosnovskaya, 2009, p. 68)

All players begin the game at Level 1 and gradually gain the appropriate amount of experience to move from one level to the next. New players spend months building up their characters while avoiding being killed (called "ganked" in WoW) by more experienced players. As a player advances in the game, the challenges become more difficult, and the rewards become more substantial. The initial version of WoW offered 60 levels, but this was increased to 70 levels with the Burning Crusade expansion. After months of play, the good players get to Level 60 where they join with other players in guilds and undertake intricately planned raids on dungeons to kill dragons and engage in massive rumbles against other guilds.

The game-playing experience involves the completion of "quests," the discovery of new territories, and combat with the enemies created by the game designers. Quests are frequently the most efficient means of gaining experience, and they often provide substantial material rewards, such as clothing, magical items, or weapons. There are more than 2,000 quests currently available in the game, and they require players to successfully complete unique tasks. Each of these adventures reflects different types of quest modes. For example, collection quests require players to investigate Azeroth and collect specific items, while delivery quests enlist players to act as couriers of messages from one region to another. Discovery quests involve seeking out specific territories or locations, killing quests require a specific number of enemies to be slain, and dungeon quests are composed of a combination of types (Boyns et al., 2009).

Over time as other MMORPGs have grown in popularity, the intense competition among MMORPGs for players has reduced the number of WoW's regular players significantly to about 5 million players in 2018, and this downward trend was forecast for at least the next 5 years (Statistica, 2018).

DIGITAL GAMES AS SPORT

Digital gaming has become so popular that it has grown into a major sport. Many colleges now recruit digital game players and offer them athletic scholarships worth up to $19,000 per year. Varsity digital game players wear team jerseys displaying the logos of their sponsors. Team members are required to engage in daily practicing, which can range up to 5 hours per day. The Collegiate StarLeague now has 450 schools and 10,000 players, including well-known universities such as Harvard, Stanford, and Georgia Tech. They compete in the North American College Championship (NACC), where the winning team earns $30,000 in scholarship money (Gregory, 2015).

There are also professional leagues of video gamers, and these contests are regularly televised on major cable channels such as ESPN. According to SuperData Research, 93 million people watched an e-sports event in 2015. When the League of Legends held its pro World Championship in October 2013, it drew a viewership of 32 million, which was a much larger audience that the 26.3 million people who watched Game 7 of that year's NBA Finals (Gregory, 2015). By 2018, the viewership of all e-sports on television had grown to 380 million, and it was expected to grow to more than 550 million viewers by 2021 (Koch, 2019).

Some players of digital games have gotten so good that they have attracted fans who pay to watch them compete. There are even websites (Twitch and Mixer) that are dedicated to fans who want to watch people play digital games. In 2018 viewers spent 8.4 billion hours watching gamers being live-streamed on Twitch, which is a company that Amazon bought in 2013. One gamer, known as Ninja, attracted 14 million followers on Twitch (Video games, 2019, p. 32).

"Our culture loves video games, and it's difficult to imagine what our lives would be like without them," explains Barton (2017). "After the 'Great Video Game Crash of 1983,' prognosticators were all too ready to declare that the 'fad' of video games was over. Obviously, that didn't happen, and video games have only gotten bigger and better since the glorious days of *Pac-Man*, *Space Invaders*, and *Donkey Kong*."

Effects on Individuals

Research on the effects of digital gaming on individuals is, of course, relatively new, but already there are some clear patterns of findings emerging. Most of those patterns reflect effects on individuals' behaviors, affects, and cognitions.

BEHAVIOR

Researchers have found that the experience of competing in digital games can lead to several behavioral effects, including increased attraction to competition, displacement of nongaming activities, aggression, addiction, and influencing other real-life behaviors.

Attraction

Humans have been attracted to games for as long as civilization has existed (Huizinga, 1949). That attraction has increased with the easy availability of digital games now provided on platforms that allow people to play against a computer or to play against (and with) players all over the world.

Attraction to digital game playing has been linked to the ability of these games to satisfy the need that many people have to socialize with others on a common task. Boyns et al. (2009) explain, "The unique design of WoW transforms the game into much more than a 'game space,' it is also a sociological space that facilitates a complex array of social interactions and opportunities for sociability" (p. 68). Also, an online survey of 399 U.S. adults aged 18–75 found that playing the augmented reality (AR) game Pokémon Go was associated with friendship formation and friendship intensification (Bonus, Peebles, Mares, & Sarmiento, 2018).

Displacement

Another behavioral effect of playing MMORPGs is displacement, which is engaging in one activity to the extent that it takes away time and interest from engaging in other activities. Digital games provide players with a cyberworld that is often much more attractive than their real worlds, so players shift their time and resources into these cyberworlds, thus displacing the time they used to spend in their real worlds. For many players, the cyberworlds offer experiences they cannot get in their real world, so players move into the cyberworld and live their lives there, where they create economies, political systems, friendships, romantic attachments, and careers. In his book *Synthetic Worlds*, Edward Castronova (2005) argues that

> the synthetic worlds now emerging from the computer game industry . . . are becoming an important host of ordinary human affairs. There is much more than gaming going on there; conflict, governance, trade, love. The number of people who could be said to "live" out there in cyberspace is already numbering in the millions; it is growing and we are already beginning to see subtle and not-so-subtle effects of this behavior at the societal level in real Earth countries. (p. 2)

Williams (2006) conducted a one-month panel study of online digital game playing and found some displacement effects. He found that exposure to entertainment messages was reduced as digital game-playing time increased.

Scholars typically expect that the playing of digital games displaces real-world interpersonal relationships, but research on this is contradictory. For example, a longitudinal study examining gaming- and non-gaming-related friendships and social support among a representative sample of social online players (i.e., people who play online video games with others) found that playing digital games with online or offline friends is not related to perceived social support, positively or negatively, cross-sectionally or longitudinally (Domahidi, Breuer, Kowert, Festl, & Quandt, 2018). In contrast, Williams (2006) found that some kinds of existing friendships eroded and the most social players became more insulated from one another, which has been referred to as "**cocooning**." Also, some people are able to use digital game playing to improve their interpersonal skills and then use those improved skills successfully in developing interpersonal relationships in the real world.

Aggressive Behavior

In a major review of video game play research, Jones and colleagues (2014) found that playing violent digital games was related to increases in aggressiveness. This finding is not surprising given that many digital games are designed to put players in situations requiring them to engage in physical conflict in order to survive or advance in the game. Game designers build in levels where a player must fight off increasingly stronger opponents to get their rewards, and this conditioning during game playing spills over into players' real lives.

Addictive Behavior

Polls find that 90% of American children under the age of 18 play video games (Kamenetz, 2018). This widespread use has led social critics to claim that digital game playing will lead to considerable numbers of people becoming addicted. There is some evidence to support this claim. Kamenetz (2018) has found that about 8% of all digital game players meet the conditions for addiction. Also, Castronova (2005) conducted a study of users of these games and found that about 57% said they would quit their real-world job and work in the cyberworld if they could make enough money there to support themselves, and three quarters of players wished they could spend all of their time in the cyberworld of the game.

Fear of addiction has been directed especially at MMORPGs (Yee, 2002). Alter (2017) explains why MMORPGs are so addictive when he says, "Many players band together to form guilds—teams of allied avatars—which is part of what makes the game so addictive. It's hard to sleep at night when you know three of your guild-mates in Copenhagen, Tokyo, and Mumbai are on an epic quest without you" (p. 17).

Games like WoW "attract millions of teens and young adults, and a considerable minority—up to 40%—develop addictions" (Alter, 2017, p. 17). Alter (2017) calls WoW "one of the most addictive behavioral experiences on the planet. Almost half of all players consider themselves 'addicted.' An article in *Popular Science* described WoW as 'the obvious choice' when searching for the world's most addictive game. There are support groups with thousands of members, and more than a quarter of a million people have taken the free online World of Warcraft Addiction Test."

There are examples of digital game players becoming so addicted to playing these games that it has led to their death. For example, a Korean player was found dead of exhaustion after spending 80 continuous hours in Lineage without a break. An EverQuest user committed suicide triggered by a feeling of desperation conditioned by events within the game world (Castronova, 2005).

China is so concerned about digital game addiction that it has asked designers of digital games made in the United States to build tools into their games to track how much time minors spend online playing these games so that the games will cut off access to people who try to play more than 2 hours a day. In response, Riot Games has added an anti-addiction system to the Chinese version of its League of Legends to comply with China's new regulations (China's video game surveillance, 2019, p. 20).

Real-Life Behaviors

The research shows that playing digital games in some circumstances influences players' real-life behaviors while, in other circumstances, it does not. Thus it is too simple to conclude from the research that digital game-playing behavior always influences real-life behaviors. One finding from the research is that different types of games exert different degrees of influence. For example, in a study of digital game playing and its relationship to risky behaviors in real life, Gilbert, Giaccardi, and Ward (2018) conducted a survey of 273 undergraduate men at a large Midwestern university. They found that playing sports video games was associated with greater alcohol use, drug use, and delinquent behaviors. However, they found that playing action-type games—in contrast to sports-type games—was negatively associated with real-life use of alcohol and drugs.

Research has also found that the type of avatar is related to different levels of influence on players' real-life behaviors. For example, when game players design an avatar in a way that players think they ought to be, they are likely to change their behavior later in real life to conform to how they thought the avatar ought to act. Sah, Ratan, Tsai, Peng, and Sarinopoulos (2017) designed a study where female participants ($N = 133$) customized an avatar in a digital game to reflect their actual self, an ideal self, or a self they felt they ought to be. Participants then selected food items for their avatar within the digital game as well as food items for themselves to eat afterward. The results of this study showed that only using the "ought-self" avatar in playing a game influenced real-world behaviors. That is, research participants who designed an avatar to behave in a game in a way that participants thought they ought to behave (were conscious of their health) demonstrated an influence on their real-world behaviors. No such effect emerged for participants who used an ideal-self or actual-self avatar, indicating that participants formed the goal of being healthy only with regard to the ought-self. This study demonstrates that the way avatars behave in a digital game can lead to players adopting those same behaviors in their real life—but only under certain conditions.

AFFECT

Designers of digital games carefully consider the game's affective tone as a way of triggering particular emotions in people as they play their games. There is a range of emotions open to game designers.

Emotional Arousal

People play games in order to feel aroused and to experience strong emotions. Games can arouse players and can trigger emotions when they are both losing (frustration, humiliation, and anger) and winning (joy and elation). These emotions are often more intense than the emotions normally triggered in a person's real life, especially when players are fully immersed in competitive situations.

One factor that has been found to increase emotional intensity in digital game playing is the use of musical sound tracks (Klimmt et al., 2019). In one experiment, young males ($N = 68$) played Assassin's Creed: Black Flag with the original soundtrack music either present or absent, and then reported their enjoyment of the game-playing experience. In a second study, young males ($N = 59$) played an episode of Alien: Isolation with soundtrack music present or absent and reported their horror experience. The results of both studies show that the soundtrack served to intensify emotional reactions.

Feelings of Well-Being

In a major review of video game play research, Jones and colleagues (2014) concluded that moderate to low levels of game play can have a positive influence on players and their feelings of well-being. The researchers said that video game play has been shown to improve mood, reduce emotional anxiety, improve emotional regulation, increase feelings of relaxation, and reduce stress. Also, moderate play has been shown to be associated with better health outcomes than either excessive video game play or no play at all. The experience of feelings of competence, autonomy, and relatedness during video game play has been linked with higher self-esteem and certainly to greater success in life. A person's mood can also be improved by digital game play when players experience success (Koban et al., 2019).

Enjoyment

Even though MMORPGs are highly competitive, enjoyment is increased when players band together into teams and develop strong attachments to their team members (Schmierbach et al., 2012). Also, an online survey of 399 U.S. adults aged 18–75 found that playing the AR game Pokémon Go increased positive affect, such as nostalgic reverie (Bonus et al., 2018).

Emotional Desensitization

In a longitudinal experiment, Grizzard, Tamborini, Sherry, and Weber (2017) examined (a) whether repeated violent game play led to emotional desensitization and (b) whether desensitization generalized to other play and real-life experiences. Participants played alternate versions of the same violent game for the first four days of the experiment; on these days, some participants played the game as a United Nations soldier (moral condition), while other participants played the game as a terrorist soldier (immoral condition). On Day 5, all participants played a novel game as a terrorist. Results indicated two things. First, habituation occurred over repeated game play, that is, repeated exposure decreased the ability of the players to experience a feeling of guilt. Second, the decreased ability to elicit guilt was found to be generalized to other game-playing experiences, that is, the guilt that was elicited by the novel game on Day 5 was reduced more for the immoral character condition compared to the moral character condition. These findings provide causal, longitudinal evidence that playing digital games can lead to emotional desensitization.

In their review of digital game play research, Jones and colleagues (2014) found that playing violent video games was related to desensitization to the suffering of victims of violence under certain conditions. Specifically, the playing of digital games can reduce a player's feelings of guilt about behaving in antisocial ways. When feelings of guilt are reduced, players feel less sympathy for victims of harm.

COGNITIONS

Playing digital games has been found to lead to a variety of cognitive effects, including learning game rules, immersion, perceptions of control, perception of competency, type of intelligence, and self-objectification.

Learning Game Rules

As players experience a digital game, they learn what the rules of the game are. In general, designers typically build their games around six rules that are designed to reduce the risk that players will reject their games. First, there must be some reward to the player, and the rewards must go to only the good players. Bad players should be punished, but the punishment should never be for something that happened outside a player's control. Second, the game should be relatively easy to learn. Of course some games are very complex, but the complexity is not revealed to a player in the beginning. Instead, the complexity is gradually revealed step-by-step as the player moves through the game. Third, the game should be predictable. The game should follow logical rules so that players can predict the outcome of their actions. Fourth, the game should be consistent. The outcome of a particular action must always be the same. Fifth, there should be a fair degree of familiarity. This means that designers should consider what players bring to the game and use it. And sixth, the game should be challenging. If it is too simple, players will quickly lose interest. Instead, designers must build in layers where players advance to greater and greater challenges to keep them playing.

Immersion

Digital games, especially MMORPGs, have been found to trigger perceptions in players that they are immersed in an intense situation. Games do this by setting up sequences of challenges that pull players deeper and deeper into the action and thereby motivate players to continue playing. For example, Castronova and colleagues (2009) explain that MMORPGs

> start players with only a fraction of the game play options and abilities that they will have at the end of the game. A newly created player character starts with the most rudimentary abilities and will later gain additional advancements through exploring the world and accomplishing various tasks. One type of character advancement is the acquiring of "innate" abilities—abilities that allow the character to attack in a certain way, heal other characters, or accomplish any number of actions in the world. The second type of advancement is the acquiring of items more "external" to the player character—armor, weapons, and tools that enhance a character's innate abilities. . . . There are three main reasons that items are valuable: some items, such as arrows or food, are constantly being used up and need to be replaced; other items are made valuable by the amount that they increase a character's abilities; and other items are valuable simply because they are

hard to obtain and anyone who acquires the item gains social prestige with the other players. (pp. 167, 168)

Psychologists who study how people play digital games have come up with two terms to describe the experience of immersion: flow and telescoping. Flow is a term coined by the social psychologist Mihaly Csikszentmihalyi (1998) to refer to the cognitive state of being so involved in a task that people lose all sense of place and time. With digital games, players often become so involved in a game that it is as if they enter the world presented on the screen and lose the sense that they are in the real world. Players become so focused on meeting the immediate challenges presented by the game that other needs (such as thirst, sleep, and hunger) become secondary, that is, satisfying those secondary needs gets put off in the interest of satisfying the primary need of achieving the next objective in the game. The expectation of successfully completing the next objective in the game is so pleasurable that everything else is forgotten while in the **flow state**.

Flow has typically been viewed as a solitary experience in the literature, that is, flow isolates individuals from one another. But recently scholars have been examining it in the context of social interaction in gaming (Borderie & Michinov, 2017; Sawyer, 2007; Walker, 2010). Research has found that when players are strongly bound together in achieving a task, they can all share the feeling of flow.

Telescoping refers to the way digital game players focus on the steps within the process of moving through a game (Johnson, 2005). At any given point in a digital game, the player must focus on an immediate objective that follows from previous objectives that were successfully achieved and lead to upcoming objectives that take the player to the end of the game. This focusing on the immediate objective is viewed as the foreground, and all the other objectives are pushed into the background where they are used as only context for the foregrounded objective. Thus game players must keep the big picture in mind as they concentrate on achieving their immediate objective. When they meet their immediate objective, they do not stop playing; instead, they suddenly feel propelled onward to the challenge of achieving their next objective. Johnson says that "talented gamers have mastered the ability to keep all these varied objectives alive in their heads simultaneously" (p. 54).

Telescoping is not the same as multitasking. Multitasking is handling an assortment of unrelated objectives at the same time, such as talking on the phone, instant messaging friends, listening to music on an iPod, and googling topics. Telescoping focuses more on how people navigate through a sequence of ordered tasks one at a time to progress to the end point of that sequence.

Game-playing immersion through the cognitive states of flow and telescoping is strongly associated with affective effects, because they reward players with feelings of pleasure. These cognitive states can act like a narcotic that continually draws players back to gaming for a repeat of the experience. And once players feel the experience, they want it to continue uninterrupted. When game play is interrupted, players want to get back to the game as quickly as possible.

Digital game immersion can lead to players becoming more detached from objective reality (Aardema, O'Conner, Cote, & Taillon, 2010). This can lead to altered perceptions of one's body such that over time players perceive themselves as having the same characteristics as their avatars (Banakou, Groten, & Slater, 2013; Kilteni, Groten, & Slater, 2012; Normand, Giannopoulos, Spanlang, & Slater, 2011).

Perception of Control

Playing digital games often triggers a perception of control in players. Many of us feel a lack of control over events in our real lives where we seem to continually work at things that fail to deliver adequate rewards. We sometimes feel that our lives are so routine that we never seem to make any progress, which Castronova (2005) refers to as the **Sisyphus problem**. Sisyphus was a character in Greek mythology who was doomed to push a heavy boulder up a hill, and each time as he neared the top, he would weaken from the exertion and the boulder would roll back down the hill. Sisyphus would have to start all over again, day after day. Castronova (2009) explains that many people feel like some burdens of their everyday life are too onerous to push over the top of a hill, so they play digital games where they can be successful and metaphorically get that boulder all the way to the peak so it will roll down the other side. When people are able to successfully accomplish tasks in a game world, they are rewarded with a perception that they are in control of events and outcomes.

Perception of Competency

Playing electronic games also satisfies the cognitive need for competence. We all want challenges to motivate us, and we also want the experience of meeting those challenges so that we can feel successful. Digital games offer a sequence of gradually increasing challenges that begin with fairly easy tasks that we can finish quickly. The completion of these initial tasks makes us feel competent, and this motivates us to continue toward more challenging tasks with increasing confidence. As we complete these more challenging tasks, the feeling of reward intensifies and our confidence builds, which propels us toward even more challenging tasks.

Type of Intelligence

Digital game playing has been found to be related to players' **fluid intelligence** but not to their **crystalline intelligence**. This is the finding of a longitudinal study conducted to investigate the relationship between children's digital game use and type of intelligence (Fikkers, Piotrowski, & Valkenburg, 2019). Using data from 934 children aged 3 to 7 years (52% girls) across four waves with 1-year intervals, the researchers also found no relationship between type of intelligence and attraction to digital game playing, that is, people high on either type of intelligence were not found to be more attracted to playing digital games. However, people high in fluid intelligence were found to be more facile at learning the rules of the game on their own and at figuring out ways around obstacles better than players who were high on crystalline intelligence.

Self-Objectification

Playing digital games with a sexualized avatar has been found to increase **self-objectification** among adolescents. Vandenbosch, Driesmans, Trekels, and Eggermont (2017) conducted an experiment to examine the effects of playing sexualizing video games on adolescent boys' and girls' self-objectified body image. Participants were early and middle adolescents ($N = 115$) who played a digital game with either a male or a female sexualized avatar. Researchers found that playing the digital game with a sexualized avatar increased self-objectification. This effect occurred regardless of the gender of the adolescent.

PHYSIOLOGY: BRAIN ACTIVITY

Research has found that brain activity changes when people play digital games and enter a state of flow, which is characterized by high cognitive control accompanied with a low degree of mental effort. Using functional magnetic resonance imaging (fMRI) while their research participants played a video game that was manipulated in terms of task difficulty, Huskey, Wilcox, and Weber (2018) found that when the game tasks matched their participants' game-playing ability, there was a high degree of brain activity in the fronto-parietal control network, which indicated cognitive control. They also found a corresponding low degree of global brain activity, which indicated low metabolic cost. This brain pattern indicates a state of flow.

Conclusions

Digital games offer competitive experiences that lead to a wide range of effects, especially behavioral, affective, and cognitive. Although research into the phenomenon of digital games is relatively new, there is already a considerable amount of evidence that these games trigger attraction to them and that continual game playing reinforces this attraction even to the point of addiction. The games are emotionally arousing as players are drawn deeper into the play and experience feelings of enjoyment and aggression. The game-playing experience also triggers all sorts of cognitions, especially perceptions of immersion, flow, control, and competency.

CHAPTER 10

Effects on Institutions

As you have seen in the previous chapters, digital media have been exerting all kinds of influence on individuals that have led to a wide variety of effects. Now in this chapter, we examine how digital media's influence has been affecting institutions. Most of the research on this topic has concentrated on three institutions: the economy, politics, and religion. This chapter presents some research that shows that the institutions of health care, families, and communities have also been influenced by digital media.

The Economy

The rise of digital media has significantly influenced the institution of the economy, especially in three ways. First, it has created virtual economies that influence real-world economies. Second, it has changed retailing. And third, it has altered the way analog media do business.

VIRTUAL ECONOMIES

Digital media have made it possible to create virtual economies. Recall from Chapter 8 ("Effects of Living in Virtual Worlds") and Chapter 9 ("Effects of Competing in Digital Games") that the last few decades have seen the creation and growth of internet plat-forms that attract millions of people who each spend considerable amounts of time on a regular basis in these virtual worlds where users continually engage in resource exchanges. These virtual worlds attract users who exchange their resource of time (and sometimes money) in order to receive the cooperative and competitive experiences that these digital platforms offer. Many of these digital platforms also offer users opportunities to engage in exchanges of virtual goods and services both with the platforms and with other users. These systems of exchange have developed into quite elaborate economies.

One example of a virtual world with a well-developed economy is Second Life. When people join Second Life and become a "resident," they need to acquire clothing, living accommodations, and many other goods and services. Ethnographer J. Sonia Huang (2009) talks about when she first entered Second Life: "I noticed that a basic avatar had very limited movements (i.e., walk, run, fly, and sit down). If I wanted my avatar to hug, dance, or express an emotion, I would have had to purchase so-called 'scripted attachments' or 'animation overidders,' which then would allow my avatar to be more humanized in SL" (p. 193). She continues, "Unlike other virtual worlds where game creators are also the main suppliers of in-world goods and services, SL's technology allows residents to build anything imaginable—from clothes, vehicles, houses, to buildings. Most importantly, SL residents retain full ownership of their virtual creations. In other words, they are free to buy and sell anything they own in SL" (pp. 193–194). Therefore, in Second Life, residents can buy things with their time and money and also sell things to other residents, which makes for a more dynamic and extensive economy.

Digital gaming platforms have also created virtual worlds with elaborate econo-mies. MMORPGs (massively multiplayer online role-playing games) such as EverQuest and World of Warcraft attract millions of players from all over the world who continu-ally participate in economic exchanges as part of the game play. Players are given op-portunities to engage in work-like tasks in order to earn some type of "coin of the realm" for this work. Players can then use this currency to buy necessities and even luxuries to enhance their game-playing experience. They can also barter exchanges of goods with other players. In these ways, players can gradually amass wealth within the game.

While many of these exchanges of resources take place exclusively within those virtual worlds, much of that economic activity crosses the boundaries of those virtual worlds and moves into real-world economies. For example, in the early 2000s, some players of MMORPGs began trying to sell the resources they earned within game worlds to people in the real world for real-world currencies. For example, players of EverQuest would work at menial tasks in that particular cyberworld where they were paid around 300 platinum pieces an hour on average. Some of these players sold their platinum pieces on eBay to other EverQuest game players for U.S. dollars. The exchange rate at the time was about $3.50 U.S. for 300 EverQuest platinum pieces (Castronova, 2005). Of course, $3.50 an hour is far below the minimum wage in America, but in other countries it is a good income. Some ambitious people in poor third world countries entered the EverQuest cyberworld every day to work at tasks like hammering metal into suits of armor by clicking a mouse all day; they then sold those virtual suits of armor on eBay to EverQuest game players who were willing to pay for the virtual armor with real-world currencies. As of 2004, eBay was hosting about $30 million of annual trade for goods that only exist in virtual worlds. Much of this trade was for real currencies, meaning that eBay was in the foreign-currency exchange market (Castronova, 2005, p. 149).

Many of these virtual world platforms have established their own currency exchanges where users can trade the cryptocurrencies they earn in those virtual worlds (such as platinum pieces in EverQuest and Linden Dollars in Second Life) into real-world currencies (such as dollars or euros). By the end of 2017, the exchange market for cryptocurrencies was averaging daily trading volumes of more than $50 billion, which was more than the daily trading volume of the New York Stock Exchange (Williams-Grut, 2017).

Not only have people been moving resources from virtual worlds into the real world, but also real-world companies have been trying to market their products within virtual worlds. For example, Adidas had sold more than 21,000 virtual shoes to Second Life residents; these are shoes that avatars wear in the virtual worlds, not shoes the players of those games wear in the real world. Toyota created a futuristic urban island called Scion City within Second Life. Toyota opened a virtual dealership in Second Life where residents can buy Toyota vehicles and even take them for test drives on Toyota's racetrack. AOL launched an interactive mall dubbed AOL Pointe, where residents can buy clothes for their avatars, skate in a park, and watch videos together. And in October 2006, Reuters, one of the oldest existing news agencies in real life, chose to station a full-time reporter in Second Life in order to cover events in that virtual world and then disseminate those stories along with real-world news feeds to residents of Second Life (Huang, 2009). Entrepreneurs have even started consulting businesses (e.g., Millions of Us and Rivers Run Red) that help real-world companies establish retail outlets within these virtual worlds (Dai, 2009, p. 209).

RETAILING

With the rise of digital media, retailers have opened stores on the internet, and people have been shifting from buying products in brick-and-mortar stores to buying products online. Although this e-commerce is relatively new, it already accounted for $304 billion by the end of 2014, which was 6.4% of all retail sales in the United States that year. It continues to grow and was expected to reach $587 billion in sales by 2019, which would account for about 11% of all retail sales in that year (Lipsman, 2019). According to eMarketer, 91% of internet users are digital shoppers, defined as internet users who have browsed, researched, or compared products digitally via any device whether or not they bought digitally.

Online Retailers

Two of the dominant platforms for e-commerce are Amazon and eBay. The pioneer in online retailing is Amazon.com, which was created by Jeff Bezos in 1994 and went online the following year as a website for selling books. The company began diversifying beyond selling printed books by also producing readers for electronic books called Kindle. Then over the years it has continued to expand its offering of products until now it also sells video, software, electronics, apparel, furniture, toys, jewelry, and even food.

Amazon.com was built with a business model that emphasized convenience, variety, and low prices. Consumers could find the books (and later other products) they were looking for more easily and then order those products online for quick delivery. Because it had no brick-and-mortar stores and a small inventory, Amazon's overhead costs were fairly low. Its high volume of business allowed it to keep prices low and even offer free delivery of products.

As of 2012, Amazon's "market value had reached $80 billion, which was 60 percent higher than the combined value of two large and successful offline retailers, Target and Kohl's, who had almost 2,900 stores between them" (Lieber & Syverson, 2012, p. 189). By 2018, Amazon had become the largest internet-based retailer in the United States and was generating revenues of $232.9 billion with net income of $10.1 billion (Market Mogul Team, 2018). Amazon now controls almost 40% of all e-commerce in the United States. It is responsible for 42% of all books sold and a third of the market for streaming video. More than 1.9 million small businesses in the United States now use Amazon as a place to sell their goods and services, and in 2018 about 200,000 of those vendors generated sales of at least $100,000 each by using Amazon (Amazon, 2019, p. 20).

eBay was launched in September 1995 by Pierre Omidyar as an online auction site where anyone who wanted to sell household items could post pictures and descriptions of their items online and allow viewers to bid on those items. When sellers accept a bid, they arrange for the sale of the item through eBay and then mail the item to the buyer. Within two years, eBay had accounted for more than 1 million items sold. In 1998, the company went public selling stock as a public corporation. By 2007, it had a quarter of a billion registered users worldwide, with 100 million items on sale at any given time, ranging from items selling for a few dollars to a Gulfstream II business jet that sold for $4.9 million in 2001 (The basics of selling on eBay, 2007). By 2013, its annual revenue had increased to $16 billion, but then it declined to about $9.5 billion in 2018 (MarketWatch.com, 2018).

Advantages for Shoppers

Online retailers offer some clear advantages to shoppers that make their services superior to brick-and-mortar stores. These advantages are convenience, greater choice, customer service, and customization.

Convenience   Online retailers have streamlined the shopping experience. People with a mobile device connected to the internet can shop anywhere anytime. Shoppers do not need to go to a physical location, and they do not need to wait for a store to open. When they buy a product, shoppers do not need to carry it back home, because it will be delivered instead, often with no fee for delivery.

Greater Choice   Online retailers offer a much wider selection of products than do brick-and-mortar retailers, which are limited by the physical size of their store. For example, a big brick-and-mortar store like Walmart has about 120,000 different products for sale on its shelves, while Amazon offers more than 353 million different products for sale.

Many shoppers feel overwhelmed by too many choices offered by digital retailers, so many of these retailers have developed recommendation systems that narrow each shopper's choices down to a manageable number by using algorithms that consider each shopper's past retail behaviors. These recommender systems arrive at their suggestions in two different ways. One way is for the recommender system to access data about the shopper's personal tastes, their buying history, and even their browsing history. This information is then used to suggest products that the shopper is most likely to want. A second way is for the recommender system to wait for a shopper to buy a product and then recommend additional products that other shoppers have typically bought at the same time (Jian & Mackie-Mason, 2012).

A great deal of research goes into continually improving recommender systems. Some companies have the goal of improving their recommender systems to such a high degree of precision that their systems will be able to guess what each shopper wants and make a recommendation before those people even begin shopping.

> Recently Amazon was awarded a patent for what it calls "anticipatory shipping." Essentially Amazon wants to start shipping you a package before you officially clicked "buy." The retailer would predict what you want before you actually buy it by relying on—what else?—digital data. Factors such as previous orders, product searches, historical purchasing behavior, demographics, and wish lists among any number of other categories of data, could help inform algorithms designed to predict your next purchase before you actually make that purchase. (DuBravac, 2015, pp. 111–112)

While recommender systems reduce choices to a manageable number for shoppers, this reduction in choice comes with a risk of consumers being manipulated unfairly by retailers. Fudenberg and Villas-Boas (2012) point out that with the developments in information technology, firms have more detailed digital information about their prospective and previous customers, which provides new mechanisms for price discrimination. In particular, when firms have information about consumers' previous buying or search behavior, they may be able to use that information to charge different prices to consumers with different purchase histories. This form of differential pricing is already being used in several markets, and may become increasingly prevalent as companies use greater amounts of consumer data to market their products more aggressively.

Customer Service   When companies have websites, they make themselves constantly available to consumers. Social media is the most preferred communication channel for customers to reach a company customer service representative. Most social media users expect a response from a business in under four hours, and 42% expect a response within one hour (Tuten & Solomon, 2018).

> Brands that respond quickly and effectively can turn complaints into positive experiences and compliments into delight. Sadly, most brands don't. Though as much as half of the social media posts directed to brands requested a response, less than 15% of those messages got a response from the brand in question. For those that did get a response, the average response time was more than eight hours. Being ignored is an insult in the conversational realm of social media. And customers respond in-kind: 36% of shunned customers say they will try to shame the company online, 29% intend to switch to a competitor of future purchases, and 14% say they write negative reviews. (Tuten & Solomon, 2018, p. 293)

Another form of customer service is for retailers to provide shoppers with lots of information and pictures about their products so shoppers can make easy comparisons on their screens. Comparison shopping is also aided by online sites that allow users of products to post reviews. Research shows that these review sites are very popular, with 95% of consumers reporting having read reviews prior to making a purchase decision; two thirds of consumers read between one and ten reviews before making a purchase (Tuten & Solomon, 2018). Also, a study of Yelp reviews posted by buyers of products from more than 4,000 small businesses found that the unsolicited organic Yelp reviews were associated with increases in revenue of about $8,000 annually on average across all companies. Another study found that for independent restaurants, an increase in a Yelp rating by even one star was associated with an annual increase in sales revenues of 5% to 9% (Tuten & Solomon, 2018).

However, there is reason to be skeptical of many reviews, because a high proportion of the reviews on well-known sites are either fraudulent or incentivized. It has been found that as much as 30% of online reviews are fraudulent, which means that the review was either written by people who had not actually bought the product they were reviewing or written by the marketers of their own products (very positive review) or for competing brands (negative review; Tuten & Solomon, 2018).

Incentivized reviews are generated by "opinion influencers," who are people who have blogs with thousands or even millions of followers and who are paid to promote a particular product. Product sellers who use online sites frequently solicit five-star reviews and even offer to pay for them with free products or even cash (Reviews, 2019, p. 33).

While many retailers who provide opportunities for consumers to review their products online often enforce strict guidelines for reviewers and even check those reviews for honesty, many reviews can mislead consumers before they are identified as being fraudulent. For example, one journalist told a story about buying an iPhone charger that had received "3,971 five-star reviews" on Amazon. "When it arrived, the charger broke within minutes, I reached out to Amazon and those thousands of five-star reviews for the charger disappeared. The product now has 11 reviews and holds a rating of 2.5 stars. But before all those [reviews] disappeared, how many shoppers spotted this $13.99 charger page on Amazon's first-page results and fell for the scam?" (quoted in Reviews, 2019, p. 33).

Comparison shopping across different retailers is also enhanced by **shopbots**, which are electronic intermediaries that assist buyers when they search for product and price information on the internet. Shopbots, which have been operating on the internet since the late 1990s, do not sell items themselves—instead they gather and aggregate price, product, and other relevant information from third-party sellers and present it to the users in an accessible way so consumers can easily compare offers. Shopbots also display links to vendors' websites to help shoppers quickly go to those sites that offer the best deals (Moraga-Gonzalez & Wildenbeest, 2012).

Customization   Digital retailers are also moving toward customizing products themselves to make them more useful for individual users. DuBravac (2015) predicts that there will soon be a "fully personalized economy. Products, up till now mass-produced, will be produced specifically for the individual who buys them" (p. 124). Until the industrial revolution in the mid-nineteenth century, products were made one at a time to custom-fit the needs of each customer. For example, tailors made clothes from scratch to fit the body shape of each individual. With the industrial revolution, products were mass produced to standard sizes so people had to fit the products. Now with digitization there is mass customization of products (DuBravac, 2015, p. 267). This digital customization incorporates the advantages of mass production of products while giving consumers the ability to request alterations of standard products in order to meet their specific needs.

Advantages for Retailers

The advantages of online retailing are not limited to shoppers; retailers also experience considerable advantages. These include reduced overhead costs, reduced risk, greater ability to target particular consumers, and turning consumers into prosumers.

Reduced Overhead   The major economic advantage for online retailers is that it greatly reduces overhead. Building and maintaining brick-and-mortar stores is expensive, especially with the cost of inventory and sales staffs. With online merchandizing, retailers can avoid tying money up in inventory until they have made a sale.

Reduced Risk   A major marketing advantage for online retailers is that they can reduce their risk of offering products that might not sell. Retailers use digital media to monitor consumers' past purchases to predict what they might buy now. Also, by monitoring conversations on social media, they can identify consumer needs as soon as they arise. Retailers can then use all this information to build recommender systems to direct prospective customers to particular products and to set prices in a way to motivate sales.

Now with the Internet of Things, retailers have access to even more information as all sorts of objects become connected to the internet (e.g., cars, household appliances, and fitness trackers). In 2008 the number of things connected to the internet surpassed the number of people on the planet, and that number was expected to grow to more than 50 billion things by 2020. And as these connected devices get smaller, faster, and more affordable, their market penetration is poised to take off. Shawn DuBravac, the chief economist for the Consumer Electronics Association, explains:

> Your devices, from your smartphone to your tablet to your car to your entertainment system, will have near-complete knowledge of you as we move towards 2025. They will know your identity in the literal sense of the word. Some of them will have picked up the data about you in the traditional way—because you've chosen to input it—but most will automatically capture the data, because their primary input system will be sensors and they will be tied into additional sensor systems. You won't have to manually input much, if anything at all. The sensors will capture most of it and then—there's the really interesting part—will be able to share that information across devices and platforms via the Internet of Things. Because all "things" will be connected, they will all be able to exchange data about you, improving their delivery of whatever services they offer. (2015, pp. 116)

Targeting   Retailers collect a great deal of information from digital media that help them identify who their customers are and why they buy the products they do. This information gathering has gotten so extensive and so sophisticated that retailers can now fill in the gaps in their databases. For example, in 2012, Twitter began giving advertisers the ability to target promotions by gender, but in no place does Twitter ever ask their users to self-identify gender. Instead, Twitter reports they are able to infer a person's gender with 90% accuracy by observing how people use Twitter. And digital companies are working on algorithms to predict just about everything else—not just gender—about everyone (DuBravac, 2015).

Prosumers   Online retailers use digital market techniques to turn consumers into prosumers, by identifying who their consumers are and then conditioning them to do more than simply buy and use their products; retailers are now focused on getting their consumers to tell their friends about their products through postings on social media and posting high ratings of their products. Thus ambitious marketers are conditioning people to be positive representatives of their products without having to pay them to do so (Chayko, 2018).

MEDIA BUSINESSES

Digital media have created a new business model that has been so successful that it has attracted audiences and revenues away from analog media and forced those analog media to make major changes to their business model in order to survive. Perhaps the most dominant characteristic of the digital media business model is that it regards people as individuals requiring different treatments, rather than regarding people as members of broad demographic groups where they are all treated the same. Digital media collect a great deal of data from all people and use this information to identify each person's needs. To satisfy those needs, digital media have broken large conglomerated messages and services down into small message units and service units to give consumers more control over selecting only those they want.

Analog media have typically bundled many messages together and forced audience members to buy the entire bundle. For example, newspapers and magazines required people to buy an entire issue of each publication, rather than allow users to access and pay for only the particular stories they want. Cable systems required people to subscribe to tiers of bundled channels, rather than pick only those individual channels they wanted. When people subscribed to a movie channel, they had to pay for access to the whole channel, rather than pay for only the movies they wanted. Recording companies required people to buy an entire CD of songs, rather than only the particular songs they wanted. In contrast, digital media unbundle messages and services so individuals can buy access to just the messages and services they want (Simon, 2014).

Another feature of the digital media business model is that they allow for users to create and disseminate content. This is very different from the analog media model, where gatekeepers control which messages get produced and disseminated. With digital media, anyone can be a novelist, a songwriter/musician, or a video storyteller. Of course, most of these digital messages that are created by individuals attract only tiny audiences. However, the few messages that break through the clutter and attract large audiences get the attention of large media companies that then try to buy the distribution rights and help those producers attract an even larger audience.

A third characteristic of the digital media business model is that it relies much more on charging businesses for particular services in accessing audiences, rather than on charging them for audience exposures to advertising messages, which is characteristic of the analog media business model. This appears to be a global trend. For example, Ji (2019) conducted a major analysis of the aggregate revenue of all major media industries, across 51 countries, from 2009 to 2013, and found that the use of digital media has led to a shift in the balance of revenue away from advertising and toward direct payments. This means that businesses that used to heavily advertise their products in analog media have been shifting revenue away from paying to expose their target audiences to their general advertising messages. Now those companies are shifting their advertising budgets into digital media where they are charged only when their prospective customers do something (such as using particular keywords on search engines, clicking on a hot button link, or visiting a particular website).

As many retailers have been shifting away from using analog media for advertising and instead using digital media, there have been big winners and losers among the media. Spending on online and social media sources has increased dramatically, especially since the recession of 2008. Television generated more advertising revenue than any other medium until 2017, when digital media's advertising income surpassed that of television for the first time (McAllister & Orme, 2017). Digital advertising has come a long way since the first banner ad appeared on a website in 1994 (Singel, 2010). In 2017, global online advertising spending reached $209 billion and accounted for 41% of all advertising spending (Kafka & Molla, 2017).

The ten largest digital firms have always dominated digital advertising, taking three quarters of ad dollars since at least the mid-1990s. But the shift to mobile and video has intensified concentration at the very top. As of mid-2016, Google and Facebook together combined for more than 73% of digital advertising in the United States, a remarkable duopoly over a 60 billion-dollars-a-year industry.

Newspapers

The biggest losers have been the print media, especially those involved in journalistic activities. Advertising spending on newspapers slipped from nearly $49 billion in 2000 down to only $19 billion by 2015, a time when the newspaper industry has experienced a decline in number of newspapers and number of employees.

The newspaper publishing sector of analog media is in transition. Its legacy business (print version) is declining, which has motivated many newspapers to add an online service. This change has helped many print newspapers to survive as their digital platforms have been able to attract a different kind of news consumer. Leurdijk, Nieuwenhuis, and Poel (2014b) explain,

> Consumers benefit from the increased availability of "free" news and the options to tailor news consumption according to one's own preferences. There is some concern, however, as to whether the market can also sustain the desired quality of the output, and the ability of some vulnerable news genres, such as investigative journalism, sustained reporting on local government and local politics, or foreign new reporting, to survive. (p. 161)

Even in China, analog newspapers are also under pressure to change their business model. Wang and Sparks (2019) reviewed the impact of digital technologies on Chinese newspapers and found that the diffusion of the smartphone has precipitated severe economic problems for the printed press. There have been decreases in both readership and advertising revenues, which have had an effect on the structure of provincial-level press groups. The decline in economic viability has been felt most acutely by the commercially oriented titles, while the more politically oriented papers have led the way in finding new sources of funding. However, these political sources of support tend to tie journalism more tightly to political and economic power, and lead to commercial goals replacing journalistic ones. This shifting balance of economic power has important consequences for the viability of independent and critical journalism.

Music

After a period of increases in sales and revenues following the introduction of the CD in the late 1990s, the music industry faced substantial revenue losses in subsequent years. Digital media have fundamentally transformed the music industry by forcing a shift in music distribution, sales, and consumption. Leurdijk, Nieuwenhuis, and Poel (2014a) explain,

Users and artists benefit from the new and varied ways of communication and transaction that are enabled by the Internet. They also benefit from cost reductions that are inherent in the evolution from physical goods to online services. Consumers have gained greatly in ease of use, flexibility, added services and more variety in pay modes. But at the same time they are paying for this with data about their identity, linked to their online behavior and consumption patterns, and they risk being locked in (by switching costs) by some of the new series when they increasingly rely on one provider for a range of different services, including music, and switching to other services becomes increasingly complex. (p. 145)

Books

The book publishing model has changed. It used to be dominated by the giants in publishing (e.g., Bertelsmann and Hachette), but now it is dominated by online book distributors (especially Amazon). "The digitization of book publishing generates a shift from the central role and domination of the book value chain by the publisher toward a downstream domination by the new entrants (distributors)" (De Prato, 2014, p. 98).

Politics

Digital media have also been changing political institutions, primarily by shifting power away from traditional authorities and toward individuals. Altenhofen (2019) explains: "New media promote a decentralization of power and undermine established patterns and systems of authority because communication technology has become faster, more flexible, and ubiquitous, therefore threatening traditional hierarchies of authority already established off-line" (p. 97). Some of these changes have been positive, but others have been negative.

POSITIVE EFFECTS

Scholars have focused their research on examining three positive effects that digital media have been exerting on the institution of politics. These positive effects are mobilizing communities, crowdfunding, and data-driven decisions.

Mobilizing Communities

The widespread use of digital communication platforms—such as Twitter, Facebook, Instagram, YouTube, and Tumblr—is changing the way political groups attract members and exert power both in the United States and globally (Barker-Plummer & Barker-Plummer, 2019). Because these digital forms of communication are available to anyone with access to the internet, they are powerful tools for sharing information and building political communities around particular issues. Before the rise of digital media, citizens who wanted to advocate for change typically depended on traditional media to build public awareness, so they had to create public events such as protests, marches, and sit-ins in order to attract media coverage. These advocates could produce their own media such as newsletters or videos, or they could engage in strategic interactions with journalists to try to shape the way their issues and events were communicated to the public. Now engaged citizens and social change groups have access to platforms with the potential to reach large audiences directly.

"Since its founding, Twitter has emerged as an especially popular platform for activists, journalists, elected officials, and others interested in social justice and social change, and identifiable clusters of speakers have emerged around particular social issues—for example, 'Black Twitter,' 'Feminist Twitter,' 'Green Twitter,' and so on" (Barker-Plummer & Barker-Plummer, 2019, p. 80). A particularly useful digital tool for building communities quickly has been Twitter's hashtags (e.g., #YesAllWomen), which allows Twitter users to link their comments to those of others. "When large numbers of people join a conversation, the hashtag trends and is highlighted by Twitter and often covered by journalists."

Researchers have conducted a variety of studies to look at how social media are used to mobilize communities on various social issues so that they generate enough power to influence audience thinking on a particular issue. For example, social media has been used successfully to mobilize communities to deal with poverty (Vincent & Straub, 2017); Twitter has been used to build and maintain a community of people interested in protecting the environment (Breideband, 2019); Twitter with the hashtag #YesAllWomen has been used to attract hundreds of thousands of citizens and motivate them to speak out against violence and harassment against women (Barker-Plummer & Barker-Plummer, 2019); and Twitter was used by the Tea Party to mobilize against President Obama and his Affordable Care Act (Richardson, 2019).

One of the most successful uses of digital media to create a political community was the 2016 presidential campaign of Bernie Sanders. Penney (2017) explains, "While the 'official' Sanders organization built digital applications to transform supporters into a tightly controlled distribution network for its social media messaging, this was complemented by 'unofficial' grassroots networks that circulated more informal and culturally oriented appeals" (p. 404).

Crowdfunding

The technique of **crowdfunding** was originated by brand-new businesses that needed to raise a large amount of start-up capital to fund their business activities. These startups posted appeals on social media platforms to get large numbers of people to each invest a relatively small amount of money in their business. Because this technique was often successful, people running political campaigns began using it to get large numbers of people to donate money to candidates running for office.

Political fundraisers have recognized an opportunity to appeal to citizens who are more interested in donating to particular causes than to political parties. That is, fundraisers can target potential donors more precisely using digital media and then assure these people that their donations will only go to the causes they care about.

To illustrate this innovation, Williams (2019) highlights a crowdfunding example of campaign funding (if.then.fund):

> Rather than donating to a party or an individual candidate, these platforms encourage users to tie their money to issue statements. If.then. fund makes visible a particular action a congressperson can take (like a particular bill introduction or a vote), briefly explains the position, then asks for a contribution. When a bill or action comes up for a vote, collected funds are distributed evenly among the officeholders who took the donor's desired stance. (p. 34)

Data-Driven Decisions

By using digital data, political campaigns can better (more quickly and more precisely) recognize the changing concerns of the electorate and then craft particular messages to appeal to the emerging needs. Lanius (2019) explains that

> digital data technologies for political participation can be used to accomplish two major goals: (1) to expand the number of individuals represented in politics by collecting their preferences on key public issues, and (2) to reach currently underrepresented populations to understand their perspectives then integrating them into the political process. Data analytics that are used to investigate political questions often rely upon data from social media platforms and networked communication technologies to generate an image of how the populace is feeling at a given moment in time. (p. 64)

However, she also states, "While these goals are commendable, it is important to be cautious in relying on new technologies for something as important as political representation. Good intentions can pave a dangerous road" (Lanius, 2019, pp. 63–64).

NEGATIVE EFFECTS

Digital media have also exerted influence on the institution of politics that many critics regard as negative. These effects include polarization, hacktivism, and clicktivism.

Polarization

The use of digital media has increased the degree of political polarization. For example, Lelkes, Sood, and Iyengar (2015) conducted a study to examine the relationship between internet access and political polarization. They found that greater access to the internet turned out to be associated with increased partisan hostility. In other words, this study found evidence for a causal relationship between the arrival of the internet in a community and the exacerbation of political differences within that community. This dynamic is explained by Darr, Hitt, and Dunaway (2018), who found that when local newspapers go out of business, people seek their national news from cable TV channels and websites, which are typically partisan. Thus people are less likely to get balanced coverage of events and instead get news that is more one-sided, which reinforces their existing political orientation rather than helping expand their minds by exposing them to a wider range of points of view. This narrowing of people's political perspective serves to fragment the population into insular groups of people who then are more likely to vote a straight ticket rather than split their vote across partisan lines.

Hacktivism

Hacktivism is defined as the nonviolent use of illegal or legally ambiguous digital tools in the pursuit of political ends. Baybars-Hawks (2015) explains:

> Hacktivism is a controversial term, and can often be misconstrued as cyberterrorism. What separates hacktivism from cyberterrorism is a distinctly political or social cause behind the "haction." Some argue that it was coined to describe how electronic direct action might drive social change by combining programming skills with critical thinking. Others use it more or less synonymously with malicious, destructive acts that undermine the security of the Internet as a technical, economic and political platform. (p. 4)

One of the most destructive forms of hacktivism is denial of service (DoS) attacks that paralyze websites, financial networks, and computer systems. With DoS, hackers get into an organization's website code and remove enough of that code so that users can no longer access the website.

Clicktivism

Clicktivism is the practice of supporting political or social causes by using the internet (e.g., social media or online petitions) in place of real-world participation (attending political meetings, rallies, and demonstrations) that would require more effort.

Clicktivism has been criticized for several reasons (Williams, 2019). One criticism is that clicktivism gives people a sense of active political participation even when their participation is superficial. Thus clicktivism reduces real political engagement. Another criticism is that clicktivism turns political messages into a commodity where people simply click on the positions they like, much like clicking on products they wish to purchase online.

While these criticisms may have validity, the research to date does not support them. For example, Moeller, Kühne, and De Vreese (2018) conducted a study to find out why youth turnout at European parliamentary elections has been dwindling. Their study used a data set that combined content analysis of news stories ($N = 769$) about the EU and a multiple-wave panel survey ($N = 994$) over 6 months. They found that while exposure to news from traditional media sources had no significant effect on participation, exposure to news from digital media positively affected turnout.

Clicktivism has been shown to have advantages.

> By moving public discourses online, thus lowering the barriers to entry and the costs of producing and distributing content, we are unlocking a

post-geographic information sharing and activism potential that is largely untapped in the political realm. Individuals may gain international notoriety in hours. Words written in the morning can be uploaded, instantly translated and remediated, bounced from multiple satellites to reach a reader in every country on earth before evening. Alliances and movements are organized along lines far more personally significant than geographic location or national origin. Enormous amounts of money are raised for causes, individuals, and organizations, from millions of scattered strangers and small donors who find a momentary empathetic or strategic alliance. (Williams, 2019, p. 25)

Religion

In their four-volume handbook, *Religion and Media: Critical Concepts in Religious Studies*, Kirby and Cusack (2017) argue that the study of how media have shaped the institution of religion is "central to any understanding of religion in the contemporary world" (p. 1). The media, especially digital media, have been found to transform the practice of religion in two major ways. One way is that media have offered traditional religions a means to grow their value by serving more needs of their members as well as reaching out to a wider range of people. The second way is that digitization has led to the creation of virtual worlds where people can go to create alternative religious practices and celebrations.

ENHANCING ESTABLISHED RELIGIONS AND PRACTICES

Many scholars have criticized digital media for exerting a negative effect on established religions, and some researchers have found support for much of this criticism. For example, research has shown that digital media have been influential in decreasing attendance rates of mainstream religions (Bouma, 2006), increasing the visibility and the intensity of various fundamentalist sects (Almond, Appleby, & Sivan, 2003), and contributing to a substantial rise in atheism, secularity, and nonreligious groups (Bullivant & Lee, 2012). However, the majority of research has shown that digital media offer tools to help established religions fulfill their purposes better by providing their believers with more information and helping them sustain a stronger feeling of religious community (Campbell, 2012; Sawin, 2018).

Sharing Information

One way digital media have been changing the institution of religion is they give established religions more tools for sharing information with their believers. Grant and Stout (2019) explain,

> The advent of the Internet and social media broke the access barrier, offering virtually any organized (or unorganized) faith the opportunity to share

endless information to members, prospective members, and anyone who might be interested in learning more about that religion. This social dimension has provided opportunities for the sharing of prayer, inspiration, homilies, and scripture, as well as more mundane information such as schedules and appeals for financial support. (Grant & Stout, 2019, p. 4)

For example, during the late 1990s and into the 2000s, as many as 10,000 houses of worship were launching websites each year (Farquhar, 2019). During an average week, one in five Americans were sharing religious faith online (Pew Research Center, 2014). Also, established religions have created apps to serve the needs of their believers, with one estimate claiming that there were more than 6,000 religious-themed apps available in the iTunes store alone (Buie & Blythe, 2013). Some of these apps simply provide people with information, while others help users engage in religious practices (guiding prayer, meditation, ritual, engaging with sacred texts, and playing religious games; Campbell, Altenhofen, Bellar, & Cho, 2014). And even the pope uses both Twitter and Instagram, with the Instagram account being the fastest growing in the history of that platform (Boyle, Hansen, & Christensen, 2019). Twitter's microblogging format along with hashtags makes it especially useful for "finding related individuals who share similar interests on Twitter," which gives users the ability "to find and communicate with others of their faith" (Boyle et al., 2019, p. 16).

With digital media, sharing of information is two-way. Blossom and colleagues (2019) explain that religious organizations are gathering a good deal of data about their parishioners and their evolving needs so they can provide better religious experiences to them.

Supporting Existing Practices

Before mass media, religious ceremonies took place primarily in sacred places, built and consecrated by the faithful. It was a ritual to go to a special physical space—perhaps a church, synagogue, or mosque—and practice one's religion. With the rise of analog media of radio and then television, religious organizations could broadcast their worship services to people who were unable to attend those sacred places in person. Now with the internet, worshipers do not need to wait for a broadcast; they can access services any time, day or night. Also, cyber churches have evolved from web forums into fully interactive sites where members can view and engage in a service online.

Users of virtual worlds have brought established religious practices into those worlds. Geraci (2014) explains, "Thanks to virtual worlds, many religious practitioners now reimagine their traditions and creatively work to restore them to 'authentic' sanctity or replace religious institutions with virtual world communities that provide meaning and purpose to human life" (p. 12). He continues,

> Residents of virtual worlds orient themselves through space and time, a fact that can be turned into religious participation online. In virtual worlds, we gain a sense of embodiment that is critical to religious participation. While there is no question that we might challenge the extent to which such embodiment realizes the full potential of human life, we cannot pretend that

there is nothing new or interesting about walking avatars through temples, churches, and even fantasy landscapes. Life in a virtual world has a visceral quality that helps ensure we will engage the questions of meaning, purpose, and value that are crucial to religious life. (p. 6)

Established churches with declining memberships have been found to use digital platforms for making their worship services more widely available. One example of this is illustrated by a study of how the Swedish national church (Svenska kyrkan) has extensively used digital media to address the problem of its declining membership (Hutchings, 2017). Two notable uses of how they used digital media are the digital-physical technology installation in cemeteries and a series of posts about death and sadness on Facebook. In both projects, the church presented emotion as a universally shared experience that could be used to bring together its religious and nonreligious audiences.

Processing the emotion of grief has also been helped by digital media. An ethnographic study of funeral industry conventions found many examples of funeral planning tools, funeral service mediation, and memorialization products that use digital media (Nansen, Kohn, Arnold, van Ryn, & Gibbs, 2017).

Reinforcing Religious Identity

Campbell (2017) says that research has found that the internet "empowers religious internet users to create and perform religious identity online" and that "online religious practice may create new, dynamic opportunities for self-expression of belief and religious lifestyle practice" (p. 15). She says, "The fluidity and transience of online environment poses challenges to traditional authority structures, roles, and tools. The result has been the internet is framed both as a threat to certain established roles and hierarchies and as a tool of empowerment for others" (p. 17).

Social media have been found to be a valuable tool for people to reinforce their religious faith even when they leave their homes and migrate to other countries. In one study, Souza (2018) found that Pentecostals used Facebook to develop and maintain transnational networks where they could use their original language to support their religious beliefs. Digital media have been found to be used to support practices of all sorts of religions, including the Ifa sect of the Yoruba religion in western Africa (Salami, 2018), use of Yiddish in the Jewish religion (Soldat-Jaffe, 2018), Christian evangelism (Omoniyi, 2018), Muslims in America (El Naggar, 2018), Hindus in America (Pandharipande, 2018), and the Sufi sect of Islam (Rosowsky, 2018).

Building Community

Farquhar (2019) explains that when religious bodies use social media to interact with members, those members experience more emotional support and a greater sense of community. Because digital media allow members to communicate and support one another, this leads to a greater sense of community that goes beyond religious leaders providing only one-way communication from authorities.

Campbell (2017) argues that the research shows that religious communities that form online "function quite differently than traditional religious institutions and structures. Rather than operating as tightly bounded social structures, they function as loose social networks with varying levels of religious affiliation and commitment" (p. 13). "One of the clearest examples of networked community is seen in the rise of cyberchurches, entities that create spaces for people to engage in worship-based activities online," such as in Second Life, "where individuals construct virtual 3D architectures meant to mirror traditional church or temple structures where religious practices can be simulated. . . . What makes cyberchurches a form of networked community are the ways these settings can supplement or extend people's offline religious participation, by offering intimate fellowship with others or providing connections to a like-minded theological context" (p. 14).

CREATING ALTERNATIVE RELIGIOUS EXPERIENCES

Digital media have fostered a proliferation of new and alternative religions and spiritualities by giving people the ability to create virtual worlds, which often stimulates them to explore the meaning of life, sometimes in religious ways (Partridge, 2004). Geraci (2014) adds, "Virtual worlds . . . make way for new religious opportunities: they allow us new ways of expressing old religious practices and beliefs, but they also offer new ways of circumventing those traditions" (p. 1).

"Certainly, there are many people who continue to rely on traditional stories as the bedrock for their beliefs," Geraci (2014) explains, "but at the same time many others have gone in search of new stories that will give the world meaning, help them to interpret the world, and make life worth living" (p. 5).

Virtual worlds are rearranging or replacing traditional religious practices. They do this by presenting users with fresh new worlds that stimulate people to think about alternative answers to fundamental questions that humans have been asking for millennia. Where did we come from? Why are we here? What is the purpose of life?

In an in-depth study of two of the most popular virtual worlds (World of Warcraft and Second Life), Geraci (2014) examined why people who spent time in these worlds create and engage in religious rituals. He explains,

> *World of Warcraft* has an entire lore, a vast historical narrative that ultimately ground everything the player does. The game is a sweeping battle of good against evil, which provides plenty of space for players to recognize their own essential heroism. According to the lore, when the Titans traveled the universe creating life and making it good, they found an evil source of demons in the universe. They sent one of their own—Sargeras, the best and strongest of them all—to fend off the demons and protect the order they had founded. But like more conventional angels in our Western traditions, he fell from grace. Corrupted by the very demonic powers he had set out to resist, Sargeras turned on his former fellows, took command of the demons, and sent them forth to dismantle the cosmos. *World of Warcraft* players are at the heart of Sargeras's conflict with the Titans. They live (most of the time)

on Azeroth, a planet that Sargeras has tried and failed to corrupt and that continues to be a locus for the activities of his Burning Legion. . . . Players lead their people in this battle against the Burning Legion. (p. 7)

Geraci (2014) argues that even when virtual worlds lack epic narratives, they provide opportunities for their users to create one.

> In *Second Life*, a world where everything is the responsibility of those who log in, religious stories have exploded into being. On occasion these are created ex nihilo, as new religions that may not even be possible to think through in a conventional reality. More often, though, they are formed by reframing and reconstructing the old religious ways and ideas. Many people come to *Second Life* to live out their religious lives in a new world: they build churches, temples, mosques, and even forest glades in virtual reality. They gather and celebrate together, often with neither permission from, nor relationship to, their communities' conventional counterparts. Instead of letting the old hierarchies dictate who they are, what they must believe and do, and where they must go, these virtual world residents are happily rearranging and reassembling religious life and telling entirely new stories about gods, providence, and themselves. . . . To a considerable extent, the story of *Second Life* is, itself, a story of religious redemption: for founders and residents alike, *Second Life* could offer a new, better world. This operates on two levels: first, the practice of traditional religions can provide new opportunities to the faithful; and second, life there can, itself, be a religious opportunity. Inspired by science fiction and popular science books about artificial intelligence and virtual reality, many *Second Life* residents believe that the world is a template for the eventual uploading of immortal human minds into a virtual reality paradise. As such, to think through it as a place where some residents wish to escape the limitations of their bodies is to think about a modern religious institution. (p. 8)

Geraci (2014) explains that "virtual worlds provide a multiplicity of religious opportunities that can be absolutely vital to residency in those worlds" (p. 23). Larchet (2019) argues:

> The new media are seen as a way to a new world and a new man, the ideal of all religions. The adoption of the new media by the people is preached for reasons that go beyond the commercial aim of selling devices, software, and applications, and the political aim of boosting the economy. (p. 137)

In summary, Geraci (2014) explains that virtual worlds provide religions with two kinds of opportunities to help their members.

> First, they provide new places to practice old religions; this is important because their very newness gives users hope that in them old religions can overcome the age-old handicaps of prejudice and ignorance. . . . Second, they provide new locations for the creation of meaningful lives without recourse to traditional religious communities. (pp. 11–12)

Health Care

The institution of health care has been profoundly influenced by the rise of digital media. "The storage, management, and transmission of health-related data now increasingly occur digitally. Technology also supports and influences clinical decision-making and facilitates patient care, often from a distance" (Chayko, 2018, pp. 160–161).

MONITORING ONE'S BODY

Mobile digital devices are available to monitor all sorts of characteristics about a person's health. For example, you can use these devices to check your blood pressure and heart rate. Also, there is an FDA-cleared mobile EKG monitor that allows you to track your heart health anytime, anywhere. When coupled with its dedicated app, Kardia Mobile delivers a medical-grade electrocardiogram (ECG) to your smartphone in just 30 seconds. Alcohoot is a small device that connects to your smartphone and helps you keep track of your blood alcohol levels using police-grade technology and works in tandem with an Android/iOS app. Muse is a headband with seven electroencephalography (EEG) sensors that monitor your brain activity during meditation and transmits the information to your computer, smartphone, or tablet via Bluetooth.

These devices are typically inexpensive and easy to use. When they are connected to smartphones, the information can be uploaded to medical professionals.

SEEKING HEALTH INFORMATION

Many people use digital platforms for seeking information about health. In 2013, Pew Research reported that 59% of Americans had looked online for health information in the past year (DuBravac, 2015).

With all this medical information now available, it is not surprising that people are using it to self-diagnose. In a recent survey, 35% of respondents said they have looked up health information on the internet and used that information to diagnose illnesses for themselves and others. Also, it was found that 41% of the self-diagnosers had their condition confirmed by a physician—a number that suggests people aren't as bad at self-diagnoses as perhaps many doctors believe. Still, six in ten Americans incorrectly self-diagnose themselves (DuBravac, 2015).

SEEKING TREATMENT

People can use digital platforms to seek medical treatment without having to go to a medical facility and waiting to see a doctor in person. **Telehealth** services give people the opportunity to share their symptoms online with a doctor and be given a diagnosis within 10 minutes. There are health services where people can text a photo of a cut, a rash, or a bug bite to a doctor and within minutes receive a diagnosis that tells them whether professional medical treatment is necessary (DuBravac, 2015).

With digital tools, doctors are becoming more efficient. They are able to take on more patients, even while reducing their per-patient hours. A study conducted in Britain looked at the effects of telehealth technology on 6,000 patients with chronic diseases and found that applying telehealth tools to this population reduced admissions to the emergency room by 20% and mortality by 45% (DuBravac, 2015).

Family

The institution of family has been affected by digital media in several ways. Some of these ways serve to increase family connections, while other ways serve to fragment the family.

Digital media offer many opportunities for family members to stay in close touch with each other. Family members can use digital media platforms to communicate with others even when they are separated geographically. They can use apps like FaceTime to have face-to-face conversations. They can use texting and email to send tailor-made messages of words and images to family members. And they can use SNSs to post more general messages about themselves so that family members—and others—can keep up with the developments in their lives. Parents can track the activities of their children with nanny cams and GPS trackers on smartphones.

Digital media, however, can also exert a fragmenting influence on families. In tech-rich societies, many families invest in multiple **internet-connected technologies (ICT)** that can be found in nearly every room of the house. In addition to computers (desktop and laptop), tablets, and cell phones or smartphones, homes may contain multiple televisions, digital cable boxes, gaming consoles, video recorders, and DVD or Blu-Ray players. This allows for each family member to engage in very different interactions with these devices as well as other people in remote locations, which means that over time the proportion of shared experiences across family members erodes. With less common ground, there is less content to motivate interpersonal conversations.

This reduction in shared family experiences is not new with digital media; instead, it began with the analog medium of television. In the early days of television broadcasting, television viewing was a shared experience as family members gathered each evening in front of the single TV set and watched the same programs together. But with the rise of cable television with their offerings of scores and then hundreds of channels, individual family members developed their own personal viewing repertoires that substantially differed from other family members'. Households invested in multiple television sets, which were then placed in different parts of a house and led to individualized viewing experiences. And now with the rise of digital media where individual family members each have their own viewing devices (smartphones, tablets, and laptop computers), sharing viewing experiences across family members is more rare (Chayko, 2018).

People's devotion to digital screens is so profound that they lose touch with the real world around them, especially to the people who are the closest to them geographically, that is, their family members. This type of negative effect is a concern of even the most tech-savvy people. For example, Alter (2017) tells a story about when Steve Jobs introduced the iPad. "For ninety minutes, Jobs explained why the iPad was the best way to look at photos, listen to music, take classes on iTunes U, browse Facebook, play games, and navigate thousands of apps. He believed everyone should own an iPad. But he refused to let his kids use the device" (p. 1).

Communities

Digital media are reshaping communities. Geography used to be an essential factor in the formation of communities; that is, people had to live relatively close to one another in order to gather together in groups and form communities. Now, with the proliferation of digital platforms on just about every conceivable concern, people can join communities based solely on interest. Geography has almost disappeared as an important factor that explains how communities are formed.

The interactive nature of digital media has stimulated the rise of a **participatory culture** where more people are connecting with others who share their special interests. The members of each of these communities take an active part in the creation and consumption of their cultural products and are expected to share them freely and widely. "The participatory culture is also an economy in which content, goods, time, effort, and money are, to one degree or another, shared, exchanged, and spent. This kind of sharing economy transcends the internet" (Chayko, 2018, p. 67).

Some scholars have conducted case studies to determine how digital media have been used to build virtual communities around common civic interests and strengthen those communities in Argentina (Schwarz, 2015), Kenya (Nyaole-Kowuor, 2015), Palestine (Farah, 2015), Greece (Gerodimos, 2015), China (Bogen, 2015), and Mexico (Guerrero & Luengas, 2015). What all of these case studies show is that digital media make previously inaccessible forms of information available to the public through viral sharing of the information horizontally (across members of the public) rather than vertically (from experts down to members of the public). When the information exposes a problem or corruption, it can mobilize people to discuss the problem and propose courses of action. This builds communities that involve people in civic action by tweeting, demonstrating, and putting pressure on elected officials to address those issues. For example, Mihailidis (2015) shows how social media were used by organizations and individuals in the aftermath of the 2013 Boston Marathon bombing to help guide runners to safety, to contact their family and friends. Runners used text messaging, Twitter, Facebook, and Instagram to obtain updates and information. The Boston Police Department also used Twitter to communicate with the community in real time, offering important updates on the safety of Boston as well as to solicit information about what happened in order to identify the perpetrator. Other scholars have shown how social media have been used to strengthen a sense of community when public tragedies strike—for example, how people in Buenos Aires used social media to share information and grieve when a train crash killed 52 people and injured hundreds in 2012 (Schwarz, 2015).

Shumow (2015) argues that from studies, we have learned that digital media provide people with greater opportunities to build communities and to engage in "democratic organizing, protest, and mobilization in the digital age; like the technologies themselves, these movements are emerging and transforming at a rapid pace, toppling dictators and authoritarian regimes nearly overnight" (pp. 202–203). But there is also an irony, as Shumow points out when he says, "At no point in history have we had more opportunities for seeking out and sharing information; at the same time, those choices are obscured, not through scarcity or lack of access, as may have been the case in the past, but through ubiquity and abundance" (p. 203).

Conclusions

Digital media have been found to influence many institutions. Some of these influences have led to positive effects by strengthening those existing institutions and allowing them to serve the needs of society in better and more numerous ways. However, other digital influences have led to negative effects by reducing some of the positive functions of those institutions and/or leading people to behave in ways that they begin disregarding the value of those institutions.

Research on this topic is relatively sparse compared to the amount of research that examines how digital media exert influence on individuals. One reason for this sparseness is that research that examines institutions typically takes longer to conduct because changes take longer to manifest themselves in a clear way with large aggregates than they do with individual people. Even so, a clear picture is beginning to emerge, and that picture tells us that the influence of digital media is at least as strong as the influence has been from analog media.

Further Reading

Baybars-Hawks, B. (Ed.). (2015). *New media politics: Rethinking activism and national security in cyberspace.* Newcastle upon Tyne, U.K.: Cambridge Scholars Publishing. (272 pages)

This is an edited book of 17 chapters written by an international group of scholars who are concerned with how people have been using the internet legally and illegally to increase the power of social movements.

De Prato, G., Sanz, E., & Simon, J. P. (Eds.). (2014). *Digital media worlds: The new economy of media.* London: Palgrave Macmillan. (221 pages, including references and index)

This edited volume of 10 chapters is a bit dated now with most of the facts and figures from the late 1990s and early 2000s, but the patterns that the authors document illuminate how digital media have quickly attracted audiences and advertisers away from traditional media. The majority of chapters are detailed case studies of individual analog media industries—book publishing, television, film, music newspaper, and video games.

Geraci, R. M. (2014). *Virtually sacred: Myth and meaning in World of Warcraft and Second Life.* New York: Oxford University Press. (348 pages with a methods appendix, endnotes, references, and index)

The author is a religious studies professor who immersed himself in two of the most popular virtual worlds—World of Warcraft and Second Life—in order to examine how and why people who spent time in these worlds created and engaged in religious rituals. Geraci's perspective on what constitutes religion is broad, that is, he is not focused on looking for evidence of particular practices from religions established in the real world. Instead, he looks for how people construct spiritual meanings in their virtual lives, how they represent those meanings to others, and how they celebrate those meanings.

Hindman, M. (2018). *The internet trap: How the digital economy builds monopolies and undermines democracy.* Princeton, NJ: Princeton University Press. (240 pages with endnotes, bibliography, and index)

This book takes an economic approach to explain two negative trends in the development of the internet. One trend is the rise of monopolies as successful internet companies increase their dominance. The other trend is the undermining of democracy by destroying local news journalism and replacing it with stories that news organizations think people would find most interesting rather than information that would challenge them or educate them broadly about the important issues of the day.

CHAPTER 11

Broad Effects

The previous seven chapters each focused on effects that researchers have found to arise in people from exposure to a different kind of digital media experience—news, advertising, entertainment, social networking sites, virtual worlds, and competing in games—as well as the effect on institutions. In this chapter, we turn our attention to the research that documents effects from exposure to digital media in general. These are broad effects because they arise from exposure to any kind of digital media content or platform. That is, these effects are not limited to just one type of digital media experience.

These broad effects are presented in two sets. The first set includes what I call **unit effects**. Much of the media effects literature is composed of research studies that test

169

whether exposure to digital media in general (regardless of content) can lead to one type of effect (on a person's physiology, feelings, cognitions, beliefs, and attitudes). I refer to these as unit effects, because the research focuses on only one type of effect. However, the research literature also includes studies that have tested to see whether when a particular type of effect occurs it leads to another type of effect or even to a series of types of effects. This type of research goes beyond a unit approach, where different types of effects are tested one at a time in isolation from each other, and instead looks for clusters of effects in sequences over time. For example, a particular effect might start out as a cognitive-type effect, where a person acquires some new information, which then alters an existing attitude that then triggers a behavior. I refer to this as a **cascade effect**, because it is not a simple one-step effect but instead is better understood as a process that progresses through several interrelated steps over time.

Unit Effects

This section presents a review of the research about how exposure to digital media can result in a particular type of effect: physiological, affective, cognitive, and attitudinal.

PHYSIOLOGICAL

There seem to be five major physiological effects that have been found to be widespread across all digital media exposures. These are dopamine production, rewiring the human brain, loss of sleep, stress, and obesity.

Dopamine Production

Dopamine is released when the brain seeks, detects the possibility of, and receives a novel reward. Kamenetz (2018) found that dopamine production in individuals' brains is stimulated by exposure to videos because of the way video uses constant motion (within shots as well as the quick pacing from shot to shot).

Brain Rewiring

Research has shown that brains can get wired a certain way through conditioning by variable reinforcement (Brooks & Lasser, 2018). In his book *The Shallows: What the Internet Is Doing to Our Brains*, Nicholas Carr (2010) explained that the human brain is enormously plastic, and although this plasticity diminishes with age a bit, it is still a major characteristic of the brain. This means that experience shapes our brain functioning by creating paths of firing among neurons. Habits are developed by continually using the same path of neuron firings. Thus our mental activity can alter our neural circuitry. Carr continues:

If, knowing what we know today about the brain's plasticity, you were to set out to invent a medium that would rewire our mental circuits as quickly and as thoroughly as possible, you would probably end up designing something that looks and works a lot like the Internet. It's not just that we tend to use the Net regularly, even obsessively. It's that the Net delivers precisely the kind of sensory and cognitive stimuli—repetitive, intensive, interactive, addictive—that have been shown to result in strong and rapid alterations in brain circuits and functions. With the exception of alphabets and number systems, the Net may well be the single most powerful mind-altering technology that has every come into general use. At the very least, it's the most powerful that has come along since the book. (Carr, 2010, p. 116)

Loss of Sleep

The American Medical Association says teens need 8 to 10 hours of sleep each night, but the National Sleep Foundation found that 90% of teens 15 to 17 reported getting less than 8 hours of sleep per night and 56% reported getting less than 7 hours per night. Furthermore, the loss of sleep has been attributed to screen time (Brooks & Lasser, 2018).

This loss of sleep due to screens has been traced to both psychological and physical causes. Psychologically, the way digital media have conditioned us for constant exposure makes it difficult for individuals to cut off their exposure even when they are tired and need to sleep. Physically, digital screens emit a blue light that decreases melatonin production, which is a hormone that helps regulate the sleep–wake cycle. Therefore, heavy screen use—especially close to bedtime—can interrupt normal sleeping rhythms (Brooks & Lasser, 2018). Alter (2017) points out that 95% of adults use an electronic device that emits light in the hour before bed, and more than half check their emails throughout the night. Also, 60% of adults between the ages of 18 and 64 keep their phones next to them when they sleep, which helps explain why 50% of adults claim they don't sleep well—because they're always connected to technology. Sleep quality has declined dramatically in the past half century, particularly over the past two decades, and one of the major culprits is the bluish light that emanates from many of these electronic devices (Alter, 2017, p. 69).

Stress

While stress could be categorized as an emotional effect because it manifests itself as a feeling, it is more helpful to think of it as a physiological effect because the cause of the feeling of stress is the body's increase in levels of cortisol.

A representative survey of 1,557 German internet users between 14 and 85 years of age found that perceived stress was related to communication load resulting from private emails and social media messages as well as internet multitasking. Perceived social pressure and the fear of missing out on information and social interaction were key drivers of communication load and internet multitasking, with younger users reporting more stress than older users (Reinecke et al., 2017).

Obesity

Across all age groups, more than 2 hours a day of watching videos doubles the risk of obesity in kids. The average time preschoolers spend watching videos is more than 4 hours per day (Kamenetz, 2018).

The reason that digital media exposure has been blamed as a contributing factor to obesity, especially among children, is that the media present a constant stream of ads for unhealthy foods high in fat, salt, and sugar. Also, 90% of the foods marketed to kids are unhealthy. People are constantly being presented with appeals to eat, so many people overeat. In addition, the deeply passive state of watching videos burns fewer calories than any other waking activity (Kamenetz, 2018).

AFFECTIVE

Feelings of happiness, impatience, loneliness, and depression have been found to result from various experiences with digital media in general.

Happiness

In the short term, the use of digital media continually triggers feelings of happiness in users as they successfully satisfy their immediate needs (Erreygers, Vandebosch, Vranjes, Baillien, & De Witte, 2017). However, over the long run, the constant use of online platforms to interact with other people is damaging to an individual's happiness because it pushes out real-world interactions and in-person contact. Happiness requires "meaningful, positive, need-satisfying relationships" (Brooks & Lasser, 2018, p. 10).

Impatience

Larchet (2019) is a Swiss philosopher who argues in *The New Media Epidemic: The Undermining of Society, Family, and Our Own Soul* that the rise of digital media has created a generalized sense of impatience among users of digital media. He observes, "The new media are the means of getting everything right now. They turn us into spoilt children with desires and fancies that if they cannot be satisfied at once, make us burst with intolerance and frustration" (pp. 28–29). He continues, "Far from freeing up time, the new media simply shrink time and speed up everything. The result is a world without duration, because everything is always changing and there is no more space between temporal markers (p. 31).

Loneliness

Larchet (2019) argues that digital media have served to increase loneliness by the way they give us a feeling of connecting with others, but this feeling of connectedness turns to loneliness when we realize that the interpersonal relationships we develop through digital media are not meaningful or substantial.

> Connected man's hyper-communication, by emphasizing the form (communication itself) over content (the message), shows quite clearly its main aim: to be a way of escaping loneliness. It is hardly surprising that the new media, which allows communication at will, have developed in a society like ours where social bonds are much weaker than in a traditional society. There is conflict between generations; families are dispersed; marriage is in crisis and unions are unstable; and more and more people, especially in cities but also in the country, live alone, not only in old age but also when still young. People are physically and psychologically isolated. Their loneliness is reinforced by misunderstandings between generations. Changes in society, of values and of technology, take place rapidly, and the parents adapt to them much less easily than their offspring. . . . Paradoxically, hyper-communication does not cure the problem of loneliness, but to some extent makes it worse because it encourages superficial relationships that fail to help people deal with their loneliness in more constructive ways. (p. 39)

Depression

Another widespread emotional effect often examined by researchers is depression. Often researchers will point out that during the past several decades as people have been increasing their use of digital media. Also, rates of clinical and subclinical mental health problems have also been growing, particularly among adolescents and young adults who are the heaviest users of digital media. There has been an increase of 37% in major depressive episodes from 2005 to 2014, and this is likely to be an underestimate (Brooks & Lasser, 2018). Also, the number of Americans on prescriptions for antidepressant medication has gone from 6.8% in 1999 to 13% in 2012, while the suicide rate is increasing for every age group (Brooks & Lasser, 2018).

One plausible reason for the growth of depression among users of digital media is that the emotions they feel initially are realized to be false over the long haul, that is, when people interact with computers, they cannot have satisfying emotional exchanges, and this leaves them feeling depressed. In her book *Alone Together: Why We Expect More From Technology and Less From Each Other*, Sherry Turkle (2011) tells a story about how people develop attachments to even simple computer programs, such as ELIZA, which was a computer program developed in the 1970s that allowed people to ask questions and have the computer respond with preprogrammed statements that gave users the sense they were talking with a friend or a psychotherapist. So if a person typed "I am angry with my mother," ELIZA would respond with something like "Tell me more about your mother" or "Why do you think you are so angry?" Thus this exchange appeared to be an interpersonal conversation. However, ELIZA was not really conversing, nor was it expressing emotions, although the exchanges were interpreted by users that way at times. Since then computer programs have gotten a lot more sophisticated, but none of them can communicate in a truly human manner; however, many appear to do so by simulating emotions that make users believe digital devices are actually thinking, conversing, and feeling.

COGNITIVE

Exposure to digital media has greatly enhanced users' learning of new information, but it has also resulted in less obvious cognitive effects, such as fostering an awareness deficit, leading users to create hybrid identities, and increasing narcissistic thought patterns.

Learning

Because digital media offered features that analog media could not, many scholars believed digital media would elevate the general level of learning in the population. For example, many educators once believed that hypermedia (multimedia triggered by hot buttons in text) "would provide a richer learning experience for readers," and would

> deepen comprehension and strengthen learning. The more inputs, the better. But this assumption, long accepted without much evidence, has also been contradicted by research. The division of attention demanded by multimedia further strains our cognitive abilities, diminishing our learning and weakening our understanding. When it comes to supplying the mind with the stuff of thought, more can be less. (Carr, 2010, pp. 129–130)

Larchet (2019) adds, "Most studies agree that using the new media brings about a deterioration in school results both short and long term" (p. 111). Some recent research has shown how the more video that children watch before the age of 3, the less they attend to their schoolwork at the age of 10. Participation, effort, and curiosity are all diminished. Two-thirds of all children under 6 years of age live in homes where the TV is on at least half the waking hours, even when no one is present to view. One third live in homes where the TV is on most or almost all of the time. And more than 65% of children were found to have a TV in their bedroom. Children in this group were found to read less than other children and to be slower to learn to read. There are now dozens of studies showing language delays from too early and too much screen exposure (Kamenetz, 2018).

In a meta-analysis of 63 studies (N = 13,484) that examined the extent to which web interactivity could affect various psychological outcomes, Yang and Shen (2018) found that interactivity did not necessarily increase cognitive elaboration, knowledge acquisition, and information recall.

There appear to be three reasons to explain why this massive exposure to digital media has not resulted in people, especially children, using this rich source of information as a way to increase their knowledge. One reason is that digital media eat up time. "Taken together, . . . they reduce by between 28% and 36% the time devoted to lessons and homework" (Larchet, 2019, p. 111).

A second reason is that exposure to digital media often increases tiredness by burning up the user's energy and by reducing the time and quality of sleep. This has an impact on wakefulness, attention, and memory, and on mental development in general. A sleep-depriving mechanism that is caused by screens is the overproduction of cortisol, the stress hormone. Because screens are emotionally arousing, they serve to generate cortisol in the human body. This constant triggering of cortisol leads to a "roller coaster effect" where people are constantly going from tired to wired and back to tired (Kamenetz, 2018).

A third reason that digital media use does not lead to higher amounts of learning is that it diminishes rather than increases people's attention. Digital media use has been found to reduce the user's attentiveness and concentration (Larchet, 2019). It appears that typically when people use their digital devices, they do so with a low level of attention. Instead, their activity falls largely into a category of automaticity, where they perform mundane habits of which they are unaware. "The Net's cacophony of stimuli short-circuits both conscious and unconscious thought, preventing our minds from thinking either deeply or creatively. Our brains turn into simple signal-processing units, quickly shepherding information into consciousness and then back out again" (Carr, 2010, p. 119).

Awareness Deficit

Research has shown how each hour spent watching screens between the ages of 5 and 11 increases by 50% the probability of attention deficit at the age of 13. Yet more research shows that each hour spent with screens at 14 years of age increases the probability of attention deficit at 16 by 44%. And recent research shows that children between the ages of 3 and 5 spend 4.1 hours on screens daily (Kamenetz, 2018).

People are largely unaware of how much time they spend with the media. For example, a recent study comparing actual phone use to estimated phone use found that young adults checked their phones twice a much as they estimated (Brooks & Lasser, 2018). Much of media exposure consists of mundane behaviors, that is, our behaviors are governed by automatic routines that we have gradually developed over time. These routines run automatically without our conscious awareness, so we have no specific memory of each exposure. When we are asked about our exposures (such as how many sites we visited during an internet search), we have no recollection of those exposures so we cannot provide an accurate answer; instead, we must make wild guesses that are often huge underestimations or overestimations.

Hybrid Identities

Schultze (2014) points out,

> That we rely increasingly on digital bodies to interact with the world implies that our identities (i.e., who we are) are increasingly hybrid, simultaneously performed in physical and in digital spaces. We are cyborgs, that is, human beings whose bodies are extended through technology and whose identities are entangled with technology. As such, we find ourselves having to construct and manage who we are in a space where distinctions between the real and the virtual are increasingly blurred. (p. 53)

Narcissism

A personality trait that has been shaped by digital media is narcissism. Narcissism is defined as an excessive interest in oneself and one's appearance, self-centeredness arising from failure to distinguish the self from external objects. Turkle (2011) explains,

> In the psychoanalytic tradition, one speaks about narcissism not to indicate people who love themselves, but a personality so fragile that it needs constant support. It cannot tolerate the complex demands of other people but tries to relate to them by distorting who they are and splitting off what it needs, what it can use. So, the narcissistic self gets on with others by dealing only with their made-to-measure representations. (p. 177)

A study of U.S. college students found a significant increase in scores on the Narcissistic Personality Inventory between 1982 and 2006, which coincides with the rise of the internet (Aiken, 2016). While this study only demonstrates correlation rather than causation, there are valid arguments that give us reasons to believe that the rise of digital media has influenced the increase in narcissism. Larchet (2019) explains,

> The new media allow you to photograph yourself, to video yourself, to record yourself. Furthermore, they allow all these representations of yourself to be edited with various applications and to be posted on various social media, such as Facebook, or on Internet sites dedicated to their transmission, like YouTube for videos. Anything goes if it will set you apart from the rest, be it fringe, eccentric, extreme, or dangerous. You can be a hero for a day by making a record-size pizza, by driving a car at 125 mph down a city street or by downing several bottles of spirits, one after the other. Provocative tweets or short, cutting phrases on blogs, Facebook, or Twitter are also ways to make yourself heard, to create a buzz, and to make people speak about you. (p. 97)

Turkle (2011) argues that digital media guide youngsters "into narcissistic ways of relating to the world" (p. 179). These media condition people to interact with their surroundings in a particular way that enables them to feel in control and spend much energy on constructing and then maintaining a highly manicured online self-narrative.

ATTITUDINAL

Most people have a positive attitude about the internet. In February 2014, a Pew Research Project "found that 90 percent of internet users say the internet has been a good thing for them personally. Only 6 percent say it's been a bad thing and 3 percent say it's been both. Similarly, 76 percent of internet users believe that it has been a good thing for society, while 15 percent say it's been a bad thing and 8 percent say it's been both" (DuBravac, 2015, p. 265).

Cascade Effects

Sometimes it is easy to understand a particular effect because there is a clear manifestation of what the effect is, and it is easy to categorize it as behavioral, physiological, affective, belief, attitudinal, or cognitive. But oftentimes effects are more complicated, such as when the effect itself is a complex of several things, for example, an alteration of cognitions that leads to the acquisition of a belief that then over time continually triggers a behavioral pattern. I refer to this kind of effect as a cascade effect because in order to understand its nature, we need to consider how media influence sets off a progression of effects where the occurrence of one type of effect triggers the occurrence of another type of effect and so on. In this section we will unpack the sequences in five cascade-type effects: concentration, choice, connectedness, disinhibition, and addiction. With each of these five cascade effects, notice how media influence first triggers one type of unit effect that then triggers another type of unit effect in a progression.

Before we examine each of these five cascade effects in some detail, there are a few things you need to understand about them. First, each cascade begins with a simple drive, that is, users have a need that they want to satisfy so they seek out digital messages to satisfy that need. For example, we may have a need to connect with people, to influence others, to experience competition, to shop for goods and services, to get information in general or on a particular topic, or to avoid boredom. Our needs set us on a path that begins with exposure to digital media and then progresses through a sequence of subsequent effects. Rather than consider each of these effects separately, they are better understood as a set of effects where each earlier one triggers a subsequent effect.

Second, as people interact with digital media to satisfy a particular need, they typically do not experience a single effect; instead, during their exposure they make a series of decisions that delineate a path where a sequence of effects unfolds. Think of these decision points as forks in the road; the decisions people make determine the path they take.

Third, some of these paths have a positive trajectory, that is, the decisions people make take them along a path that continually satisfies their needs in a better and better way. In contrast, other paths have a negative trajectory, that is, the decisions that people make take them down a path that serves to satisfy the needs of other people or companies at the expense of satisfying the person's own needs. Also, there are paths of effects that exhibit both a positive and then a negative trajectory. The key to the direction of the effects trajectory is the degree of mindfulness that people maintain when progressing down a path. **Mindfulness** is "the awareness that emerges through paying attention, on purpose, in the present moment, and nonjudgmentally to the unfolding of experience moment by moment. Mindfulness is not about emptying our minds; it is about focusing our attention. Mindfulness is about training ourselves to maintain focused, conscious awareness on one thing that we choose" (Brooks & Lasser, 2018, p. 12).

When we are mindful, we maintain an awareness of our needs that guides us through decisions that we consciously make to satisfy those needs. When people are mindful in making these decisions, they can stay on a positive path and fashion a progression that continually satisfies their evolving needs. But when people are not mindful, their decisions are made by default and their resulting actions get routinized into habits that often serve the needs of message providers much more than the needs of the users. When this happens, people move through the progression in a negative manner as they get further and further away from satisfying their own needs, which results in them becoming more unhappy, frustrated, bored, or anxious that something is just not going well.

Fourth, designers of digital platforms have their own needs. When their needs are the same as those of the users, then it is easier for users to stay on a positive effects trajectory because they are not being distracted by other forces manipulating them. But often, the two sets of needs are different. If users stay mindful of their own needs and manage their digital exposure to satisfy their own personal needs, then the trajectory stays positive for them. But when users lose mindfulness, other factors take over, and those factors that are purposely planted in the digital messages and platforms serve to satisfy the needs of other people and organizations. Those factors are designed to distract users from satisfying their own needs and condition them to satisfy the needs of the message producers. This conditioning leads to automatic habits that are the defaults users follow when they are not mindful.

In summary, each of the five progressions begins as a simple drive we experience as a desire to satisfy a particular need. As we interact with digital media in a process of satisfying these needs, we are faced with a series of decisions that can keep us on one path or take us far afield as we branch off from the central need-satisfying path. When we are mindful, our decisions are made consciously and strategically to satisfy our needs. But when we lose mindfulness, we default to automatic routines that have been programmed by people and organizations that are working to use you to satisfy their needs.

CONCENTRATION PROGRESSION

When we expose ourselves to digital media, we often have a drive to experience a high degree of concentration that is achieved when the digital exposure takes us into either transported state or a flow state—sometimes called "being in the zone." Both states are highly pleasurable. The pleasure comes from our feeling that the costs of exposure are low (it's easy to continue in the exposures) relative to the high amount of payoff (completely holding our attention such that we strongly desire it to continue; Brooks & Lasser, 2018).

The **transported state** of exposure is achieved when a media exposure pulls us so completely into the experience that we lose track of time and place (Potter, 2019). For example, we watch a movie or video that is so engrossing that we are fully pulled into the action by strongly identifying with the characters so that we vicariously feel their emotions and actually feel we are part of the action. The flow state is similar to the transported state in the sense that we lose track of time and place, but with the flow state we are engaging in a challenging task that requires us to make decisions to complete tasks, such as when we play online games or when we get fully involved in internet searches for particular information that we can use in term papers or on exams.

Positive Trajectory

A positive trajectory starts when we recognize that we have a need to experience pleasure from being "swept away" deeply into a digital experience—such as entering a fantasy world, playing an engrossing digital game, being submerged in an online shopping experience for "retail therapy," or engaging in an intense, extended texting exchange with a close friend. We want to experience physiological arousal and affective pleasure. When we do achieve this pleasure state, we trigger the formation of a positive attitude (or if this is a repeated activity, we reinforce the existing attitude) about the experience that makes us want to continue with the experience. As we continue in the experience, we exhibit a behavioral effect that can develop over time into a positive habit.

When we are in a transported state, the challenge is to avoid distractions so we can continue in this state. Let's say you are in a movie theater or at home watching a movie streaming on a big-screen television. You are totally into the action; then your phone rings to interrupt this pleasurable state. You feel disappointed or angry. If you are able to ignore the distraction and return to the transported state, then the trajectory of your exposure stays positive because it continues to satisfy your need as it continues to deliver pleasure.

Negative Trajectory

When a positive trajectory is suddenly interrupted with distractions, this can set us off on a negative trajectory if we succumb to those interruptions. Interruptions destroy our concentration by tempting us to switch our exposure to some other digital message. The more interruptions we experience, the harder it is to get back to a state of high concentration.

When we are on one digital media platform, other platforms continually try to attract our attention to their platforms by using **push notifications** (Liebold, Brill, Pietschmann, Schwab, & Ohler, 2017). These push notifications are sounds (pings, rings, etc.) and sights (pop-up windows, etc.) that rely on the brain's **orienting reflex**, which is hardwired into the human brain as a way to ensure the survival of the species. The more primitive parts of our brains have been hardwired to monitor threats to us from our environment. That is, our attention is automatically triggered by stimuli that are either novel or salient, or both. When we respond to these triggers, dopamine is released in the brain and we feel pleasure (Gazzaley & Rosen, 2016). The orienting reflex kicks in when a novel stimulus occurs, and the brain automatically diverts attention to the source of that stimulus in order to make sure it is not coming from a threat to the person. When we succumb to these temptations introduced by the push notifications, we tend to get distracted away from consciously satisfying our needs and instead end up spending our time and energy satisfying needs that are not ours.

When we continually experience interruptions in our everyday lives, our ability to concentrate erodes, which leaves us with a lowered ability to achieve concentration with anything because we fully expect to be interrupted no matter what we do. This is especially a problem with digital messages because so many of them bombard us with push notifications that are sent to us to alert us to something wanting our attention. When we respond to these interruptions, it is an indication that we believe what we are currently doing is less important than the unknown of what could get our attention next (Brooks & Lasser, 2018). Over time, we come to believe there is always a better alternative to what we are currently doing. This leads us to constantly feel anxious and frequently feel frustrated when we cannot locate that "better" alternative. These feelings create—and then continually reinforce—a belief that there is always something better out there somewhere, and this belief reduces our ability to feel satisfied with what we are currently doing. Over time we develop the behavioral habit of continually searching. This searching is mindless because we do not have a clear idea of what we are searching for and instead are motivated by irrational and anxious feelings. As we consistently respond to distractions that promise something new, we erode our ability to fully immerse ourselves in tasks that require deep concentration.

In their book *The Distracted Mind: Ancient Brains in a High-Tech World*, Gazzaley and Rosen (2016) argue that the current information culture continuously presents so many distractions that it is impossible for people to concentrate adequately on tasks, and this is harming our ability to function well. This leads to compulsively checking our screens to make sure we are not missing anything. None of these checks by themselves is a problem, but cumulatively, it is death by a thousand paper cuts (Brooks & Lasser, 2018).

We are so programmed to deal with interruptions that we often interrupt ourselves even without external factors interrupting us. And perhaps the most harmful aspect of this problem is that we are unaware of it. We greatly underestimate how many interruptions to our concentration we really experience in our everyday lives. For example, a study comparing actual phone use to estimated phone use found that young adults checked their phones twice a much as they estimated (Brooks & Lasser, 2018).

> Dozens of studies by psychologists, neurobiologists, educators, and Web designers point to the same conclusion: when we go online, we enter an environment that promotes cursory reading, hurried and distracted thinking, and superficial learning. It's possible to think deeply while surfing the Net, just as it's possible to think shallowly while reading a book, but that's not the type of thinking the technology encourages and rewards. (Carr, 2010, pp. 115–116)

In order to maintain concentration, many people engage in multitasking. They believe that it requires a higher degree of concentration to multitask, so they think they are forcing themselves into higher levels of concentration by multitasking. Furthermore, they believe that the rewards of multitasking are significantly higher, that is, it is better to finish three tasks in a unit of time rather than only one task in that same unit of time.

These beliefs that multitasking stimulates a higher degree of concentration and delivers more rewards are faulty according to psychological studies about the effectiveness of multitasking. These faulty beliefs arise from thinking that the human brain performs like a computer. Modern-day computers are amazing multitaskers because they are able to handle many processing tasks at exactly the same time by using parallel processing. Computers can divide their processing power into many sectors with each sector processing a different task at the same time in a parallel fashion.

Brains have evolved to allow humans to engage in more than one goal-directed activity at a time, switching back and forth among multiple goals—thus multitasking. But let's examine what multitasking really means for the human brain, that is, can the human brain multitask like computers? In some ways, the human brain is like a computer. For example, parts of the human brain can parallel process information just like computers, that is, the brain is constantly monitoring all sorts of body systems (such as breathing, blood circulation, and digestion). However, when it comes to the cognitive part of the brain governing attention, humans are not able to process in a parallel fashion, because attention is a very limited resource where we can only focus our attention on one thing at a time. Instead, people process in a serial manner, that is, we switch our attention from one task to another, where we pay attention to only one thing at a time. When we switch, we focus on one thing and ignore all others, even if only for a very brief time (Gazzaley & Rosen, 2016).

When we watch people multitask, it looks as if they are working on several things simultaneously, but this is not what is really going on. During multitasking, people pay attention to one thing for a few seconds and then shift attention to something else for a few seconds and on and on; brains are constantly switching attention. This is serial processing, not parallel processing. If we have a good goal management system (like a traffic controller), then we make progress on multiple tasks in a serial fashion as our attention is constantly switched from task to task (Gazzaley & Rosen, 2016). However, switching across tasks in a serial manner increases—rather than decreases—the expenditure of cognitive resources. Each time we switch, we need to make decisions about where to leave off on one task, which task to engage with next, and remember where we were on that new task when we last switched away from it. The continued switching can be exhausting and reduces concentration.

With the many forms of stimuli that media—especially digital media—provide, multitasking has become popular. Gazzaley and Rosen (2016) point out that 95% of people report multitasking each day and that this multitasking consumes more than one third of their day. Also, the typical teen and young adult believes he or she can juggle six to seven different forms of media at the same time. Gazzaley and Rosen (2016) argue that in our information-rich culture with so many distractions, we are constantly switching our attention because so many stimuli appear to be novel and salient. "We have adopted a style of 'everyday media multitasking'—which is just a generous way of saying that we have lost our awareness of what is necessary and what is simply reflexive responding as thought prodded by a sharp stick" (Gazzaley & Rosen, 2016, p. 123).

The idea of multitasking has been perceived in very different ways over time. Turkle (2011) explains,

> Subtly, over time, multitasking, once seen as something of a blight, was recast as a virtue. And over time, the conversation about its virtues became extravagant, with young people close to lionized for their ability to do many

> things at once. Experts went so far as to declare multitasking not just a skill but *the* crucial skill for successful work and learning in digital culture. There was even concern that old-fashioned teachers who could only do one thing at a time would hamper student learning. . . . When psychologists study multitasking, they do not find a story of new efficiencies. Rather, multitaskers don't perform as well on any of the tasks they are attempting. But multitasking feels good because the body rewards it with neurochemicals that induce a multitasking "high." The high deceives multitaskers into thinking they are being especially productive. (pp. 162, 163)

Research into multitasking has not found it to be a way to increase a person's productivity. To the contrary, multitasking has been found to reduce productivity because all the switching between tasks reduces the brain's ability to complete tasks well (Gazzaley & Rosen, 2016). These studies were conducted at all levels of educational settings, in the workplace, and in all kinds of interpersonal relationships. Research has also found that the negative effects of multitasking showed up in all age groups, but they were strongest in younger people because they had grown up in the situation where information-saturated culture was stronger and there were more salient distractions, such as SNSs and texting.

What those studies continually find is that multitasking is associated with all sorts of negative effects (Chang, 2017; McGregor, Mourão, Neto, Straubhaar, & Angeluci, 2017), especially in the area of political participation (de Zúñiga & Liu, 2017; Lin & Chiang, 2017). And multitasking has been found to lead to other negative effects, such as lower rates of sleep, lower levels of mental health, and higher rates of ADHD, depression, anxiety, and narcissistic personality disorder (Gazzaley & Rosen, 2016).

Perhaps the most negative effect of multitasking is that it greatly reduces people's ability to concentrate over time. In a recent study, Rosen (cited in Gazzaley & Rosen, 2016) observed students (middle school through university level) working on a 15-minute task and found the typical student could not stay focused on the task for more than 3 to 5 minutes. He also found that lower student GPAs were related to time spent on task and total time spent with media on a typical day, especially whether they frequently accessed Facebook. And in another study, the median time before a switch occurred was only 11 seconds (Yeykelis, Cummings, & Reeves, 2018).

Gazzaley and Rosen (2016) argue,

> The truth is that we are mostly oblivious to the toll that constant task switching generates. We convince ourselves that we can handle it because we mistakenly believe that we possess a brain that is built for multitasking; or, because we do it all the time, we feel that we must have become really good at it . . . [but] people who believe that they are good at multitasking actually tend to be those who do the worst on laboratory tests of multitasking. (p. 177)

Herbert Simon (1971), the Nobel Prize–winning economist, argued that a world rich in information actually creates a poverty of attention because when people are presented with so many choices, they tend to resist investing the considerable work required to sort through all the choices to make the best selections. Instead people default to automatic routines that make the selections for them without having to exert the effort to pay much attention to them.

CHOICE PROGRESSION

Digital media constantly present us with an overwhelming number of choices. When we make our choices consciously, we are likely to set out on a positive trajectory. But when we make those choices unconsciously—typically by defaulting to habits—then we increase the probability that we set out on a negative trajectory.

Positive Trajectory

The more we know about our needs, the better choices we can make. When we are mindful, we begin by recalling what digital media we used in the past to satisfy our needs and remember which choices worked best. If we were unsatisfied by all our previous choices (i.e., none seemed to satisfy a particular need well), then we undertake a strategic search of alternatives that have a chance of satisfying this particular need better. If we stay mindful during our search, it is likely we will find a digital experience that will satisfy our need better than in the past.

During our search, we are sensitive to the characteristics of salience and novelty. Salience refers to the perceived match between a person's need and the observable characteristics of the message. Novelty refers to the message's freshness. The human brain is hardwired to explore new environments and experiences primarily for the purpose of finding food. This exploring is pleasurable because it stimulates dopamine production in the brain. But in the modern age, we are exploring for information, and this exploration still stimulates dopamine production (Gazzaley & Rosen, 2016). Novelty activates the same reward centers in the brain as does food.

Salience and novelty trigger physiological effects; they also require perceptions, so this progression involves cognitions and beliefs. These cognitions are compared to a person's beliefs about what salience and novelty are. Then a judgment is made about the value of a choice (attitudinal effect). The option that gets the highest value judgment is then selected, and exposure results (behavioral effect).

When we engage this searching process in a mindful manner, we are conscious of how we are making our choices so that we can use salience and novelty to maximize the pleasure of a physiological effect. We are aware of our beliefs and how we use them as standards for making judgments of value, thus maximizing the attitudinal effect. Then we follow through on shaping our exposures to maximize the behavioral effect, that is, using particular exposures to satisfy our needs more completely.

Negative Trajectory

This **choice progression** can also have a negative trajectory. The factors that take us on a negative trajectory are impulsivity, fear, and especially habits.

Impulsivity is a personality trait characterized by the urge to act spontaneously without reflecting on an action and its consequences (Aiken, 2016). People who are impulsive are impatient with long, involved thinking procedures, so they prefer to make decisions quickly. Thus they are more interested in efficiency (making decisions quickly and then moving on) instead of effectiveness (making decisions that have the greatest chance of satisfying their needs).

When we have too many choices, we get fatigued and even paralyzed. Barry Schwartz in *The Paradox of Choice* argues that often people have too many choices, and this tends to make them fearful rather than happy. When people have only two or a small number of choice options, they can usually select the best one easily and move on. But when they are given many options to choose from, they feel pressure to consider them all in detail to ensure they are choosing the best one, and when they finally do make a choice, they experience a fear that they might not have considered all the variables of all the choice options well enough to have truly made the best selection. When people are continually presented with many choices, they constantly feel overwhelmed, and this feeling of fatigue drives many people to rely on past exposure habits that allow them to make choices automatically without having to go through the hassle of evaluating each alternative carefully.

Exposure habits are automatic routines we have learned through past experience. Habits give us the ability to avoid having to deal with each decision in our everyday lives as if it were the first time we encountered the need to decide. But there are two major problems with relying on habits. One problem is that the habits that were originally created to satisfy our needs in the best way possible are likely to have lost their ability over time to satisfy those needs well—or at all—but the habit still guides our behavior, and we continue to expose ourselves to choices that have little value in satisfying those needs.

Another major problem with habits is that they have often been shaped and reinforced by other people or organizations to satisfy their needs instead of our needs. Media organizations are in the business of constructing audiences and conditioning them for repeated exposures. Digital businesses are very sophisticated with their methods and very successful in conditioning us. To see more detail on this point, read *Hooked: How to Build Habit-Forming Products* by Nir Eyal (see Box 11.1).

When we are presented with choices, we could choose not to act reflexively and consciously consider the advantages as well as the disadvantages of the alternative choices. The human brain has evolved a critical time delay that disrupts the purely reflexive nature of the perception–action cycle so that people can evaluate the stimulus and decide what to do. This delay allows for attention, which is "a complex set of integrated processes with multiple subcomponents." The fundamental feature of selectivity is that it allows us to direct our brainpower and in so doing allows us to maximize "the effectiveness of our neural processing and in turn optimizes our performance" (Gazzaley & Rosen, 2016, p. 30). Think of selectivity as a spotlight; it directs our attention to things to focus on (Gazzaley & Rosen, 2016). But if we do not think about how we pay attention to things and instead automatically process stimuli, we fail to take advantage of this ability to mindfully make decisions and instead we stay on a negative trajectory.

Box 11.1. How to Hook People Into Forming Habits

In *Hooked: How to Build Habit-Forming Products* (2014), Nir Eyal tells media managers and advertisers how to condition users of the digital media to form habits that will satisfy their business needs. He uses the findings from psychological research to create a four-step model that explains how to hook people to develop habits. The point of this model is to move people into what Eyal calls the habit zone, where the behaviors you have programmed are repeated automatically as habits. Cognitive psychologists define habits as automatic behaviors triggered by situational cues. Habits keep users loyal by reducing the costs to continue the habit and raising the costs to trying something new that would break the habit. Eyal says that a "company can begin to determine its product's habit-forming potential by plotting two factors: *frequency* (how often the behavior occurs) and *perceived utility* (how useful and rewarding the behavior is in the user's mind over alternative solutions)" (p. 29).

The four steps in his model are trigger, action, variable reward, and investment. He argues that all kinds of companies and media producers use this model to condition people into habits that benefit them.

TRIGGER

"A trigger is the actuator of behavior—the spark plug in the engine" (p. 7). Eyal makes a distinction between external triggers and internal triggers: "External triggers are embedded with information, which tells the user what to do next" (p. 41). In contrast, "internal triggers manifest automatically in your mind. Connecting internal triggers with a product is the brass ring of consumer technology" (p. 48).

ACTION

The second step is to get people to try the behavior that you want to develop into a habit. It can be simple, such as clicking on an ad. Action needs to be simple so that "any technology or product that significantly reduces the steps to complete a task will enjoy high adoption rates by the people it assists" (p. 67). Thus, plan actions that require low amounts of time, money, physical effort, and brain cycles. This is why internet sites like Facebook and Twitter, searching with Google, and taking pictures with an iPhone are so habit forming. The psychological tools that help with action are the scarcity effect (action makes you special because it is rare), framing, anchoring, and endowed progress (loyalty cards used by retailers).

VARIABLE REWARD

You need to reward the behavior, but do so in a variable pattern so that the rewards are unpredictable. You must also find the types of rewards that are of value to people you are trying to hook.

INVESTMENT

Get the person to do some work, and this will build commitment. "The more users invest time and effort into a product or service, the more they will value it" (p. 136). "The stored value users put into the product increases the likelihood they will use it again in the future" (p. 145). Thus, every time people buy a new song on iTunes, they are strengthening their ties to that service.

In summary, when we are impulsive and feel fatigued by overwhelming choice, we default to habits of exposure. Because these media exposure habits have been largely programmed by digital platforms to satisfy their own business needs, the habits that the media condition us to perform tend to satisfy their business needs much more than our own personal needs.

CONNECTEDNESS PROGRESSION

This progression starts with a drive to connect with other people. As Sherry Turkle writes in *Alone Together*, our happiness is tied to the quality of our social relationships. "We are stimulated by connectivity itself. We learn to require it" (2011, p. 227). The internet has created a participatory culture where people consider it enjoyable and creative to be a part of the online experience that connects them with other people. The members of the public take an active part in the creation and consumption of their cultural products as they connect with others (Chayko, 2018).

Positive Trajectory

Digital media offer users the opportunity to connect with many people. It is simple and convenient to create interactions with new people on social networking sites. This behavior can translate into pleasurable emotions of attachments and positive beliefs about the value of friendships.

Digital media give people an efficient way to connect with others. Efficiency becomes very important when people feel overwhelmed with all the tasks they must accomplish in their everyday lives. One set of tasks that people feel pressure to complete every day is connecting with people, so they look for efficient ways to connect in a way that gives them control over making and maintaining friendships. Turkle (2011) explains that people use digital forms of communication rather than face-to-face forms because digital forms appear to be more efficient. That is, with email and especially texting, you can send quick, short messages that tell receivers you are connected to them. In contrast, phone conversations and in-person conversations are much less efficient because they require more effort and consume more time.

Another positive trajectory of using digital media to connect with other people is for self-discovery. Turkle (2011) writes, "People don't forge online identities with the idea that they are embarking on a potentially 'therapeutic' exercise." She continues,

> Yet, in these performances . . . something else breaks through. When we perform a life through our avatars, we express our hopes, strengths, and vulnerabilities. They are a kind of natural Rorschach. We have an opportunity to see what we wish for and what we might be missing. But more than this, we may work through blocks and address insecurities. People can use an avatar as "practice for real life." (p. 212)

Some people are so fragile that they need a safe place where they can develop social skills with little or no negative consequences until their social skills are strong enough to try out with actual people in the real world. With online anonymity, internet users tend to trust people easier and they disclose information about themselves more quickly. This leads to faster friendships and quicker intimacy (Aiken, 2016).

Yet another positive trajectory is to give people a greater sense of control. Turkle (2011) explains, "In text, messaging, and e-mail, you hide as much as you show. You can present yourself as you wish to be 'seen'" (p. 207). And because these messages endure on the internet, their archiving value can add to a person's sense of control. Turkle (2011) says, "I interview couples who tell me that they text or e-mail each other while in bed. Some say they want to leave a record of a request or a feeling 'on the system'" (p. 208).

In all of these positive trajectories, people start with a personal need (increase their efficiency in dealing with mundane tasks, find a safe place to develop social skills, and increase their sense of control) and then strategically and mindfully use digital media to satisfy that need.

Negative Trajectory

A positive trajectory strategy can turn into a negative trajectory habit when people begin to rely too much on digital technology to make friends and build friendships. As people spend more time with technology rather than in direct contact with people, their connections often weaken. When we use a "quantity over quality" strategy to develop more "friendships," we begin to expect more from technology and less from each other. Eventually the *number* of friendships is what is most important and we spend considerable effort increasing that number. We end up having a long list of many, many friends but none that we really know or on whom we could really depend. This leads us to become less satisfied in our friendships so we try to develop more, looking for that super friend (Brooks & Lasser, 2018). Turkle (2011) relates a story about a 17-year-old high school girl who said, "I come home from school and go online, and I'm feeling okay, and I talk for two hours on the Web. But then I still have no friends. I'll never know the people I spoke to. They are 'chat people.' Yeah, they could be twelve years old" (p. 248).

In the long run, there is no adequate substitute for in-person contact with real people. Attachment theory says that we all need to feel significant attachment to family and close friends in order to feel secure and happy. This requires lots of touching and undivided attention where we feel the other person regards us as important and worthy to them (Brooks & Lasser, 2018). Also, studies show that in-person friendships decrease cortisol (the stress hormone) while increasing oxytocin (hormone associated with bonding and pleasure; Brooks & Lasser, 2018).

At the extreme of this negative trajectory, connectivity becomes a craving; when we receive a text or an email, our nervous system responds by giving us a shot of dopamine. We are stimulated by connectivity itself. We learn to require it, even as it depletes us. Turkle (2011) explains that when we are overwhelmed "by the volume and velocity of our lives, we turn to technology to help us find time. But technology makes us busier than ever and ever more in search of retreat. Gradually, we come to see our online life as life itself" (Turkle, 2011, p. 17).

Thus, the more we use digital platforms to connect with others, the less connected we feel in a satisfying way and the stronger we crave connection.

In an interesting ethnographic study, Ito and his colleagues (2009) hung out with American children and teenagers over a three-year period to study why they spent so much time with interactive media. The researchers made several major observations. First, they observed that interactive media offer two strong attractions for today's youth: friendship-driven participation and interest-driven participation. Second, the researchers observed that interactions with media vary by degree of involvement. The least engaging degree of involvement is "hanging out" with friends and extending social networks.

Turkle (2011) argues that over time as people use the digital media, they become flattened into personae, that is, the depth of detail that elaborates each human as unique is missing.

If we use these opportunities to reflect and are mindful of our digital exposures, we can get on a positive trajectory. But if we are overwhelmed and default to habits to avoid reflection, then we are likely reinforcing a negative trajectory.

DISINHIBITION PROGRESSION

This progression begins with a drive to push ourselves beyond the limits imposed upon us by socialization. We learn these limits as social norms that show us where the line is between what is acceptable behavior in society and what is not. As we grow up—especially during adolescence—we have a drive to test the boundaries of the social norms that we have learned. Years of socialization have inhibited us from performing certain behaviors (i.e., cross the line of social acceptability). So we go online to experience things we cannot experience in our real life, especially those things we cannot experience without sanctions in our real life. We are motivated to push the lines, but we need to be disinhibited to do so. Digital media give us a relatively safe, nonthreatening place to test these boundaries.

Online disinhibition is enhanced by a variety of factors. "Disinhibition is facilitated by the environmental conditions of cyberspace—by the perceived lack of authority, the anonymity, as well as the sense of distance or physical remove" (Aiken, 2016, p. 21). This condition makes it possible for people to do things on digital platforms that they would ordinarily prevent themselves from doing in their real lives.

Positive Trajectory

When people go online and are aware that they are testing the boundaries of social norms, then their online behaviors can have a positive trajectory. People use digital media in an anonymous way to test the lines with personal consequences that are fairly minor. By using texts and blog postings, people can push the boundaries and observe how others react. Also, people can enter fantasy worlds and try out behaviors to see how they feel about performing those actions. These testings of boundaries are a form of exploration where people are able to experience interactions with types of people that they cannot experience in their real lives. They are able to try out risky behaviors in virtual worlds where the consequences of creating harm are less serious than in the real world.

Sometimes people will have irrational fears that inhibit them from trying out new behaviors in their real life. They can enter a virtual world where they are likely to be disinhibited enough to try out a range of behaviors and learn a lot about how they feel when performing those behaviors. This procedure is successful in getting people to overcome irrational fears by practicing more constructive behaviors in virtual worlds with low negative consequences. Then when their confidence is increased to an acceptable level, they can begin performing those more constructive behaviors in the real world. An example of this is with shy people who have an irrational fear of rejection when trying to meet new people. This fear prevents them in real life from starting conversations with strangers whom they would like to meet. These people can enter a fantasy world such as Second Life and use their avatars to practice meeting other avatars. If they get rejected, it is no big deal because it is just an avatar that was rejected, not them as a person. But if they are accepted and form a friendship, people can learn from this experience and try to replicate it in real life.

Negative Trajectory

There is always a risk of going too far in testing boundaries with digital messages. One example is cyber-exhibitionism, where people will post sexually suggestive or even pornographic pictures of themselves online. Typically, these people are simply trying to stimulate an immediate reaction from particular individuals. However, whatever goes out on the internet can become public and lasts forever. Images and texts can easily be duplicated and endlessly disseminated. The sender loses control over those postings.

Another negative trajectory for disinhibition is when people engage in unhealthy behaviors on the internet and find these behaviors very pleasurable, in part because there are very minor, if any, negative consequences in virtual worlds. If those people then begin engaging in those same (or similar) behaviors in real life, they are likely to experience strong negative consequences. For example, let's say a timid adolescent boy wants to learn how to push the boundaries so he can feel strong and powerful. He begins playing highly violent digital games and is continually rewarded for being aggressive, and the more aggressive he is, the more reward he gets in the game. The boy then begins acting highly aggressive in real life. Because these behaviors are typically over the line of acceptable human behavior, he will likely not get real-life rewards and is more likely to experience severe punishments.

ADDICTION PROGRESSION

The **addiction progression** has no positive trajectory because addiction is always a negative effect. The cascade to digital addiction begins innocently enough with a drive to find digital experiences that are better in some way (e.g., more emotionally intense and satisfying) than people can find in their real lives. When people find such an experience—from gaming, connecting with others on a social networking site, or acquiring a product or service online—they feel happy and rewarded, so they repeatedly perform those behaviors in the hope of continuing to experience those rewards.

Addiction to media is not an immediate effect but takes a long time to evolve as people move through a cascade of effects from displacement to dependency and then to addiction. Not everyone who is attracted to media ends up enslaved by an addiction effect, but many people do, as you saw in Chapter 3.

Displacement

As experiences with digital media are rewarded over time, people gravitate to these digital exposures and experience a displacement effect where digital experiences increase and crowd out other kinds of experiences. People begin decreasing the time they spend with nonmedia activities as their time with media continues to increase. Thus people stop relying on media to add to their total set of real-world experiences and instead use media exposures to substitute for real-world experiences. For example, television was found to displace book reading through two mechanisms: it deteriorates attitudes supporting book reading, and it diminishes children's ability to concentrate on reading (Koolstra & Van der Voort, 1996).

It appears that many people are experiencing displacement due to media exposures. For example, Alter (2017) found that the average American aged 8 to 18 "spends more time communicating through screens than she does with other people directly, face-to-face. Since the turn of the new millennium, the rate of non-screen playtime fell 20 percent, while the rate of screen playtime increased by a similar amount" (p. 237).

Displacement by itself can be a positive effect if the growing amount of media experiences serves a person's needs better than the alternative experiences they are replacing. However, it can also be a negative effect if the displacement primarily serves the needs of the media at the expense of the person, especially if it moves on to dependence and eventually addiction.

Dependence

The next step along the addiction cascade is reached when displacement turns into a **dependence effect** where people develop a reliance on particular digital experiences; that is, people not only prefer these digital experiences but also require them. This is typically a negative effect when people reach a point where they begin to lose control over their exposures and habitually seek out particular kinds of digital exposures without considering whether those exposures are satisfying their needs or not. At this point, media conditioning has become so successful that people mindlessly continue with repeated exposures without evaluating the degree to which those continued exposures are useful in satisfying their needs.

This dependency effect is explained by how people allow the media to reinforce their exposures into a habit and then into dependency (Ball-Rokeach & DeFleur, 1976; Sears & Freedman, 1967; Himmelweit et al., 1980; LaRose & Eastin, 2002; Lazarsfeld, Berelson, & Gaudet, 1944; McIntosh et al., 2000; Shah et al., 2001; Sherry, 2001; Slater, 2003).

Addiction

People have progressed all the way to addiction when they realize that their behavioral patterns of exposure to particular digital media no longer deliver positive experiences and yet they are unable to eliminate or even alter those behavioral patterns. They have reached a point where exposure to particular media experiences (e.g., competing in digital games, contacting virtual friends, and buying products online) no longer triggers positive emotional states, such as happiness, but people continue performing their exposure habits even though those habits now typically trigger negative emotional states, such as disgust or loathing. At this point, people realize they no longer *want* to perform the behavioral sequence but continue to do so anyway because they have lost control over their behavior; this is the clearest signal that a person is addicted to the behavioral sequence. "Even as you come to loathe Facebook or Instagram for consuming too much of your time, you continue to want updates as much as you did when they still made you happy" (Alter, 2017, p. 87).

This addiction cascade is primarily behavioral, but it typically involves affect—the emotions we feel for reward. It also involves physiological elements of arousal that come from engaging in behaviors with the expectation of reward (increases in dopamine and/or adrenaline).

The path to addiction is long and relies on many factors to continue its progression. Research has shown that the most influential factor in this progression is reward—as long as that reward is variable. To illustrate this idea, think about some behavioral pattern you have developed with digital media. Perhaps it is using social media to check on friends. Perhaps it is competing on digital games. Or perhaps it is shopping online. Think about how you feel when you engage in this habit; that feeling is likely to be very pleasant, which makes the experience rewarding to you. Now think about how often you feel that rewarding emotion. If you feel it every time you engage in this digital exposure behavior, then you will get bored. And over time, you will get bored more quickly. But what if you do not feel rewarded during each exposure? When rewards are withheld, we develop a drive to continue with exposures until we get that feeling of reward again. This pattern is called a **variable reward schedule**, because we experience times of reward interspersed with times of no reward.

This is why digital game playing is so addictive to many people. If the games were so simple that players always won, then the drive to compete would wear out soon as we learn that it does not matter how well we play because we will always win. But games that have increasing levels of difficulty ensure that players will often run into problems they cannot solve, so they need to work harder to figure out the barriers to reward so they can achieve those rewarding feelings once again. With a variable reward schedule, the reinforcement of exposure behaviors is particularly strong, because even losing is a motivator, that is, when players fail to experience a rewarding feeling, their motivation to continue playing gets stronger because they are seeking the next thrill that is triggered by winning.

Over time, people's behavioral patterns are strengthened by a variable reward sequence, and those behaviors become even more fixed, that is, harder to alter (Aiken, 2016). What makes the variable reinforcement schedule so powerful is not the rewards but the failures that become motivators to keep trying for the rewards. Coming off a recent loss is deeply motivating. "To some extent we all need losses and difficulties and challenges, because without them the thrill of success weakens gradually with each new victory. That's why people spend precious chunks of free time doing difficult crosswords and climbing dangerous mountains—because the hardship of the challenge is far more compelling that knowing you're going to succeed" (Aiken, 2016, p. 169).

These variable reward schedules are used with all digital media, not just gaming. For example, Facebook has a "like" button where users can provide feedback about whether they like something that is posted on a Facebook site. Alter (2017) argues,

> It's hard to exaggerate how much the "like" button changed the psychology of Facebook use. What had begun as a passive way to track your friends' lives was now deeply interactive, and with exactly the sort of unpredictable feedback that constitutes a variable reward schedule. . . . Users were gambling every time they shared a photo, web link, or status update. A post with zero likes wasn't just privately painful, but also a kind of public condemnation: whether you didn't have enough online friends, or, worse still, your online friends weren't impressed. (p. 128)

While Facebook was the first major social networking force to introduce the like button, now this function is common among digital platforms. Alter (2017) explains, "You can like and repost tweets on Twitter, pictures on Instagram, posts on Google+, columns on LinkedIn, and videos on You Tube" (p. 128).

If we are mindful of our media exposures and take control over our decision-making, we can avoid addiction. However, the media are working hard to prevent us from thinking too much about our choices; they prefer we default to habits that they can program and control. In his book *Irresistible: The Rise of Addictive Technology and the Business of Keeping Us Hooked*, Adam Alter (2017) puts it succinctly: "In 2004, Facebook was fun; in 2016, it's addictive" (p. 5).

Conclusions

This chapter focused your attention on the broad media effects that can arise from exposure to any kind of digital media. This is in contrast to the effects that arise from exposure to one type of digital content as presented in the previous six chapters. This chapter first presented an inventory of unit effects. These are effects that focus on only one type of effect: physiological, affective, cognitive, and attitudinal.

A second kind of effect illuminated in this chapter is the cascade type of effect, which is a path illustrating a sequence of unit effects that can have either a positive or a negative trajectory, depending on how people make decisions throughout the progression. This section examined five progressions: concentration, choice, connectedness, disinhibition, and addiction.

Further Reading

Kamenetz, A. (2018). *The art of screen time: How your family can balance digital media and real life*. New York: PublicAffairs. (266 pages, including endnotes and index)

The author, a digital education correspondent for National Public Radio, takes the position that while digital media present some risks of negative effects to children, digital media effects are overwhelmingly positive. The book is an easy-to-read description about what is known about how digital media affect children and about what parents can do to help their children benefit from digital media.

Larchet, J.-C. (2019). *The new media epidemic: The undermining of society, family, and our own soul*. Jordanville, NY: Holy Trinity Publications. (197 pages with endnotes and index)

The author is a Swiss philosopher who argues that the rise of digital media has created many problems for individuals and society. His criticism focuses on the destruction of interpersonal relationships, increase in unhealthy behaviors and mental disorders, abolition of privacy, dumbing down of the human mind, and the impoverishment of spiritual life.

CHAPTER 12

Big Picture Issue: Control

The phenomenon of digital media is still very new, and the research that has been conducted to examine it is even newer. As you have seen in the previous chapters, researchers have already generated a considerable amount of knowledge about digital media and how they are affecting individuals and institutions. However, there are also many gaps in our understanding of this quickly growing phenomenon, and these gaps raise important issues for us to consider. The most fundamental of all these issues is control. Because mass media are essentially tools, it is important to think about who gets to control these powerful tools. This leads to the question, Are people controlling their use of media, or are media controlling users?

Digital media offer users many opportunities to control information that analog media do not. For example, over the last several centuries, analog media have exercised considerable control over what was presented to the public as news each day. There was a small set of professional journalists (at television networks and a handful of influential newspapers) who decided each day which events to cover, whom to interview as sources, and how to structure their daily stories. These elites set the news agenda that other journalists typically followed (McCombs, 2005). Now with digital media, there is a large number of news platforms, each exercising its own judgments about what is important, so there is a much wider variety of news stories. Each person has the opportunity to select which news provider satisfies his/her need for information best. Digital media have also expanded the number of entertainment options, thus giving each person more control over making choices about entertainment messages.

Digital media have also removed limits on the kinds and amounts of information users can access as well as when and where they can access it. And perhaps even more importantly, digital media provide people with the tools to create their own messages and instantly make those messages available to particular people or even to anyone anywhere in the world. Thus, digital media have given everyone much more opportunity to control how they interact with information and entertainment messages and thereby influence how those messages influence them.

Digital media, however, have also given media themselves more power of control—but in less obvious ways. That is, media companies now have new tools to attract and condition audiences as well as control information that has previously been kept private. This chapter will show you how these new tools have greatly increased the media's power to control your access to messages and to gather information about you that you may have thought was kept private.

Access to Information

Digital media make available an incredibly wide variety of information, which makes it seem as if we are required to exercise a greater amount of control in order to wade through all the choices to find the information we really want. The media have developed search tools to help us navigate through all the choices more efficiently. However, while those search tools—especially recommender systems—provide users with more efficiency, they also provide digital media with a means of exercising greater control over users. And when users depend on recommender systems in their many searches, they lose control over their choices and increase their risk of experiencing a negative effect of ending up in an echo chamber where they are limited to hearing the same things over and over.

RECOMMENDER SYSTEMS

Recommender systems were originally developed by digital platforms that offered their users a huge number of choices that those platforms felt might overwhelm their users. So these platforms began collecting data on their users' preferences and past behaviors, and then employed these data to try making user choice more efficient. For example, Netflix offers its users thousands of movies and videos to provide enough variety of entertainment that could satisfy the various needs of millions of different customers. But this number of choices could overwhelm users, so Netflix developed a recommender system to reduce the number of choices down to a manageable amount to help each individual user make his/her selections more efficiently. Netflix's recommender system gathers information about each user (primarily their preferences and their history of selecting movies) and then uses that information to narrow down the number of choices to a small set of movies that the system predicts will be of greatest interest to that user.

Online retailers also use recommender systems. For example, Amazon.com offers more than 600 million products to its customers. While Amazon organizes products by type (books, electronics, clothing, etc.), its primary tool for making the buying experience more efficient for customers is its recommender system. Amazon gathers information about its customers' shopping habits, such as which products they have searched for in the past, which products they have bought, and which products are typically bought together. Amazon uses this information to rank order products by potential interest for each customer, so that when a user conducts a search in a particular product category, Amazon's recommender system ranks all the products in that search category and presents the customer with a screen displaying only the highest-ranked products based on its best guess about which products would interest that customer the most.

Digital platforms also use recommender systems to drive their users to news sites. For example, Google and Facebook are digital platforms that do not generate news stories for their users, but they know many of their users want news, so they use recommender systems to refer their visitors to particular news sites that they believe their visitors would find valuable and interesting. These news recommender systems are based not on journalistic criteria but instead on what these digital platforms have determined individuals would find most interesting. Google News has been called a pioneer in replacing editorial judgment with algorithmic decision-making. In 2007, Google researchers released a paper detailing the company's internal work in news personalization. In some ways recommending news stories is similar to recommending movies. Most users, most of the time, arrive at a news site without knowing which specific articles they would like to see. As Google's researchers put it, "User attitudes are dominated by the demands to 'show us something interesting'" (Hindman, 2018, p. 53).

When recommender systems drive users to news platforms, serious problems can arise. This is what happened in the 2016 presidential election where Facebook's recommender algorithms could not distinguish accurate news from inaccurate news and drove many people to news sites where the news was not credible and sometimes even totally fabricated. Thus many voters were being continually exposed to a faulty base of information, which those people used to make their voting choices. Following the election, Facebook received a great deal of criticism that led it to change its recommender algorithm.

> In the immediate aftermath of Trump's election it was social media companies such as Facebook which came in for particular and persistent criticism for their role in the way that fake news was being spread. Most of the solutions that were proposed in the media for tracking the perceived problem therefore focused on what Facebook should do to change its service, the main argument was as follows: the personalisation algorithm that shapes the way people experience the site is responsible for creating "**filter bubbles**," which shield users from views they disagree with, and allow fake news and highly partisan opinions to circulate unchecked. (Seargeant & Tagg, 2018, p. 180)

In response to the criticisms that the company was being responsible for the spread of false news, Facebook radically changed how it drove traffic to news sites. Facebook altered its recommender algorithm to remove the economic incentives that advertising revenue provided to **fake news mills**, which are "news" sites that purposefully posted fabricated and sensational articles as a means of generating advertising revenue from high levels of clicks. Another thing Facebook did was to create some tools to help users make "more informed" decisions about the content they encountered. In April 2017, Facebook launched what it referred to as an "educational tool" intended to help users identify suspect stories and flag them as unreliable (Seargeant & Tagg, 2018, p. 183). This educational tool is simply a list of bullet points that Facebook "hopes will help guide users through their online news consumption" by reminding them of "things such as being skeptical of headlines, checking the URL and source of an article, examining the genre (formatting, use of images, whether it is meant as satire, etc.), looking at the evidence cited, and cross-referencing with other articles on the same topic." The list ends with the advice to "think critically about the stories you read, and only share news that you know to be credible" (Seargeant & Tagg, 2018, p. 183).

As a result of these changes, traffic from Facebook to news sites declined dramatically from its peak in 2015. Some sites were even forced to shut down. For example, LittleThings, which was a site focusing on sharing feel-good news on social media, shut down after seeing its traffic fall by 75% after the early 2018 Facebook algorithm change (Hindman, 2018).

Recommender systems for news do not consider how important stories are or how accurate the facts are in those stories; they only consider the degree of appeal those stories might have for users based on what news stories those users have selected in the past. Also, recommender systems for news tend to narrow users' perspective on the world, rather than opening it up. By making news selections based on a person's past selections, these recommender systems tend to show people the same things over and over rather than help them explore new ideas. This leads to a fragmenting of society that is composed of individuals each locked into a different niche of information based on their past interests. These recommender systems erode away the probability that people across niches will share information and thus develop a common perspective on the world. The fragmentation divides people into smaller and smaller niches where people in one niche regard people in other niches as being wrong in their perceptions about what is important.

This problem becomes even more serious when inaccurate information gets reported as facts in some news sources and not others. Thus some niches are constructed and reinforced with inaccurate information. Beliefs formed from this inaccurate information get amplified and solidified over time.

While recommender systems offer the significant advantage of efficiency to users, they also serve to limit user choice. For example, users with a long history of buying products on Amazon are continually presented with the same few product choices when they search on Amazon; they are rarely if ever shown much range of choice beyond those products in their past purchase habits—unless they continue to search beyond the first few screens of search results. If buyers are only concerned with efficiency, then this is not a problem. But if buyers are bored with the products they typically buy and find that those products no longer satisfy their needs, then this limiting of their choice prevents them from seeing the kinds of alternatives that may satisfy their needs better.

ECHO CHAMBER

Recommender systems tend to isolate people by putting them in echo chambers where they tend to hear the same things again and again. By filtering information for each individual based on a person's past interests, recommender systems tend to reinforce a person's existing knowledge base rather than expanding it.

> A new generation of filters looks at the things you seem to like—the actual things you've done, or the things people like you like—and tries to extrapolate. They are prediction engines, constantly creating and refining a theory of who you are and what you'll do and want next. Together, these engines create a unique universe of information for each of us . . . which fundamentally alters the way we encounter ideas and information. (Pariser, 2011, p. 9)

Recommender systems keep us in a comfortable cocoon as defined by our initial interests so that we keep getting the same kind of information based on those interests and are therefore not likely to get the variety of information that would help us understand things outside our narrow niche. When we are not aware that recommender algorithms have isolated us inside a niche, we falsely think that the information and opportunities we see represent an objective and complete picture of what is happening in the world.

When people inside a niche only hear one type of news over and over, their preexisting opinions get reinforced continually to the point where people have no toleration for other opinions. When people are not exposed to a diversity of opinions, like what was more common with analog media sources of news, these people come to believe that other opinions do not exist, or if those opinions do exist, very few people hold them. Inside their echo chamber they only hear a narrow perspective. And because they hear that narrow perspective over and over, they fail to see the diversity that older forms of journalism provided.

While digital media offer people a hugely expanded variety of entertainment options, products, and news, everyone has been given the opportunity to exercise a far greater degree of control over their choices. But other factors about digital media serve to limit people's choice to a far greater degree than ever. The widespread use of recommender systems that are designed to provide users with greater efficiency has led to the creation of many individual echo chambers that significantly fragment the population into hundreds—if not thousands—of tiny niches.

Privacy

What does privacy mean in a world of digital media? How much privacy do you have when your every action with digital media is recorded and assembled into huge databases? How much privacy do you have when any business, government, organization, or individual can buy access to those huge databases? And how much privacy do you have when companies that know your patterns of thinking and behaving use that knowledge to influence you to serve their needs?

The place to start your deliberations about how to answer these questions is to examine how you think about privacy. If you are like most people, you think of privacy as a kind of bubble where you are in the center of that bubble. You let a few people—your very closest friends—into that bubble where you share all your most personal thoughts; you trust that these close friends will not share your secrets with anyone without your permission. Our natural inclination is to think that when we share some personal information with particular people, we are bringing them into a kind of bubble of privacy. When we tell a close friend something very personal, there is typically an implied understanding that our friend will not share that information with someone else without our permission.

The idea of privacy is simple when we think of it as an "invasion." When someone invades a bubble without our permission, accesses some information inside that bubble, and then shares it with people outside that bubble, this is an invasion of our privacy. However, the idea of privacy becomes very complicated when we think of it as "boundaries." We have all created a complex set of boundaries for sharing information about ourselves. There is not just one bubble; instead, there are many bubbles, each with its own boundary. Those boundaries vary by type of information and about the type of relationship we have with different types of people. For example, when you go to a medical doctor and tell her about your embarrassing symptoms, you expect her to keep that information private. The information you tell your doctor is very different than what you share with a best friend, a parent, your boss, a coworker, a financial advisor, a therapist, and a religious counselor. The information you share with each person in your life is different. Also, the limits of sharing you put on each person are different. Sometimes when you share information with a particular person, you ask him to not tell anyone, or to tell only one particular person, or to tell everyone. You can probably remember an instance when a close friend violated your trust and shared some very personal information with people outside your bubble. Can you think of any instances when one of your bubbles of privacy was invaded by an outside person or organization? If you cannot think of an example, that does not mean no such invasions ever occurred; instead, it means you are likely not aware how much information has been collected and shared about you by **big data**.

BIG DATA

Digital media make it easy for companies to record any thought you express (emails, texts, social media posts, etc.) or action you take (appointments, financial transactions, shopping experiences, whereabouts through GPS, etc.). Digital companies compile a great deal of information from across all kinds of digital sources into something called "big data." Recuber (2017) defines big data as "the continuously generated, exhaustive, and fine-grained data that is created today by things such as mobile media devices, banking and retailing transactions, and social networking sites, which is beyond the scale or scope of older ways of knowing about these aspects of the social world" (p. 47). Lanius (2019) extends this definition by saying that it refers to "data sets that are too large or complex for common computer platforms and software solutions to handle. With big data, new techniques have been engineered to support data collection, storage, and the analytical capacity to generate insight from data resources" where the goal "is to continuously predict future behaviors" (Lanius, 2019, pp. 63–64).

How do digital media get access to so much personal data about all of us? The answer to this question is that we grant them permission—although we are typically unaware that we have done so. For example, every time we download a digital platform (any app for social media, internet search, retail store, financial institution, etc.), we must activate it. The only way we can activate such apps is to sign off on a lengthy legal document that grants permission to the company providing the platform to record all our activity on that platform, save all that information, and sell that information to third parties.

The apps that we download, however, are not the only way that digital media record our personal information. Another, and particularly intrusive, way we allow digital media to invade our privacy is when we use certain things known as "personal assistants," such as Amazon's Alexa, Google's Assistant, or Apple's Siri. These devices are constantly listening and waiting for users to ask them questions. Users find these devices very convenient because they can ask any kind of question—about the weather, phone numbers, addresses, store hours, and facts found in dictionaries and encyclopedias—and immediately get an answer. However, this service comes with a cost to their privacy, because these devices constantly record what they hear. However, some of these devices are more egregious invaders of our privacy than are other devices. For example, while Google's Assistant records everything it hears, users can request that Google not store those recordings. Amazon's Alexa allows you to listen to its archive on all the comments you have made, and Amazon allows you to delete your recording history. But Apple's Siri does not give users the ability to review what it has kept or the option not to store recordings (Listening to Alexa, 2019, p. 20).

Another way big data gathers information about you is through the devices you use in your everyday lives. Now most devices with electronic components (such as automobiles and household appliances) come with the capability to connect to the internet and regularly transmit data about how they are used to their manufacturers. These inanimate objects that constantly communicate are referred to as the "Internet of Things."

The Internet of Things is fairly new but has already grown very large. There are more than seven inanimate objects connected to the internet for every person alive today, and that number of connected devices is growing fast. DuBravac (2015) predicted that by

> 2025 electronic devices connected to the Internet and equipped with powerful sensors will be ubiquitous, surrounding us at all times, acquiring and analyzing data, not only to give us what we need the moment we need it, but to acquire more information on our true identity continuously. Algorithms

utilizing this data will constantly be improving themselves to better understand and anticipate our actions. In short, our digital destiny means that there will no longer be a wall separating our offline and online selves. Nearly every action we perform will be captured, analyzed and filtered. (pp. 118–119)

As the number of things connected to the internet increases, the amount of information collected about each individual grows exponentially.

Our privacy is eroded not just by all the surveillance but also by how companies use the information to focus our attention on particular issues and product choices. For example, in 2016 Facebook sold the information it was constantly collecting on its 87 million U.S. users to a company named Cambridge Analytica, which used the data to provide political parties with a service that would influence opinion through the social media. Political parties used those data to send targeted messages to particular Facebook users in order to influence the way they voted in the American presidential election. This caused a scandal because Facebook users were not told that information from their private postings on Facebook was being sold and analyzed in a way to manipulate their political opinions and behaviors (Larchet, 2019).

PUBLIC AWARENESS

Researchers who survey digital users typically find that most people are unaware of how their use of digital media invades their privacy by collecting their personal information (Baruh, Secinti, & Cemalcilar, 2017; Metzger & Suh, 2017; Turow, Hennessy, & Draper, 2018; Vishwanath, Harrison, & Ng, 2018). This ignorance explains why so many people continue to share sensitive private information online, especially on social media platforms. For example, surveys have found that 32% of youth (10–23) have posted private personal information (e.g., social security number) online, 32% have posted their phone number, and 11% have posted their home address (Brooks & Lasser, 2018).

Information is the most valuable commodity in our economy and society. Therefore, big data will grow more powerful each year. Thus the most important questions for you to consider are the following. What does big data already know about me? What kind of information do I want big data to add about me in the future so that I can use digital media more for my own purposes and avoid being manipulated by others for their purposes? Is there information about me that I want to keep private? And if so, how can I share that information with people I want to have it without that information being recorded by big data?

Regulatory Control or Personal Control

People can deal with the issue of media control in three ways. One way is to ignore the power of digital media and continue to allow the media to collect all the information about you that they want and then use that information to direct your attention toward particular ideas and products and away from others. A second way to deal with this issue is to put pressure on regulators to rein in the growing power of the media. And a third way is to take personal control. In this section, I will present some information on the second and third options: regulatory control and personal control. Regulatory control refers to large aggregates, such as governments, creating legislation that draws a line between sanctioned practices and illegal practices, and then enforcing the legislation by stopping and punishing organizations and individuals who conduct illegal practices. Personal control refers to those things that individuals can do in their everyday lives to manage their exposure as well as the sharing of personal information.

REGULATORY CONTROL

There are two significant challenges to regulating digital media. One is to decide what needs to be regulated. The second challenge is to match a regulatory authority to the scale of digital media.

What Should Be Regulated?

This is an especially challenging question to answer, because almost all services provided by digital media have both positive and negative ramifications; regulations that impose limitations on a digital media platform in order to reduce that platform's negative influence are likely to also reduce that platform's advantages to consumers. For example, people like the convenience of using social media platforms for sharing information with friends all over the world. This is a significant positive feature that explains in large part why so many people are regular users of social media platforms. But as you saw above, these platforms have significantly reduced the amount of privacy people have. Thus it is unrealistic to expect the businesses that run these social media platforms to agree to stop recording and selling user data.

The situation is complicated because it is constructed on a network of complex exchanges of resources. So rather than taking a polarized approach to change everything or to change nothing, we need to think in terms of balances. That is, as of now, is there an unfair balance of power in favor of digital media? If so, how do we adjust that balance in a way that all parties can agree? The work required to answer these questions will be considerable.

Challenge of Scale

Almost all digital companies are global, but the regulatory bodies that are trying to control them do not exist at a global level; most exist at a national level. This creates an enormous challenge.

Currently the regulatory authorities that are attempting to control the business practices of digital companies exist at the national level, that is, a country's legislature passes laws and regulations; then that country's executive agencies enforce those laws and regulations. There are currently 197 sovereign countries in the world. If we take a national approach to regulating digital media, we need to recognize that each of these countries would have to conduct their own deliberations about where to draw the line between sanctioned and illegal activity, how to draft laws that would reduce the risk of harm to their populations without depriving their people of services they have come to rely on, and how to enforce their regulations.

There are a few supranational bodies with legislative and enforcement power. The largest of these is the European Union, which currently includes 28 countries. Therefore, the European Union has more regulatory power than does any one country, but the EU's power is still far short of being global.

Digital media are larger in scale than any country. Amazon, Alphabet, Apple, and Facebook are available to people in every country of the world, although Facebook is banned in three countries (China, North Korea, and Iran). The big digital companies are not just global; they are extremely powerful economically. For example, Alphabet is among the most valuable companies in the world, with a market capitalization of more than $860 billion, which is an amount greater than the GDP (gross domestic product) of all but 16 countries on earth. Alphabet is a conglomerate that operates more than 200 global businesses, including Google, the Chrome web browser, Gmail, YouTube, and Android.

Given the size and power of the big digital companies, it is essential to think about scale when considering how to regulate them. A system where regulation is conceptualized and enforced at a national level seems an inappropriate scale to deal with a challenge that exists on a global level, especially in terms of taxation, cybercrime, and determining fair business practices.

Taxation   One way to illustrate this problem of regulatory scale is to examine taxation. For example, in the summer of 2019, France enacted a tax of 3% on the profits of social media sites such as Facebook. But Facebook is a global company that generates revenue by selling advertising to companies all over the world so that those companies can present their ad messages to potential consumers all over the world. Because profit is the difference between how much revenue a company generates minus its expenses, the computation of profit made in France requires regulators to make many decisions to develop a tax code that has enough detail to deal with the complexity of what at first seems to be a simple 3% tax. For example, if a company in Spain pays Facebook a fee for advertising, should any of that fee be considered French revenue, even though none of the money in that exchange passed through France? If a French company pays Facebook a fee for advertising to a global audience, should all of that revenue be taxed in France, even though its purpose was largely to influence Facebook users outside of France? Also, what is to prevent Facebook from shifting its expenses away from countries where it is not being taxed to countries like France in order to report expenses in France as being higher than Facebook's revenue so it shows no profit in that country and therefore owes no tax?

Digital companies that are global can designate any location as their home country where they would then agree to abide by that home country's taxation requirements. For this reason, global companies seek to establish their home offices in countries with the most favorable taxation for them. This is why many of these global companies are based in Ireland and Luxembourg. Furthermore, global companies can use legitimate accounting practices to shift their revenue and expenses around to show profits only in countries where those profits are not being taxed.

Cybercrime   In most countries it is illegal to hack into the protected files of companies and individuals. However, hackers continually try to do just that and are often successful. There is now a computer hacked every 39 seconds globally, and since 2013, an average of 4 million records have been stolen daily through data breaches (Milkovich, 2018).

Despite most countries having laws that make computer hacking a crime, few hackers are caught because they operate in cyberspace where it is often very difficult to identify the real-life individuals who are committing these crimes. When such criminals are identified, many live in countries where either hacking is not a crime or the government does not have the resources or interest in arresting the hackers.

Fair Business Practices   Business regulators in many countries have been receiving complaints that digital companies have been violating the fair business practices established in those countries. For example, there have been many complaints that Amazon has not been treating its vendors fairly. In the United States, Congress has been holding hearings to investigate these claims of unfair business practices of Amazon. Also, the European Union has initiated an antitrust investigation over allegations that Amazon has been using data from third-party sellers on its site to create its own similar competing merchandise (Retail, 2019, p. 34). If the European Union finds that Amazon has been engaging in unfair business practices, it will likely fine Amazon and force the company to change its business practices in the 28 countries that are members of the EU. But Amazon could continue with its business practices in the other 169 countries of the world.

Trying to regulate global problems at a national level is very inefficient because it requires considerable duplication of effort, which typically results in a complexity of regulations that differ substantially across nations. This complexity makes it easy for companies to find legitimate ways to avoid being taxed. It allows companies engaged in unfair business practices to find ways to avoid sanctions and fines. And it allows cybercriminals to continue their illegal activities without being prosecuted or even caught.

PERSONAL CONTROL

People need not wait for governmental bodies to construct appropriate regulations before they take steps to avoid the risks of negative effects from digital media influence. People have the ability to make some changes in their own everyday lives and thereby exercise greater control over the influence of digital media on them. But in order to take such steps, people need to develop a good idea about how digital media are exerting their influence and which influences increase the risk of negative effects. The more you know about the risks, the more you will be motivated to control them. To illustrate this point, consider what the most knowledgeable people about digital media do. For example, Bill Gates, founder and president of Microsoft, has revealed that he has restricted his children's exposure to technology. He said that he enforces strict rules to limit the use of digital devices in his home and that when his children asked for smartphones in their early adolescence, he ignored their complaints until they were 14. Tim Cook, who followed Steve Jobs as CEO of Apple, considers that the use of technology should be limited in schools and said that he, who has no child, didn't want his nephew to use a social network. Nir Eyal, a professor at the Stanford Business School, an adviser to several companies, and author of *Hooked: How to Build Habit-Forming Products*, has described how he tries to protect his own family. He has a timer connected to the router in his home that switches off the internet at a set time every day. Chamath Palihapitiya, the former vice president in charge of user growth at Facebook, said at a Stanford Business School event, "I don't use this shit and my kids are not allowed to use this shit either" (Larchet, 2019, p. 167).

"The media landscape today is starkly different from the one that existed even a few years ago and is changing constantly," wrote Seargeant and Tagg (2018).

> Because of this, people's ability to make informed decisions about how they communicate depends on understanding not just how the technology works, but how it works *socially*. For example, it is not just a matter of knowing how to keep on top of your privacy settings; it also involves knowing the implications of what can happen as a result of choosing one setting over another. It is not just a matter of understanding how to flag something you find suspect; it is also a matter of evaluating its provenance and purpose in the first place, bearing in mind that you may have received the news via someone you trust or whose views you share—or simply from someone you know well and do not wish to offend. (p. 182)

While it is beyond the scope of this book to lay out all the strategies you could use to increase you control over the media, I can leave you with three guiding principles that can be valuable. First, use common sense as you pay more attention to your personal reactions during your exposures to digital media. Continually ask yourself, Am I getting enough from this exposure to warrant my expenditure of time and effort? If your answer is yes, then continue with those exposures because this means you have found sources of entertainment and information that are satisfying your personal needs well. But if the answer is no, then alter your exposure habit and try something new. There is a nearly infinite number of alternatives you could try, and it is highly likely that with a little effort you will find other sources of entertainment and information that will satisfy your personal needs much better.

Second, observe how other people are using digital media, and ask them about their levels of satisfaction. Be humble enough to ask lots of questions and keep an open mind rather than think you are more of an expert than you really are. For example, when parents try to control how their children use digital media, they are often unsuccessful because they fail to understand the problem they are trying to protect their children from, and as a result the regulations they impose on their children can lead to more harm than good. A survey of parents of 6- to 14-year-olds in eight European countries ($N = 6,400$) found that parents often did not try to regulate the digital media use of their children or were unsuccessful when they did because the children knew more about digital media than did their parents (Livingstone et al., 2017). Surveys in the United States generated similar findings (Hefner, Knop, Schmitt, & Vorderer, 2019; Shin & Kim, 2019).

Third, take steps now. Do not wait for governments or regulatory bodies to protect you from risks of experiencing negative effects from exposure to digital media. While many governments are working to protect individuals and society, it is likely to be a very long time until those organizations not only create useful regulations but also construct an apparatus to enforce those regulations in an adequate manner. In the meantime, your exposures continue and your risks of experiencing negative effects will grow. Patterns of behavior are much easier to alter when they are new. The longer you wait, the less able you will be able to see the dangers in the everyday things you take for granted.

Conclusions

The issues I raised in this chapter were designed to focus your attention on the most important concerns about media effects and to stimulate your thinking about who is in control. I acknowledge that I am likely leaving you with more questions than answers. My hope is that you will use the information presented in this book to start developing some answers on your own as you engage with digital media in your everyday lives. The answers you develop are likely to be different from those of other readers of this book, and that is okay. You are likely to have seen some effects that you want to take steps to avoid. You are also likely to have seen some effects that you might want to amplify because they serve to meet your own personal needs. Because each person has a different set of wants and needs, each person will likely develop a different set of opinions about where media control leads to positive effects and where it leads to effects that are considered negative. There is not one overall strategy in dealing with digital media and their effects that is likely to meet the needs of everyone.

There is one thing, however, that we all have in common, and that one thing is that we all live in a world where digital media are pervasive and powerful. We all face the same challenge. In meeting that challenge, we need to do more than simply learn how to access digital media by knowing how to download apps, knowing how to sign on to websites, and knowing how to upload information onto digital platforms. We need more than basic technical information. We also need to understand the nature of digital media, what resources digital platforms are taking from us, and how digital media are constantly shaping our attitudes, beliefs, emotional reactions, behaviors, and the ways we think about things.

Glossary

acquiring function. A category of media influence that results in an individual gaining something (e.g., information and satisfaction) from an exposure to a media message.

addiction progression. A sequence of effects on a negative trajectory that takes people to a point where they perform certain behaviors obsessively not because they want to do so but because they cannot stop themselves from doing so.

advergames. Games specifically designed and created to promote a brand, product, service, or idea.

advertorials. Advertisements camouflaged as editorial material.

altering function. A category of media influence that results in an individual having something they possess (e.g., a knowledge structure, attitude, belief, and behavioral pattern) changed in some way due to the influence of media.

analog media. Media channels that use technological means to distribute informational, entertainment, and persuasive messages simultaneously and quickly to large numbers of people. These channels, which are sometimes called legacy, traditional, or old media, include print channels (books, magazines, and newspapers), recordings, film, broadcast (radio and television), and cable TV.

automatic routines. Cognitive habits that people use unconsciously every day to help them efficiently filter messages and process their meaning.

automaticity. A mental state where people's minds run default routines without any conscious effort from them.

big data. Data sets that include thousands of data points on each of hundreds of millions of individuals; they are typically too large or complex for common computer platforms and typical software applications to handle.

binge watching. Exposing oneself to many episodes of a video series in a continuous sequence lasting hours and sometimes days.

buying funnel. An inbound advertising technique used by digital advertisers where they attract potential customers to their website and then take them step-by-step through a procedure of informing them about their products, generating positive attitudes about those products, and then triggering the buying of those products.

campaign strategy. A plan that traditional advertisers use to develop their advertising objectives from detailed research about a market, their product, and their competitors.

cascade effects. Effects on individuals that are manifested as a progression across several types of effects, in contrast to unit effects, which are manifested as occurring as only one type (physiological, affective, cognitive, beliefs, attitudinal, or behavioral).

catfishing. When a person pretends to be someone they're not on a dating site, social network, or chat site.

choice progression. A cascade of effects that is motivated by a drive to select the best digital messages for exposure from among an overwhelming number of digital messages from which to choose.

click-through rates. Number of times that visitors to a website click on a hot button that takes them to a different website.

clicktivism. The use of digital platforms, especially social media and networking sites, as a primary mode of engagement in political discourse and participation in social movements, such that people feel politically engaged in issues simply by clicking on websites instead of participating in actual political activities, such as attending political meetings, rallies, and demonstrations.

cocooning. An effect of using digital media to an extent that users become more and more isolated from all but a few people, who become so important that they are the only contacts that users need.

concentration progression. A cascade of effects that is motivated by a drive to experience the transported state and/or flow state.

connectedness progression. A cascade of effects that is motivated by a drive to use digital media to connect with other people.

copy platform. A detailed plan that traditional advertisers use to guide the design of individual ads.

crowdfunding. The use of social media and other websites to stimulate a large number of individuals to each donate relatively small amounts of money to fund business ventures and political campaigns.

crowdsourcing. Using the internet to appeal to a wide range of people to help with a task by contributing their resources of information, time, or money.

crystalline intelligence. The ability to memorize facts as well as the facility to absorb the images, definitions, opinions, and agendas of others.

cyber bullying. Using digital media to embarrass, belittle, and/or harass someone with online messages.

cyberchondria. A belief by many people that they have a serious illness based on a search of their symptoms online.

dependence effect. A step along the addiction cascade where people move from a displacement effect to a reliance on digital experiences.

digital games. Competitive platforms that allow users to compete against themselves, one other person, or many people simultaneously.

digital-native news outlets. News providers that began as internet sites rather than as add-ons to traditional media (newspapers, radio, and television) news providers.

digitization. The translation of messages into a common digital language that can be shared across a wide range of platforms.

disinhibition progression. A cascade of effects that is motivated by a drive to break with social norms and try out new behaviors risk free on digital platforms.

displacement effect. The initial step along the addiction cascade where people engage in one activity to the extent that it takes away time and interest in engaging in other activities.

Dunbar's number. A claim that the upper limit to the number of friendships that humans can adequately maintain is 150 because of the way the human brain is structured.

echo chamber. The concept that when people are continually exposed to a narrow range of information and/or opinions—either through their own choosing or by recommender systems—they tend to hear the same things over and over again and then come to believe that what they hear is all the information on that particular topic.

electronic word of mouth (eWOM). Any positive or negative statement made by potential, actual, or former customers about a product or company, which is made available to a multitude of people and institutions over the internet.

emojis. Small icons and graphics of all kinds that are used in digital messages.

emoticons. Pictures constructed from textual symbols to indicate emotional states such as smiles, frowns, and winks.

exposure habits. Behavioral patterns people develop over the course of many exposure experiences.

fake news mills. Digital platforms that appear to present news but instead purposefully post fabricated and sensational stories as a means of generating high levels of clicks, which translate into advertising revenue.

fakesters. People who do not use their real name when setting up social media accounts so that they can hide their real identity by posing as someone or something else, such as a celebrity, a pet animal, or a wholly made up person with a created identity.

filter bubble. A condition where people avoid a wide range of information in their media exposures so that the only type of information they experience in their "bubble" is that which confirms what they already believe; this filtering can be either done consciously by individuals or controlled by recommender systems.

first copy costs. The total expense of producing a single media message and disseminating it; with mass media messages, the first copy cost is much higher than the cost of all subsequent copies so there is a strong incentive to mass produce additional copies so that the first copy costs are amortized over a large number of copies.

flow state. A cognitive state where people are working on a challenging task that absorbs them so much they lose track of time and place.

fluid intelligence. The ability to be creative, make leaps of insight, and perceive things in a fresh and novel manner.

FOMO factor. The fear of missing out, which is a form of anxiety triggered in users of digital media when they realize all the messages and opportunities they may be missing because of time constraints.

friending. The practice on SNSs where a user gets other users to add them to their friends list and agrees to be on the friends list of other users.

Goldilocks syndrome. A condition where people want to attract and maintain friends who are psychologically neither too close nor too far; digital media give people an opportunity to use texting rather than phone conversations or in-person contact where the psychological distance is too close.

hacktivism. The nonviolent use of illegal or legally ambiguous digital tools in the pursuit of political ends.

hyper-localism. The trend in news coverage to focus on more specialized stories that would interest people in a relatively small niche audience.

impulsivity. A personality trait characterized by the urge to act spontaneously without reflecting on an action and its consequences.

inbound advertising perspective. A newer procedure used by advertisers who use digital platforms to interact with their potential customers while those consumers are most susceptible to persuasion.

in-game advertising (IGA). The placement of ads in existing digital games.

internet. A worldwide network of circuits and packets of data that connects countless billions of computerized devices and, thus, the people that use these devices.

internet-connected technologies (ICT). Digital devices that communicate with one another, with manufacturers of those devices, and with users by sending information through internet connections.

Internet of Things. The vast and growing set of inanimate devices that continually collect information about their usage and then share that information with other devices, the companies that manufacture them, and with others by constant connection to the internet.

lifelogging. Using SNSs to post the details of one's everyday life down to the smallest minutia.

massively multiplayer online role-playing games (MMORPGs). Digital platforms that link people together from all over the world to enable them to play a game with and against others in a fantasy world.

media effects template (MET). A two-dimensional (six types of effects by four functions) matrix that is used to organize the variety of media effects.

mere exposure effect. Just being exposed to a media message is enough to generate an effect; it is not necessary for people to pay attention to an ad or engage with it for an effect to occur.

micro-targeting. Focusing on the particular needs of relatively small numbers of individuals and continually interacting with them in special ways.

mindfulness. Conscious awareness of a person's needs and making decisions strategically to select media messages that will best satisfy those needs.

multitasking. Engaging in more than one task or exposure at the same time.

native advertising. The use of paid ads that match the look and feel of the nonadvertising content in which they are embedded.

orienting reflex. A type of automatic reflex that is hardwired into human brains so people pay immediate attention to novel stimuli that suddenly occur in a person's environment; the brain automatically diverts attention to the source of that stimulus in order to make sure it is not a threat to the person.

outbound advertising perspective. A procedure used by experts who develop an overall campaign strategy, design individual ads, and then place those ads in traditional media so their message gets to their targeted audiences.

participatory culture. The interactive nature of digital media that allows people to identify others who share their interests and to become active in communicating with them and create stronger social movements.

pornography. Printed or visual material containing the explicit description or display of sexual organs or activity, intended to stimulate erotic rather than aesthetic or emotional feelings.

push notifications. Messages sent by digital media platforms that are designed to distract us from what we are doing and to direct our attention elsewhere.

ratings services. Websites where consumers can tell marketers and the public what they think of the advertised products and services.

recommender systems. Algorithms used by digital platforms to attempt to make each user's exposure sessions more efficient by using patterns of preferences found in data gathered from users.

reinforcing function. A category of media influence that results in an individual having something they possess (e.g., a knowledge structure, attitude, belief, or behavioral pattern) gain more weight, thus making it more difficult to change.

Rorschach. A psychological test where a person is shown an inkblot that is an abstract image and then is asked what he or she sees; the way the person answers this question tell psychologists what is active in the person's mind.

search engine optimization (SEO). A technique used by inbound advertisers who continually make adjustments to their websites to make it more efficient for prospective customers to move through the buying funnel and purchase their products.

SEIM. Sexually explicit internet material.

selective exposure. A psychological concept that says people seek out information that conforms to their existing belief systems and avoid information that challenges those beliefs.

self-objectification. The viewing of oneself as an object rather than a complex human being; reducing oneself to a stereotype.

sexting. Taking and/or sending sexually explicit or suggestive photos or messages via texting or other forms of digital media.

shopbots. Online sites that assist buyers when they search for product and price information on the internet; they compile information about a wide range of products to help people comparison shop and go to the appropriate online retailers to make their purchases.

Sisyphus problem. A challenge that people continually work at but feel they make no progress; named after the character in Greek mythology who was doomed to push a heavy boulder up a hill and each time, as he neared the top, he would weaken from the exertion and the boulder would roll back down the hill, forcing him to start over again.

social media influencers. People (typically ordinary people but also celebrities) who exhibit their personal lives online as a way of attracting followers via social media; companies view these people as valuable advertising vehicles and pay them to endorse their products and services.

social networking sites (SNSs). Internet platforms that allow large numbers of people to create profiles about themselves and to continually post information about their lives in order to attract friends and interact with other users.

stickiness. Refers to a digital media company's ability to get their site's users to stay longer during exposure sessions, and then to get those users to return to the site again and again for subsequent exposures.

story formulas. The procedures that journalists learn as shortcuts to help them quickly select and write stories.

telehealth. Visiting a doctor or health-care professional online.

telescoping. A strategy players of digital games use when playing; players must focus on an immediate objective that follows from previous objectives that were successfully achieved and leads to upcoming objectives that take the player to the end of the game.

traditional media. An assortment of analog channels that use technological means to distribute informational, entertainment, and persuasive messages simultaneously and quickly to large numbers of people. These channels, which are sometimes called "legacy" or "old media," include print channels (books, magazines, and newspapers), recordings, film, broadcast (radio and television), and cable TV.

transported state. An exposure state that is achieved when a media message pulls us so completely into an experience that we lose track of time and place.

triggering function. A category of media influence that results in something (e.g., an emotion, a memory, recall of an existing belief, or a behavioral process) within an individual being stimulated.

unit effects. Effects on individuals that occur as only one type (physiological, affective, cognitive, beliefs, attitudinal, or behavioral), in contrast to cascade effects that are manifested as a progression across several types of effects.

user-generated content (UGC). Information posted on digital platforms that is created by users of those platforms rather than employees of those platforms.

variable reward schedule. A random pattern of rewarding organisms for exhibiting particular behaviors where those organisms are not rewarded each and every time they perform a particular behavior; this is an important contributing factor to an addiction effect.

virtual worlds. Environments that exist on internet servers that provide users with the means to immerse themselves in experiences that are alternatives to what they can or are willing to experience in their real lives.

wiki. A website that allows any user to add material and to edit as well as delete what previous users have contributed.

References

Aardema, F., O'Conner, K., Cote, S., & Taillon, A. (2010). Virtual reality induces dissociation and lowers sense of presence in objective reality. *Cyberpsychology, Behavior and Social Networking, 13*(4), 429–435.

Adis, A-A. A., & Jun, K. H. (2013). Antecedents of brand recall and brand attitude towards purchase intention in advergames. *European Journal of Business and Management, 5*(18), 58–68.

Aguirre, E., Mahr, D., Grewal, D., de Ruyter, K., & Wetzels, M. (2015). Unraveling the personalization paradox: The effect of information collection and trust-building strategies on online advertisement effectiveness. *Journal of Retailing, 91*(1), 34–49.

Ahlgren, M. (2020, January 20). 40+ Twitter statistics and facts for 2020. Retrieved February 7, 2020, from https://www.websitehostingrating.com/twitter-statistics

Aiken, M. (2016). *The cyber effect*. New York: Spiegel & Grau.

Ajzen, I., & Fishbein, M. (1977). Attitude-behavior relations: A theoretical analysis and review of empirical research. *Psychological Bulletin, 84*, 888–918.

Ajzen, I., & Fishbein, M. (2005). The influence of attitudes on behavior. In D. Albarracin, B. T. Johnson, & M. P. Zanna (Eds.), *The handbook of attitudes* (pp. 173–221). Mahwah, NJ: Erlbaum.

Albarracin, D., Zanna, M. P., Johnson, B. T., & Kumkale, G. T. (2005). Attitudes: Introduction and scope. In D. Albarracin, B. T. Johnson, & M. P. Zanna (Eds.), *The handbook of attitudes* (pp. 3–19). Mahwah, NJ: Erlbaum.

Albright, J. M. (2008). Sex in America online: An exploration of sex, marital status, and sexual identity in internet sex seeking and its impacts. *Journal of Sex Research, 45*(2), 175–186.

Allen, M., D'Alessio, D., & Brezgel, K. (1995). A meta-analysis summarizing the effects of pornography. *Human Communication Research, 22*, 258–283.

Allocca, K. (2018). *Videocracy: How YouTube is changing the world with double rainbows, singing foxes, and other trends we can't stop watching*. New York: Bloomsbury.

Allport, G. W. (1935). Attitudes. In C. Murchison (Ed.), *Handbook of social psychology* (pp. 798–884). Worcester, MA: Clark University Press.

Almond, G. A., Appleby, R. S., & Sivan, E. (2003). *Strong religion: The rise of fundamentalisms around the world*. Chicago: University of Chicago Press.

Altenhofen, B. (2019). The internet as religion: How online media is altering worship and belief among Catholic priests. In A. E. Grant, A. F. C. Sturgill, C. H. Chen, & D. A. Stout (Eds.), *Religion online: How digital technology is changing the way we worship and pray*: Vol. 1. *Religion in cyberspace* (pp. 97–115). Santa Barbara, CA: ABC-Clio.

Alter, A. (2017). *Irresistible: The rise of addictive technology and the business of keeping us hooked.* New York: Penguin.

Amazeen, M. A., & Bucy, E. P. (2019). Conferring resistance to digital disinformation: The inoculating influence of procedural news knowledge. *Journal of Broadcasting & Electronic Media, 63*(3), 415–432. https://doi-org.proxy.library.ucsb.edu:9443/10.1080/08838151.2 019.1653101

Amazon: The terrifying power of Jeff Bezos. (2019, October 25). *The Week.*

Anderson, S. P. (2012). Advertising on the internet. In M. Peitz & J. Waldfogel (Eds.), *The Oxford handbook of the digital economy* (pp. 355–396). New York: Oxford University Press.

Angell, R., Gorton, M., Sauer, J., Bottomley, P., & White, J. (2016). Don't distract me when I'm media multitasking: Toward a theory for raising advertising recall and recognition. *Journal of Advertising, 45*(2), 198–210.

Angwin, J. (2009). *Stealing MySpace: The battle to control the most popular website in America.* New York: Random House.

Ardèvol-Abreu, A., & Gil de Zúñiga, H. (2017). Effects of editorial media bias perception and media trust on the use of traditional, citizen, and social media news. *Journalism & Mass Communication Quarterly, 94*(3), 703–724. https://doi.org/10.1177/1077699016654684

Arenberg, T., & Lowrey, W. (2019). The impact of web metrics on community news decisions: A resource dependence perspective. *Journalism & Mass Communication Quarterly, 96*(1), 131–149.

Arendt, F., Northup, T., & Camaj, L. (2019). Selective exposure and news media brands: Implicit and explicit attitudes as predictors of news choice. *Media Psychology, 22*(3), 526–543.

Aruguete, N., & Calvo, E. (2018). Time to #protest: Selective exposure, cascading activation, and framing in social media. *Journal of Communication, 68*(3), 480–502.

Aslam, S. (2018, Feb. 5). YouTube by the numbers: Stats, demographics & fun facts. Retrieved June 10, 2018, from https://www.omnicoreagency.com/youtube-statistics

Australian Psychological Society. (2015). Stress and wellbeing: How Australians are coping with life. APA. http://bit.ly/1FPnDxS

Baek, T. H., & Morimoto, M. (2012). Stay away from me. *Journal of Advertising, 41*(1), 59–76.

Baker, C. (2003, August). Cracking the box office genome. *Wired*, p. 52.

Balbi, G., & Magaudda, P. (2018). *A history of digital media: An intermedia and global perspective.* New York: Routledge.

Ball-Rokeach, S. J., & DeFleur, M. (1976). A dependency model of mass-media effects. *Communication Research, 3*, 3–21.

Banakou, D., Groten, R., & Slater, M. (2013). Illusory ownership of a virtual child body causes overestimation of object sizes and implicit attitude changes. *Proceedings of the National Academy of Sciences, 110*(31), 12846–12851.

Bargh, J. A. (1997). The automaticity of everyday life. In R. S. Wyer (Ed.), *Advances in social cognition* (pp. 1–61). Mahwah, NJ: Erlbaum.

Barker-Plummer, B., & Barker-Plummer, D. (2019). Hashtag feminism, digital media, and new dynamics of social change: A case study of #YesAllWomen. In G. W. Richardson Jr. (Ed.), *Social media and politics: A new way to participate in the political process* (Vol. 2, pp. 78–96). Santa Barbara, CA: Praeger.

Baron, S. D., Brouwer, C., & Garbayo, A. (2014). A model for delivering branding value through high-impact digital advertising. *Journal of Advertising Research, 54*(3), 286–291.

Barton, M. (2017). *Vintage games 2.0: An insider look at the most influential games of all time.* New York: CRC Press.

Baruh, L., Secinti, E., & Cemalcilar, A. (2017). Online privacy concerns and privacy management: A meta-analytical review. *Journal of Communication, 67*(1), 26–53.

Barthel, M, (2018, June 13). Newspaper fact sheet. Pew Research Center. Retrieved June 20, 2018, from http://www.journalism.org/fact-sheet/newspapers

Basil, M. D. (1996). Identification as a mediator of celebrity effects. *Journal of Broadcasting & Electronic Media, 40*, 478–495.

Baybars-Hawks, B. (2015). Occupying cyberspace: Cyberactivism, cyber terrorism and cyber-security. In B. Baybars-Hawks (Ed.), *New media politics: Rethinking activism and national security in cyberspace* (pp. 2–14). Newcastle upon Tyne, UK: Cambridge Scholars Publishing.

Belanche, D., Flavián, C., & Pérez-Rueda, A. (2017). Understanding interactive online advertising: Congruence and product involvement in highly and lowly arousing, skippable video ads. *Journal of Interactive Marketing, 37*, 75–88.

Bell, G., & Gemmell, D. J. (2009). *Total recall: How the e-memory revolution will change everything*. New York: Dutton.

Bevilacqua, J., & Del Giudice, E. (2018, April 3). Why brands need to utilize influencer marketing in 2018. *St. Joseph Communications*. https://www.digitalinformationworld.com/2018/04/infographic-follow-the-influencer-to-follow-the-money.html

Beuckels, E., Cauberghe, V., & Hudders, L. (2017). How media multitasking reduces advertising irritation: The moderating role of the Facebook wall. *Computers in Human Behavior, 73*, 413–419.

Bialik, K., & Matsa, K. E. (2017, October 4). Key trends in social and digital news media. Pew Research Center. https://www.pewresearch.org/fact-tank/2017/10/04/key-trends-in-social-and-digital-news-media

Bleier, A., & Eisenbeiss, M. (2015). Personalized online advertising effectiveness: The interplay of what, when, and where. *Marketing Science, 34*(5), 669–688.

Blossom, H. D., Wilkinson, J. S., Gorelik, A., & Perry, S. D. (2019). Salvation by algorithm: When big data meets God. In A. E. Grant, A. F. C. Sturgill, C. H. Chen, & D. A. Stout (Eds.), *Religion online: How digital technology is changing the way we worship and pray*: Vol. 1. *Religion in cyberspace* (pp. 67–83). Santa Barbara, CA: ABC-Clio.

Blum, A. (2013). *Tubes: A journey to the center of the internet*. New York: HarperCollins.

Boellstorff, T. (2008). *Coming of age in Second Life: An anthropologist explores the virtually human*. Princeton, NJ: Princeton University Press.

Bogen, C. (2015). China: Media activism in online health communication. In M. Shumow (Ed.), *Mediated communities: Civic voices, empowerment and media literacy in the digital era* (pp. 115–136). New York: Peter Lang.

Bonus, J. A., Peebles, A., Mares, M.-L., & Sarmiento, I. G. (2018). Look on the bright side (of media effects): *Pokémon Go* as a catalyst for positive life experiences. *Media Psychology, 21*(2), 263–287.

Borderie, J., & Michinov, N. (2017). Identifying social forms of flow in multiuser video games. In R. Kowert & T. Quandt (Eds.), *New perspectives on the social aspects of digital gaming: Multiplayer 2* (pp. 32–45). New York: Routledge.

The bottom line. (2019, June 21). *The Week*.

Bouma, G. (2006). *Australian soul: Religion and spirituality in the 21st century*. Cambridge: Cambridge University Press.

Boxman-Shabtai, L., & Shifman, L. (2014). Evasive targets: Deciphering polysemy in mediated humor. *Journal of Communication, 64*, 977–998. doi: 10.1111/jcom.12116

Boyle, K., Hansen, J., & Christensen, S. (2019). Posting, sharing, and religious testifying: New rituals in the online religious environment. In A. E. Grant, A. F. C. Sturgill, C. H. Chen, & D. A. Stout (Eds.), *Religion online: How digital technology is changing the way we worship and pray*: Vol. 1. *Religion in cyberspace* (pp. 11–26). Santa Barbara, CA: ABC-Clio.

Boyns, D., Forghani, S., & Sosnovskaya, E. (2009). MMORPG worlds: On the construction of social reality in World of Warcraft. In D. Heider (Ed.), *Living virtually: Researching new worlds* (pp. 67–92). New York: Peter Lang.

Breideband, T. (2019). Caught between televisual and digital presence: Greenpeace's foray into the Twittersphere. In G. W. Richardson Jr. (Ed.), *Social media and politics: A new way to participate in the political process* (Vol. 2, pp. 43–62). Santa Barbara, CA: Praeger.

Brinson, N. H., Eastin, M. S., & Cicchirillo, V. J. (2018). Reactance to personalization: Understanding the drivers behind the growth of ad blocking. *Journal of Interactive Advertising, 18*(2), 136–147. https://doi-org.proxy.library.ucsb.edu:9443/10.1080/15252019 .2018.1491350

Brooks, M., & Lasser, J. (2018). *Tech generation: Raising balanced kids in a hyper-connected world*. New York: Oxford University Press.

Brown, W. J., Basil, M. D., & Bocarnea, M. C. (2003). Social influence of an international celebrity: Responses to the death of Princess Diana. *Journal of Communication, 53*(4), 587–605. https://doi.org/10.1111/j.1460–2466.2003.tb02912.x

Bruce, N. I., Murthi, B. P. S., & Rao, R. C. (2017). A dynamic model for digital advertising: The effects of creative format, message content, and targeting on engagement. *Journal of Marketing Research, 54*(2), 202–218.

Brummette, J., DiStaso, M., Vafeiadis, M., & Messner, M. (2018). Read all about it: The politicization of "fake news" on Twitter. *Journalism & Mass Communication Quarterly, 95*(2), 497–517.

Bryant, J., & Oliver, M. B. (2009). *Media effects: Advances in theory and research* (3rd ed.). New York: Routledge.

Brynjolfsson, E., & McAfee, A. (2014). *The second machine age*. New York: Norton.

A bubble bursts for Instagram elite. (2019, November 1). *The Week*.

Buie, E., & Blythe, M. (2013). Spirituality: There's an app for that! (but not a lot of research). In *CHI'13 extended abstracts on human factors in computing systems*. New York: ACM.

Bullivant, S., & Lee, L. (2012). Interdisciplinary studies of non-religion and secularity: The state of the union. *Journal of Contemporary Religion, 27*(1), 19–27.

Buerkel-Rothfuss, N. L. (1993). Background: What prior research shows. In B. S. Greenberg, J. D. Brown, & N. Buerkel-Rothfuss (Eds.), *Media, sex and the adolescent* (pp. 5–18). Cresskill, NJ: Hampton.

Cacciatore, M. A., Yeo, S. K., Scheufele, D. A., Xenos, M. A., Brossard, D., & Corley, E. A. (2018). Is Facebook making us dumber? Exploring social media use as a predictor of political knowledge. *Journalism & Mass Communication Quarterly, 95*(2), 404–424. https://doi.org .proxy.library.ucsb.edu:9443/10.1177/1077699018770447

Calder, B. J., Malthouse, E. C., & Schaedel, U. (2009). An experimental study of the relationship between online engagement and advertising effectiveness. *Journal of Interactive Marketing, 23*(4), 321–331.

Campbell, C., Thompson, F. M., Grimm, P. E., & Robson, K. (2017). Understanding why consumers don't skip pre-roll video ads. *Journal of Advertising, 46*(3), 411–423.

Campbell, H. A. (2012). Understanding the relationship between religion online and offline in a networked society. *Journal of the American Academy of Religion, 80*(1), 64–93.

Campbell, H. A. (2017). Understanding the relationship between religion online and offline in a networked society. In D. L. Kirby & C. M. Cusack (Eds.), *Religion and media: Critical concepts in religious studies* (Vol. 2, pp. 9–32). London: Routledge.

Campbell, H. A., Altenhofen, B., Bellar, W., & Cho, K. J. (2014). There's a religious app for that! A framework for studying religious mobile applications. *Mobile Media & Communication, 2*(2), 154–172.

Carpenter, C. J., & Amaravadi, C. S. (2019). A big data approach to assessing the impact of social norms: Reporting one's exercise to a social media audience. *Communication Research, 46*(2), 236–249.

Carr, N. (2010). *The Shallows: What the internet is doing to our brains.* New York: Norton.

Cassata, M., & Skill, T. (1983). *Life on daytime television.* Norwood, NJ: Ablex.

Castronova, E. (2001, December). Virtual worlds: A first-hand account of market and society on the cyberian frontier. CESifo working paper No. 618.

Castronova, E. (2005). *Synthetic worlds.* Chicago: University of Chicago Press.

Castronova, E., et al. (2009). Virtual world economics: A case study of the economics of Arden. In D. Heider (Ed.), *Living virtually: Researching new worlds* (pp. 165–189). New York: Peter Lang.

Chae, J. (2018). Explaining females' envy toward social media influencers. *Media Psychology, 21*(2), 246–262.

Chaiken, S., Liberman, A., & Eagly, A. H. (1989). Heuristic and systematic processing within and beyond the persuasion context. In J. S. Uleman & J. A. Bargh (Eds.), *Unintended thought* (pp. 212–252). New York: Guilford.

Chang, Y. (2017). Why do young people multitask with multiple media? Explicating the relationships among sensation seeking, needs, and media multitasking behavior. *Media Psychology, 20*(4), 685–703.

Chayko, M. (2018). *Superconnected: The internet, digital media, and techno-social life* (2nd ed.). Los Angeles: Sage.

Chen, G. M., & Lu, S. (2017). Online political discourse: Exploring differences in effects of civil and uncivil disagreement in news website comments. *Journal of Broadcasting & Electronic Media, 61*(1), 108–125.

Chen, L., & Yuan, S. (2019). Influencer marketing: How message value and credibility affect consumer trust of branded content on social media. *Journal of Interactive Advertising, 19*(1), 58–73. https://doi-org.proxy.library.ucsb.edu:9443/10.1080/15252019.2018.1533501

Chen, Z., Su, C. C., & Chen, A. (2019). Top-down or bottom-up? A network agenda-setting study of Chinese Nationalism on social media. *Journal of Broadcasting & Electronic Media, 63*(3), 512–533. https://doi-org.proxy.library.ucsb.edu:9443/10.1080/08838151.2019.1653104

China's video game surveillance. (2019, August 9). *The Week.*

Chinchanachokchai, S., Duff, B. R. L., & Sar, S. (2015). The effect of multitasking on time perception, enjoyment, and ad evaluation. *Computers in Human Behavior, 45,* 185–191.

Chiou, L., & Tucker, C. (2012). How does the use of trademarks by third-party sellers affect online search? *Marketing Science, 31*(5), 819–837.

Cho, J. (2005). Media, interpersonal discussion, and electoral choice. *Communication Research, 32,* 295–322.

Cho, J., Ahmed, S., Keum, H., Choi, Y. J., & Lee, J. H. (2018). Influencing myself: Self-reinforcement through online political expression. *Communication Research, 45*(1), 83–111. https://doi-org.proxy.library.ucsb.edu:9443/10.1177/0093650216644020

Cho, H., Shen, L., & Wilson, K. (2014). Perceived realism: Dimensions and roles in narrative persuasion. *Communication Research, 41,* 828–851.

Chun, K. Y., Song, J. H., Hollenbeck, C. R., & Lee, J-H. (2014). Are contextual advertisements effective? *International Journal of Advertising, 33*(2), 351–371.

Cingel, D. P., & Olsen, M. K. (2018). Getting over the hump: Examining curvilinear relationships between adolescent self-esteem and Facebook use. *Journal of Broadcasting & Electronic Media, 62*(2), 215–231.

Clement, J. (2018, November 29). Number of social media users worldwide from 2010 to 2021 (in billions). Statista. Retrieved July 4, 2019, from https://www.statista.com/statis tics/278414/number-of-worldwide-social-network-users

Clore, G. L., & Schnall, S. (2005). The influence of affect on attitudes. In D. Albarracin, B. T. Johnson, & M. P. Zanna (Eds.), *The handbook of attitudes* (pp. 437–489). Mahwah, NJ: Erlbaum.

Columbia Broadcasting System. (1980). *Network prime time violence tabulations for 1978–1979 season.* New York: Author.

Comstock, G. A. (1989). *The evolution of American television.* Newbury Park, CA: Sage.

Cooper, R., & Tang, T. (2009). Predicting audience exposure to television in today's media environment: An empirical integration of active-audience and structural theories. *Journal of Broadcasting & Electronic Media, 53,* 400–418.

Cortland, M. (2017, February 1). Adblock report. PageFair. https://pagefair.com/blog/2017/adblockreport

Coyne, S., & Whitehead, E. (2008). Indirect aggression in animated Disney films. *Journal of Communication, 58*(2), 382–395. https://doi.org/10.1111/j.1460–2466.2008.00390.x

Csikszentmihalyi, M. (1998). *Finding flow: The psychology of engagement with everyday life.* New York: Basic Books.

Dahlen, M., & Rosengren, S. (2016). If advertising won't die, what will it be? Toward a working definition of advertising. *Journal of Advertising, 45*(3), 334–345.

Dai, J. (2009). Virtual worlds, real brands: A critical interrogation of commodification in Second Life. In D. Heider (Ed.), *Living virtually: Researching new worlds* (pp. 209–227). New York: Peter Lang.

Dai, Y., & Walther, J. B. (2018). Vicariously experiencing parasocial intimacy with public figures through observations of interactions on social media. *Human Communication Research, 44*(3), 322–342. https://doi-org.proxy.library.ucsb.edu:9443/10.1093/hcr/hqy003

Dardis, F. E., Schmierbach, M., Ahern, L., Fraustino, J., Bellur, S., Brooks, S., & Johnson, J. (2015). Effects of in-game virtual direct experience (VDE) on reactions to real-world brands. *Journal of Promotion Management, 21*(3), 313–334.

Darr, J. P., Hitt, M. P., & Dunaway, J. L. (2018). Newspaper closures polarize voting behavior. *Journal of Communication, 68*(6), 1007–1028.

Dating Sites Review. (2018, June 10). Online dating statistics and facts. Retrieved June 10, 2018, from https://www.datingsitesreviews.com/staticpages/index.php?page=Online-Dat ing-Industry-Facts-Statistics#ref-GODI-2018-15

Davies, J. (2016, June 7). Uh-oh: Ad blocking forecast to cost $35 billion by 2020. *Digiday.* https://digiday.com/uk/uh-oh-ad-blocking-forecast-cost-35–billion-2020

Dawley, H. (2006, February 7). Time-wise, internet is now TV's equal. *MediaLife.*

DeAndrea, D. C., Van Der Heide, B., Vendemia, M. A., & Vang, M. H. (2018). How people evaluate online reviews. *Communication Research, 45*(5), 719–736. https://doi.org.proxy .library.ucsb.edu:9443/10.1177/0093650215573862

de los Santos, T. M., & Nabi, R. L. (2019). Emotionally charged: Exploring the role of emotion in online news information seeking and processing. *Journal of Broadcasting & Electronic Media, 63*(1), 39–58.

De Prato, G. (2014). The book publishing industry. In G. De Prato, E. Sanz, & J. P. Simon (Eds.), *Digital media worlds: The new economy of media* (pp. 87–101). London: Palgrave Macmillan.

De Prato, G., Sanz, E., & Simon, J. P. (Eds.), (2014). *Digital media worlds: The new economy of media.* London: Palgrave Macmillan.

de Vries, D. A., Möller, A. M., Wieringa, M. S., Eigenraam, A. W., & Hamelink, K. (2018). Social comparison as the thief of joy: Emotional consequences of viewing strangers' Instagram posts. *Media Psychology, 21*(2), 222–245.

de Zúñiga, H. G., & Chen Guest, S-T. (2019). Digital media and politics: Effects of the great information and communication divides. *Journal of Broadcasting & Electronic Media, 63*(3), 365–373. https://doi-org.proxy.library.ucsb.edu:9443/10.1080/08838151.2019.1662019

de Zúñiga, H. G., & Liu, J. H. (2017). Second screening politics in the social media sphere: Advancing research on dual screen use in political communication with evidence from 20 countries. *Journal of Broadcasting & Electronic Media, 61*(2), 193–219.

Diehl, T., Barnidge, M., & Gil de Zúñiga, H. (2019). Multi-platform news use and political participation across age groups: Toward a valid metric of platform diversity and its effects. *Journalism & Mass Communication Quarterly, 96*(2), 428–451. https://doi.org/10.1177/1077699018783960

Domahidi, E., Breuer, J., Kowert, R., Festl, R., & Quandt, T. (2018). A longitudinal analysis of gaming- and non-gaming-related friendships and social support among social online game players. *Media Psychology, 21*(2), 288–307.

Donsbach, W. (2010). Journalists and their professional identities. In S. Allan (Ed.), *The Routledge companion to news and journalism* (pp. 38–48). New York: Routledge.

DuBravac, S. (2015). *Digital destiny: How the new age of data will transform the way we work, live, and communicate*. Washington, DC: Regnery.

Duff, B. R. L., & Faber, R. J. (2011). Missing the mark. *Journal of Advertising, 40*(2), 51–62.

Duff, B. R. L., & Sar, S. (2015). Seeing the big picture: Multitasking and perceptual processing influences on ad recognition. *Journal of Advertising, 44*(3), 173–184.

Dulany, D. E. (1968). Awareness, rules, and propositional control: A confrontation with S-R behavior theory. In T. Dixon & D. Horton (Eds.), *Verbal behavior and behavior theory* (pp. 340–387). New York: Prentice Hall.

Eastman, S. T., Newton, G. D., & Pack, L. (1996). Promoting prime-time programs in mega-sporting events. *Journal of Broadcasting & Electronic Media, 40*(3), 366–388.

Eckler, P., & Bolls, P. (2011). Spreading the virus: Emotional tone of viral advertising and its effect on forwarding intentions and attitudes. *Journal of Interactive Advertising, 11*(2), 1–11.

Edgerly, S., Vraga, E. K., Bode, L., Thorson, K., & Thorson, E. (2018). New media, new relationship to participation? A closer look at youth news repertoires and political participation. *Journalism & Mass Communication Quarterly, 95*(1), 192–212. https://doi.org.proxy.library.ucsb.edu:9443/10.1177/1077699017706928

Eggermont, S. (2006). Developmental changes in adolescents' television viewing habits: longitudinal trajectories in a three-wave panel study. *Journal of Broadcasting & Electronic Media, 50*, 742–761.

El Naggar, S. (2018). American Muslim televangelists as religious celebrities: The changing "face" of religious discourse. In A. Rosowsky (Ed.), *Faith and language practices in digital spaces* (pp. 158–181). Bristol, UK: Multilingual Matters.

eMarketer. (2018, April 11). Native ad spend will make up nearly 60% of display spending in 2018. https://www.emarketer.com/content/native-ad-spend-will-make-up-nearly-60-of-display-spending-in-2018

Entertainment Software Association. (2013). Game player data. Retrieved March 31, 2013, from http://www.theesa.com/facts/gameplayer.asp

Entertainment Software Association. (2018, January 18). US video game industry revenue reaches $36 billion in 2017. Retrieved June 8, 2018, from http://www.theesa.com/article/us-video-game-industry-revenue-reaches-36-billion-2017

Erreygers, S., Vandebosch, H., Vranjes, I., Baillien, E., & De Witte, H. (2017). Nice or naughty? The role of emotions and digital media use in explaining adolescents' online pro-social and antisocial behavior. *Media Psychology, 20*(3), 374–400.

Eyal, N. (2014). *Hooked: How to build habit-forming products.* New York: Penguin.

Farah, M. (2015). Mediating Palestine. In M. Shumow (Ed.), *Mediated communities: Civic voices, empowerment and media literacy in the digital era* (pp. 75–92). New York: Peter Lang.

Farquhar, L. (2019). From Facebook to Instagram: The role of social media in religious communities. In A. E. Grant, A. F. C. Sturgill, C. H. Chen, & D. A. Stout (Eds.), *Religion online: How digital technology is changing the way we worship and pray*: Vol. 1. *Religion in cyberspace* (pp. 27–46). Santa Barbara, CA: ABC-Clio.

Feldman, L., Wojcieszak, M., Stroud, N. J., & Bimber, B. (2018). Explaining media choice: The role of issue-specific engagement in predicting interest-based and partisan selectivity. *Journal of Broadcasting & Electronic Media, 62*(1), 109–130.

Fernandez-Collado, C., Greenberg, B., Korzenny, F., & Atkin, C. (1978). Sexual intimacy and drug use in TV series. *Journal of Communication, 28*(3), 30–37.

Ferris, A. L., & Hollenbaugh, E. E. (2018). A uses and gratifications approach to exploring antecedents to Facebook dependency. *Journal of Broadcasting & Electronic Media, 62*(1), 51–70.

Festinger, L. (1957). *A theory of cognitive dissonance.* Stanford, CA: Stanford University Press.

Fikkers, K. M., Piotrowski, J. T., & Valkenburg, P. M. (2019). Child's play? Assessing the bidirectional longitudinal relationship between gaming and intelligence in early childhood. *Journal of Communication, 69*(2), 124–143.

Fishbein, M. & Ajzen, I. (1975). *Belief, attitude, intention, and behavior: An introduction to theory and research.* Reading, MA: Addison-Wesley.

Fong, N. M., Zheng, F., & Luo, X. (2015). Geo-conquesting: Competitive locational targeting of mobile promotions. *Journal of Marketing Research, 52*(5), 726–735.

Fottrell, Q. (2018, August 4). People spend most of their waking hours staring at screens. *MarketWatch.* https://www.marketwatch.com/story/people-are-spending-most-of-their-waking -hours-staring-at-screens-2018-08-01

Friedman, T. (1995). Making sense of software: Computer games and interactive textuality. In S. G. Jones (Ed.), *CyberSociety: Computer mediated communication and community* (pp. 73–89). Thousand Oaks, CA: Sage.

Frison, E., Bastin, M., Bijttebier, P., & Eggermont, S. (2019). Helpful or harmful? The different relationships between private Facebook interactions and adolescents' depressive symptoms. *Media Psychology, 22*(2), 244–272.

Fritz, B. (2009, September 9). Friends in fantasy and reality. *Los Angeles Times*, pp. A1, A8.

Fudenberg, D., & Villas-Boas, J. M. (2012). Price discrimination in the digital economy. In M. Peitz & J. Waldfogel (Eds.), *The Oxford handbook of the digital economy* (pp. 254–272). New York: Oxford University Press.

Funk, J. B., & Buchman, D. D. (1996). Playing violent video and computer games and adolescent self-concept. *Journal of Communication, 46*(2), 19–32. https://doi.org/10.1111/j .1460-2466.1996.tb01472.x

Galov, N. (2019, February 14). How many blogs are there? Retrieved July 5, 2019, from https://hostingtribunal.com/blog/how-many-blogs

Gantz, W., Wang, Z., Paul, B., & Potter, R. F. (2006). Sports versus all comers: Comparing TV sports fans with fans of other programming genres. *Journal of Broadcasting & Electronic Media, 50*, 95–118.

Gates, K. (2019). Counting the uncounted: What the absence of data on police killings reveals. In M. X Delli Carpini (Ed.), *Digital media and democratic futures* (pp. 121–142). Philadelphia: University of Pennsylvania Press.

Gazzaley, A., & Rosen, L. D. (2016). *The distracted mind: Ancient brains in a high-tech world.* Cambridge, MA: MIT Press.

Geddings, S., & Kennedy, H. W. (2006). Digital games as new media. In J. Rutter & J. Bryce (Eds.), *Understanding digital games* (pp. 129–147). London: Sage.

Geraci, R. M. (2014). *Virtually sacred: Myth and meaning in World of Warcraft and Second Life.* New York: Oxford University Press.

Gerbner, G., Gross, L., Morgan, M., & Signorielli, N. (1980). The "mainstreaming" of America: Violence profile no. 11. *Journal of Communication, 30*(3), 10–29.

Gerodimos, R. (2015). Reclaiming the urban landscape, rebuilding the civic culture: Online mobilization, community building, and public space in Athens, Greece. In M. Shumow (Ed.), *Mediated communities: Civic voices, empowerment and media literacy in the digital era* (pp. 93–114). New York: Peter Lang.

Ghose, A., Singh, P. V., & Todri, V. (2017). Got annoyed? Examining the advertising effectiveness and annoyance dynamics. In *Proceedings of the 2017 International Conference on Information Systems.* Atlanta, GA: Association for Information Systems.

Gibson, M., & Carden, C. (2018). *Living and dying in a virtual world: Digital kinships, nostalgia, and mourning in Second Life.* Cham, Switzerland: Palgrave Macmillan.

Gilbert, M. A., Giaccardi, S., & Ward, L. M. (2018). Contributions of game genre and masculinity ideologies to associations between video game play and men's risk-taking behavior. *Media Psychology, 21*(3), 437–456.

Glass, Z. (2007). The effectiveness of product placement in video games. *Journal of Interactive Advertising, 8*(1), 23–32.

Goffman, E. (1959). *The presentation of self in everyday life.* New York: Anchor.

Goh, K.-Y., Chu, J., & Wu, J. (2015). Mobile advertising: An empirical study of temporal and spatial differences in search behavior and advertising response. *Journal of Interactive Marketing, 30*, 34–45.

Goldfarb, A., & Tucker, C. (2011). Online display advertising: Targeting and obtrusiveness. *Marketing Science, 30*(3), 389–404.

Goldstein, D. G., Suri, A., McAfee, R. P., Ekstrand-Abueg, M., & Diaz F. (2014). The economic and cognitive costs of annoying display advertisements. *Journal of Marketing Research, 51*(6), 742–752.

Goodrich, K. (2014). The gender gap: Brain processing differences between the sexes shape attitudes about online advertising. *Journal of Advertising Research, 54*(1), 32–43.

Gottfried. J., & Shearer, E. (2017, September 7). Americans' online news use is closing in on TV news use. Retrieved September 6, 2020, from http://www/pewresearch.org/fact-tank/2017/09/07/americans-online-news-use-vs-tv-news-use/ft_17-09-05_platformnews_platforms

Grant, A. E., & Stout, D. A. (2019). Introduction: Religion in cyberspace. In A. E. Grant, A. F. C. Sturgill, C. H. Chen, & D. A. Stout (Eds.), *Religion online: How digital technology is changing the way we worship and pray*: Vol. 1. *Religion in cyberspace* (pp. 1–10). Santa Barbara, CA: ABC-Clio.

Greenberg, B. S. (1988). Some uncommon television images and the drench hypothesis. In S. Oskamp (Ed.), *Television as a social issue* (pp. 88–102). Newbury Park, CA: Sage.

Greenberg, B. S., Edison, N., Korzenny, F., Fernandez-Collado, C., & Atkin, C. K. (1980). Antisocial and prosocial behaviors on TV. In B. S. Greenberg (Ed.), *Life on television: Content analysis of U.S. TV drama* (pp. 99–128). Norwood, NJ: Ablex.

Greenberg, B. S., Stanley, C., Siemicki, M., Heeter, C., Soderman, A., & Linsangan, R. (1993). Sex content on soaps and prime-time television series most viewed by adolescents. In B. S. Greenberg, J. D. Brown, & N. Buerkel-Rothfuss (Eds.), *Media, sex and the adolescent* (pp. 29–44). Cresskill, NJ: Hampton.

Greenwood, D. N., & Long, C. R. (2009). Psychological predictors of media involvement: Solitude experiences and the need to belong. *Communication Research, 36*, 637–654.

Gregg, P. B. (2018). Parasocial breakup and Twitter: The firing of Barb Abney. *Journal of Broadcasting & Electronic Media, 62*(1), 38–50.

Gregory, S. (2015, March 27). Meet America's first video game varsity athletes. *Time.* http://time.com

Grewal, D., Bart, Y., Spann, M., & Zubcsek, P. P. (2016). Mobile advertising: A framework and research agenda. *Journal of Interactive Marketing, 34*, 3–14.

Grimes, T., Bergen, L., Nicholes, K., Vernberg, E., & Fonagy, P. (2004). Is psychopathology the key to understanding why some children become aggressive when they are exposed to violent television programming. *Human Communication Research, 30*, 153–181.

Grizzard, M., Tamborini, R., Sherry, J. L., & Weber, R. (2017). Repeated play reduces video games' ability to elicit guilt: Evidence from a longitudinal experiment. *Media Psychology, 20*(2), 267–290.

Gross, M. L. (2010). Advergames and the effects of game–product congruity. *Computers in Human Behavior, 26*(6), 1259–1265.

Guerrero, M., & Luengas, M. (2015). The Mexican movement #Yosoy132 as an example of Prodince's public engagement. In M. Shumow (Ed.), *Mediated communities: Civic voices, empowerment and media literacy in the digital era* (pp. 171–192). New York: Peter Lang.

Ha, L. (2008). Online advertising research in advertising journals: A review. *Journal of Current Issues and Research in Advertising, 30*(1), 31–48.

Hall, A. (2005). Audience personality and selection of media and media genres. *Media Psychology, 7*, 377–398.

Han, J., & Federico, C. M. (2018). The polarizing effect of news framing: Comparing the mediating roles of motivated reasoning, self-stereotyping, and intergroup animus. *Journal of Communication, 68*(4), 685–711.

Harms, B., Bijmolt, T. H. A., & Hoekstra, J. C. (2017). Digital native advertising: Practitioner perspectives and a research agenda. *Journal of Interactive Advertising, 17*(2), 80–91.

Harrison, K. (2006). Scope of self: Toward a model of television's effects on self-complexity in adolescence. *Communication Theory, 16*, 251–279.

Haven, B. (2007). *Marketing's new key metric: Engagement.* Cambridge, MA: Forrester Research.

Havens, T., & Lotz, A. D. (2012). *Understanding media industries.* New York: Oxford University Press.

Hawkins, R. P., Tapper, J., Bruce, L., & Pingree, S. (1995). Strategic and nonstrategic explanations for attentional inertia. *Communication Research, 22*(2), 188–206. https://doi.org/10.1177/009365095022002003

He, A. (2019, May 31). Average time spent with media in 2019 has plateaued: Digital is making up losses by old media. Retrieved October 14, 2020, from https://www.emarketer.com/content/us-time-spent-with-media-in-2019-has-plateaued-with-digital-making-up-losses-by-old-media

Hefner, D., Knop, K., Schmitt, S., & Vorderer, P. (2019). Rules? Role model? Relationship? The impact of parents on their children's problematic mobile phone involvement. *Media Psychology, 22*(1), 82–108.

Heider, D. (2009). Identity and reality: What does it mean to live virtually? In D. Heider (Ed.), *Living virtually: Researching new worlds* (pp. 131–143). New York: Peter Lang.

Hernandez, D. (2019, October 12). How much data will the Internet of Things (IOT) generate by 2020? Versa Technology. https://www.versatek.com/blog/how-much-data-will-the-internet-of-things-iot-generate-by-2020

Hillis, K. (2009). *Online a lot of the time: Ritual, fetish, sign.* Durham, NC: Duke University Press.

Himmelweit, H., Oppenheim, A., & Vince, P. (1958). *Television and the child.* Oxford: Oxford University Press.

Himmelweit, H. T., Swift, B., & Jaeger, M. E. (1980). The audience as critic: A conceptual analysis of television entertainment. In P. H. Tannenbaum (Ed.), *The entertainment functions of television* (pp. 67–106). Hillsdale, NJ: Lawrence Erlbaum.

Hindman, M. (2018). *The internet trap: How the digital economy builds monopolies and undermines democracy.* Princeton, NJ: Princeton University Press.

Hofacker, C. F., Ruyter, K. D., Lurie, N. H., Manchanda, P., & Donaldson, J. (2016). Gamification and mobile marketing effectiveness. *Journal of Interactive Marketing, 34,* 25–36.

Holcomb, J., Gottfried, J., & Mitchell, A. (2013). *News use across social media platforms.* Pew Research Journalism Project.

Hollins, P., & Robbins, S. (2009). The educational affordances of multi user virtual environments. In D. Heider (Ed.), *Living virtually: Researching new worlds* (pp. 257–270). New York: Peter Lang.

Hong, T., & Beaudoin, C. E. (2018). A behavioral function approach in predicting contribution of user-generated content. *Communication Research, 45*(5), 764–782. https://doi.org.proxy.library.ucsb.edu:9443/10.1177/0093650216644019

Horvath, C. W. (2004). Measuring television addiction. *Journal of Broadcasting & Electronic Media, 48,* 378–398.

Housholder, E., Watson, B. R., & LoRusso, S. (2018). Does political advertising lead to online information seeking? A real-world test using Google search data. *Journal of Broadcasting & Electronic Media, 62*(2), 337–353.

Huang, J. S. (2009). Real business and real competition in the unreal world. In D. Heider (Ed.), *Living virtually: Researching new worlds* (pp. 191–207). New York: Peter Lang.

Huizinga, J. (1949). *Homo ludens: A study of the play-element in culture.* London: Routledge and Kegan Paul.

Huskey, R., Wilcox, S., & Weber, R. (2018). Network neuroscience reveals distinct neuromarkers of flow during media use. *Journal of Communication, 68*(5), 872–895.

Hutchings, T. (2017). "We are a United Humanity": Death, emotion and digital media in the Church of Sweden. *Journal of Broadcasting & Electronic Media, 61*(1), 90–107.

Interactive Advertising Bureau. (2018). IAB Tech Lab solution. https://iabtechlab.com/solutions

Isen, A. M. (2000). Positive affect and decision making. In M. Lewis & J. M. Haviland-Jones (Eds.), *Handbook of emotions* (2nd ed., pp. 417–435). New York: Guilford Press.

Ito, M., et al. (2009). *Living and learning with new media: Summary of findings from the Digital Youth Project.* Cambridge, MA: MIT Press.

Ivory, J. D. (2009). Technological development in transitions in virtual worlds. In D. Heider (Ed.), *Living virtually: Researching new worlds* (pp. 11–22). New York: Peter Lang.

Jaidka, K., Zhou, A., & Lelkes, Y. (2019). Brevity is the soul of Twitter: The constraint affordance and political discussion. *Journal of Communication, 69*(4), 345–372. https://doi-org.proxy.library.ucsb.edu:9443/10.1093/joc/jqz023

James, P. D. (2009). *Talking about detective fiction.* New York: Knopf.

Jamison, L. (2018, June 10). The digital ruins of a forgotten future. Retrieved June 10, 2018, from https://www.theatlantic.com/magazine/archive/2017/12/second-life-leslie-jamison/544149

Jerath, K., Ma, L., & Park, Y.-H. (2014). Consumer click behavior at a search engine: The role of keyword popularity. *Journal of Marketing Research, 51*(4), 480–486.

Jhally, S. (1987). *The codes of advertising: Fetishism and the political economy of meaning in the consumer society.* New York: St. Martin's Press.

Jhally, S. (1987). The political economy of culture. In I. Angus and S. Jhally (Eds.), *The codes of advertising* (pp. 65–81). London: Frances Pinter.

Ji, S. W. (2019). The internet and changes in the media industry: A 5–year cross-national examination of media industries for 51 countries. *Journalism & Mass Communication Quarterly, 96*(3), 894–918. https://doi-org.proxy.library.ucsb.edu:9443/10.1177/1077699018807914

Jian, L., & Mackie-Mason, J. K. (2012). Incentive-centered design for user-contributed content. In M. Peitz & J. Waldfogel (Eds.), *The Oxford handbook of the digital economy* (pp. 399–433). New York: Oxford University Press.

Jin, S.-A. A., & Phua, J. (2014). Following celebrities' tweets about brands: The impact of Twitter-based electronic word-of-mouth on consumers' source credibility perception, buying intention, and social identification with celebrities. *Journal of Advertising, 43*(2), 941–966.

Jin, S. V., & Ryu, E. (2018). "The paradox of Narcissus and Echo in the Instagram pond" in light of the selfie culture from Freudian evolutionary psychology: Self-loving and confident but lonely. *Journal of Broadcasting & Electronic Media, 62*(4), 554–577.

Johnson, B. K., & Knobloch-Westerwick, S. (2017). When misery avoids company: Selective social comparisons to photographic online profiles. *Human Communication Research, 43*(1), 54–75. https://doi-org.proxy.library.ucsb.edu:9443/10.1111/hcre.12095

Johnson, S. (2005). *Everything bad is good for you.* New York: Riverhead Books.

Johnson, S. (2012). *Future perfect: The case for progress in a networked age.* New York: Riverhead Books.

Johnson-Laird, P. N., & Oatley, K. (2000). Cognitive and social construction of emotions. In M. Lewis & J. M. Haviland-Jones (Eds.), *Handbook of emotions* (2nd ed., pp. 458–475). New York: Guilford Press.

Jones, C. M., Scholes, L., Hohnson, D., Katsikitis, M., & Carras, M. C. (2014). Gaming well: Links between videogames and flourishing mental health. *Frontiers in Psychology, 5,* 260. https://dx-doi-org.proxy.library.ucsb.edu:9443/10.3389%2Ffpsyg.2014.00260

Jorgensen, J. J., & Ha, Y. (2019). The influence of electronic word of mouth via social networking sites on the socialization of college-aged consumers. *Journal of Interactive Advertising, 19*(1), 29–42. https://doi-org.proxy.library.ucsb.edu:9443/10.1080/15252019.2018.1533500

Jung, A.-R., & Heo, J. (2019). Ad disclosure vs. ad recognition: How persuasion knowledge influences native advertising evaluation. *Journal of Interactive Advertising, 19*(1), 1–14. https://doi-org.proxy.library.ucsb.edu:9443/10.1080/15252019.2018.1520661

Kafka, P., & Molla, R. (2017, December 4). 2017 was the year digital ad spending finally beat TV. *Recode.* https://www.recode.net/2017/12/4/16733460/2017–digital-ad-spend-advertising-beat-tv

Kaiser Family Foundation. (2003). *Sex on TV 3.* Menlo Park, CA: Author.

Kaiser Family Foundation (2005, March). Key findings from new research on children's media use. Retrieved August 23, 2009, from http://www.kaisernetwork.org/health_cast/hcast_index.cfm?display=detail&hc=1377

Kaiser Family Foundation (2010). Daily media use among children and teens up dramatically from five years ago. Retrieved June 24, 2011, from http://www.kff.org/entmedia/entmedia 012010nr.cfm

Kamenetz, A. (2018). *The art of screen time: How your family can balance digital media and real life.* New York: PublicAffairs.

Kaplan, D. (1972, July/August). The psychopathology of TV watching. *Performance.*

Kaplan, R. M. (1972). On television as a cause of aggression. *American Psychologist, 27*(10), 968–969. https://doi.org/10.1037/h0038046

Karlsson, M., Clerwall, C., & Nord, L. (2017). Do not stand corrected: Transparency and users' attitudes to inaccurate news and corrections in online journalism. *Journalism & Mass*

Communication Quarterly, 94(1), 148–167. https://doi.org.proxy.library.ucsb.edu:9443/10 .1177/1077699016654680

Karsay, K., Matthes, J., Platzer, P., & Plinke, M. (2018). Adopting the objectifying gaze: Exposure to sexually objectifying music videos and subsequent gazing behavior. *Media Psychology, 21*(1), 27–49.

Kaye, B. K., & Sapolsky, B. S. (1997). Electronic monitoring of in-home television RCD usage. *Journal of Broadcasting & Electronic Media, 41*(2), 214–228.

Keib, K., Espina, C., Lee, Y.-I., Wojdynski, B. W., Choi, D., & Bang, H. (2018). Picture this: The influence of emotionally valenced images, on attention, selection, and sharing of social media news. *Media Psychology, 21*(2), 202–221.

Kerr, A. (2006). *The business and culture of digital games: Gamework/gameplay.* London: Sage.

Kilteni, K., Groten, R., & Slater, M. (2012). The sense of embodiment in virtual reality. *Presence: Teleoperators and Virtual Environments, 21*(4), 373–387.

Kim, N. Y. (2018). The effect of ad customization and ad variation on internet users' perceptions of forced multiple advertising exposures and attitudes. *Journal of Interactive Advertising, 18*(1), 15–27.

Kim, S. J., & Hancock, J. T. (2017). How advertorials deactivate advertising schema: MTurk-based experiments to examine persuasion tactics and outcomes in health advertisements. *Communication Research, 44*(7), 1019–1045. https://doi.org.proxy.library.ucsb.edu:9443/ 10.1177/0093650216644017

Kim, Y.-C., Shin, E., Cho, A., Jung, E., Shon, K., & Shim, H. (2019). SNS dependency and community engagement in urban neighborhoods: The moderating role of integrated connectedness to a community storytelling network. *Communication Research, 46*(1), 7–32. https://doi.org.proxy.library.ucsb.edu:9443/10.1177/0093650215588786

Kirby, D. L., & Cusack, C. M. (2017). Religion and media: An introduction. In D. L. Kirby & C. M. Cusack (Eds.), *Religion and media: Critical concepts in religious studies* (pp. 1–11). London: Routledge.

Klapdor, S., Anderl, E. M., Schumann, J. H., & von Wangenheim, F. (2015). How to Use Multichannel Behavior to Predict Online Conversions. *Journal of Advertising Research, 55*(4), 433–442.

Klawitter, E., & Hargittai, E. (2018). Shortcuts to well being? Evaluating the credibility of online health information through multiple complementary heuristics. *Journal of Broadcasting & Electronic Media, 62*(2), 251–268.

Kleemans, M., Daalmans, S., Carbaat, I., & Anschütz, D. (2018). Picture perfect: The direct effect of manipulated Instagram photos on body image in adolescent girls. *Media Psychology, 21*(1), 93–110.

Klimmt, C., Possler, D., May, N., Auge, H., Wanjek, L., & Wolf, A.-L. (2019). Effects of soundtrack music on the video game experience. *Media Psychology, 22*(5), 689–713. https:// doi-org.proxy.library.ucsb.edu:9443/10.1080/15213269.2018.1507827

Knobloch-Westerwick, S., & Hastall, M. R. (2006). Social comparisons with news personae: Selective exposure to news portrayals of same-sex and same-age characters. *Communication Research, 33*, 262–285.

Knobloch-Westerwick, S., Hastall, M. R., & Rossmann, M. (2009). Coping or escaping? Effects of life dissatisfaction on selective exposure. *Communication Research, 36*, 207–228.

Knobloch-Westerwick, S., & Lavis, S. M. (2017). Selecting serious or satirical, supporting or stirring news? Selective exposure to partisan versus mockery news online videos. *Journal of Communication, 67*(1), 54–81.

Knoll, J. (2016). Advertising in social media: A review of empirical evidence. *International Journal of Advertising, 35*(2), 266–300.

Koban, K., Breuer, J., Rieger, D., Mohseni, M. R., Noack, S., Bente, G., & Ohler, P. (2019). Playing for the thrill and skill: Quiz games as means for mood and competence repair. *Media Psychology, 22*(5), 743–768. https://doi-org.proxy.library.ucsb.edu:9443/10.1080/15213269.2018.1515637

Koch, L. (2019, February 5). Esports playing in the big leagues now. eMarketer. Retrieved February 9, 2020, from https://www.emarketer.com/content/esports-disrupts-digital-sports-streaming

Koolstra, C. M., & Van der Voort, T. H. A. (1996). Longitudinal effects of television on children's leisure-time reading: A test of three explanatory models. *Human Communication Research, 23*(1), 4–35.

Kowert, R., Breuer, J., & Quandt, T. (2017). Women are from FarmVille, men are from ViceCity: The cycle of exclusion and sexism in video game content and culture. In R. Kowert & T. Quandt (Eds.), *New perspectives on the social aspects of digital gaming: Multiplayer 2* (pp. 136–150). New York: Routledge.

Krcmar, M. (1996). Family communication patterns, discourse behavior, and child television viewing. *Human Communication Research, 23*(2), 251–277.

Krcmar, M., & Greene, K. (1999). Predicting exposure to and uses of television violence. *Journal of Communication, 49*(3), 24–45.

Krcmar, M. & Kean, L. G. (2005). Uses and gratifications of media violence: Personality correlates of viewing and liking violent genres. *Media Psychology, 7*, 399–420.

Kreps, G. L. (2017). Online information and communication systems to enhance health outcomes through communication convergence. *Human Communication Research, 43*(4), 518–530. https://doi-org.proxy.library.ucsb.edu:9443/10.1111/hcre.12117

Krotz, F., & Eastman, S. T. (1999). Orientations toward television outside the home. *Journal of Communication, 49*, 5–27.

Kruglanski, A. W., & Stroebe, W. (2005). The influence of beliefs and goals on attitudes: Issues of structure, function, and dynamics. In D. Albarracin, B. T. Johnson, & M. P. Zanna (Eds.), *The handbook of attitudes* (pp. 323–368). Mahwah, NJ: Erlbaum.

Kümpel, A. S. (2019). Getting tagged, getting involved with news? A mixed-methods investigation of the effects and motives of news-related tagging activities on social network sites. *Journal of Communication, 69*(4), 373–395. https://doi-org.proxy.library.ucsb.edu:9443/10.1093/joc/jqz019

Kunkel, D., Eyal, K., & Donnerstein, E. (2007). Sexual socialization messages on entertainment television: Comparing content trends, 1997–2002. *Media Psychology, 9*, 595–622.

Kunst, J. R., Bailey, A., Prendergast, C., & Gundersen, A. (2019). Sexism, rape myths and feminist identification explain gender differences in attitudes toward the #MeToo social media campaign in two countries. *Media Psychology, 22*(5), 818–843. https://doi-org.proxy.library.ucsb.edu:9443/10.1080/15213269.2018.1532300

Kwak, N., Lane, D. S., Weeks, B. E., Kim, D. H., Lee, S. S., & Bachleda, S. (2018). Perceptions of social media for politics: Testing the slacktivism hypothesis. *Human Communication Research, 44*(2), 197–221. https://doi-org.proxy.library.ucsb.edu:9443/10.1093/hcr/hqx008

Lane, D. S., Coles, S. M., & Saleem, M. (2019). Solidarity effects in social movement messaging: How cueing dominant group identity can increase movement support. *Human Communication Research, 45*(1), 1–26. https://doi-org.proxy.library.ucsb.edu:9443/10.1093/hcr/hqy011

Lane, D. S., Lee, S. S., Liang, F., Kim, D. H., Shen, L., Weeks, B. E., & Kwak, N. (2019). Social media expression and the political self. *Journal of Communication, 69*(1), 49–72.

Lang, A., Shin, M., Bradley, S. D., Wang, Z., Lee, S., & Potter, D. (2005). Wait! Don't turn that dial! More excitement to come! The effects of story length and production pacing in local television news on channel changing behavior and information processing in a free choice environment. *Journal of Broadcasting & Electronic Media, 49*, 3–22.

Lanius, C. (2019). Big data goes to Washington: How protesters navigate aggregated social media content. In G. W. Richardson Jr. (Ed.), *Social media and politics: A new way to participate in the political process* (Vol. 2, pp. 63–78). Santa Barbara, CA: Praeger.

LaPointe, P. (2012). Measuring Facebook's impact on marketing: The proverbial hits the fan. *Journal of Advertising Research, 52*(3), 286–287.

Larchet, J.-C. (2019). *The new media epidemic: The undermining of society, family, and our own soul.* Jordanville, NY: Holy Trinity Publications.

LaRose, R., & Eastin, M. S. (2002). Is online buying out of control? Electronic commerce and consumer self-regulation. *Journal of Broadcasting & Electronic Media, 46*(4), 549–564.

LaRose, R. & Eastin, M. S. (2004). A social cognitive theory of internet uses and gratifications: Toward a new model of media attendance. *Journal of Broadcasting & Electronic Media, 48*, 358–377.

LaRose, R., Lin, C. A., & Eastin, M. S. (2003). Unregulated Internet usage: Addiction, habit, or deficient self-regulation? *Media Psychology, 5*(3), 225–253.

Larsson, A. O. (2019). News use as amplification: Norwegian national, regional, and hyper-partisan media on Facebook. *Journalism & Mass Communication Quarterly, 96*(3), 721–741. https://doi-org.proxy.library.ucsb.edu:9443/10.1177/1077699019831439

Lazarsfeld, P. F., Berelson, B., & Gaudet, H. (1944). *The people's choice: How the voter makes up his mind in a presidential campaign.* New York: Duell, Sloan & Pearce.

Lee, J. K., Choi, J., Kim, C., & Kim, Y. (2014). Social media, network heterogeneity, and opinion polarization. *Journal of Communication, 64*, 702–722. doi: 10.1111/jcom.12077

Lee, J., Kim, S., & Ham, C.-D. (2016). A double-edged sword? Predicting consumers' attitudes toward and sharing intention of native advertising on social media. *American Behavioral Scientist, 60*(12), 1425–1441.

Lelkes, Y., Sood, G., & Iyengar, S. (2015). The hostile audience: The effect of access to broadband internet on partisan affect. *American Journal of Political Science, 61*(1), 5–20. doi:10.1111/ajps.12237

Levy, S. (2007, August 27). Facebook grows up. *Newsweek*, pp. 40–46.

Li, C., Liu, J., & Hong, C. (2019). The effect of preference stability and extremity on person-alized advertising. *Journalism & Mass Communication Quarterly, 96*(2), 406–427. https://doi-org.proxy.library.ucsb.edu:9443/10.1177/1077699018782203

Li, H., & Lo, H.-Y. (2015). Do you recognize its brand? The effectiveness of online in-stream video advertisements. *Journal of Advertising, 44*(3), 208–218.

Liang, H. (2018). Broadcast versus viral spreading: The structure of diffusion cascades and selective sharing on social media. *Journal of Communication, 68*(3), 525–546.

Liang, H., & Fu, K. W. (2017). Information overload, similarity, and redundancy: Unsubscribing information sources on Twitter. *Journal of Computer-Mediated Communication, 22*(1), 1–17.

Lichter, L. S., & Lichter, S. R. (1983). *Prime time crime.* Washington, DC: Media Institute.

Lim, S. S., Vadrevu, S., Chan, Y. H., & Basnyat, I. (2012). Facework on Facebook: The online publicness of juvenile delinquents and youths-at-risk. *Journal of Broadcasting & Electronic Media, 56*, 346–361.

Leurdijk, A., Nieuwenhuis, O., & Poel, M. (2014a). The music industry. In G. De Prato, E. Sanz, & J. P. Simon (Eds.), *Digital media worlds: The new economy of media* (pp. 133–146). London: Palgrave Macmillan.

Leurdijk, A., Nieuwenhuis, O., & Poel, M. (2014b). The newspaper industry. In G. De Prato, E. Sanz, & J. P. Simon (Eds.), *Digital media worlds: The new economy of media* (pp. 147–162). London: Palgrave Macmillan.

Lieber, E., & Syverson, C. (2012). Online versus offline competition. In M. Peitz & J. Waldfogel (Eds.), *The Oxford handbook of the digital economy* (pp. 189–223). New York: Oxford University Press.

Liebold, B., Brill, M., Pietschmann, D., Schwab, F., & Ohler, P. (2017). Continuous measurement of breaks in presence: Psychophysiology and orienting responses. *Media Psychology, 20*(3), 477–501.

Lin, T. T. C., & Chiang, Y.-H. (2017). Dual screening: Examining social predictors and impact on online and offline political participation among Taiwanese internet users. *Journal of Broadcasting & Electronic Media, 61*(2), 240–263.

Lipsman, A. (2019, June 27). Global ecommerce 2019. eMarketer. Retrieved August 31, 2019, from https://www.emarketer.com/content/global-ecommerce-2019

Listening to Alexa. (2019, May 24). *The Week.*

Liu, X., Burns, A. C., & Hou, Y. (2017). An investigation of brand-related user-generated content on Twitter. *Journal of Advertising, 46*(2), 236–247.

Liu-Thompkins, Y. (2019). A decade of online advertising research: What we learned and what we need to know. *Journal of Advertising, 48*(1), 1–13.

Livingstone, S., Ólafsson, K., Helsper, E. J., Lupiáñez-Villanueva, F., Veltri, G. A., & Folkvord, F. (2017). Maximizing opportunities and minimizing risks for children online: The role of digital skills in emerging strategies of parental mediation. *Journal of Communication, 67*(1), 82–105.

Lo, V.-H., & Wei, R. (2005). Exposure to internet pornography and Taiwanese adolescents' sexual attitudes and behavior. *Journal of Broadcasting & Electronic Media, 49,* 221–237.

Logan, K. (2011). Hulu.com or NBC? *Journal of Advertising Research, 51*(1), 276–287.

Logan, K. (2013). And now a word from our sponsor: Do consumers perceive advertising on traditional television and online streaming video differently? *Journal of Marketing Communications, 19*(4), 258–276.

Lucas, K., & Sherry, J. L. (2004). Sex differences in video game play: A communication-based explanation. *Communication Research, 31,* 499–523.

Maccoby, E. E. (1954). Why do children watch television? *Public Opinion Quarterly, 18,* 239–244.

Mander, J. (1978). *Four arguments for the elimination of television.* New York: Morrow.

Mares, M.-L., & Woodard, E. H. (2006). In search of the older audience: Adult age differences in television viewing. *Journal of Broadcasting & Electronic Media, 50,* 595–614.

Marketline.com. (2019, April). Digital media in the United States. Retrieved July 21, 2019, from http://web.b.ebscohost.com.proxy.library.ucsb.edu:2048/ehost/pdfviewer/pdfviewer?vid=3&sid=0b7a0b89-3986-4f2f-83a5-1759d59ce701%40sessionmgr103

Market Mogul Team. (2018, April 3). Amazon's annual revenue over the years. Retrieved June 10, 2018, from https://themarketmogul.com/amazon-annual-revenue

MarketWatch.com. (2018, June 10). eBay, Inc. Retrieved June 10, 2018, from https://www.marketwatch.com/investing/stock/ebay/financials

Markowitz, D. M., & Hancock, J. T. (2018). Deception in mobile dating conversations. *Journal of Communication, 68*(3), 547–569.

Marr, B. (2018, May 21). How much data do we create every day? *Forbes.* https://www.forbes.com/sites/bernardmarr/2018/05/21/how-much-data-do-we-create-every-day-the-mind-blowing-stats-everyone-should-read

Marsh, K. L., & Wallace, H. M. (2005). The influence of attitudes on beliefs: Formation and change. In D. Albarracin, B. T. Johnson, & M. P. Zanna (Eds.), *The handbook of attitudes* (pp. 369–395). Mahwah, NJ: Erlbaum.

Martins, N., Weaver, A. J., & Lynch, T. (2018). What the public "knows" about media effects research: The influence of news frames on perceived credibility and belief change. *Journal of Communication, 68*(1), 98–119.

Marwick, A., & Ellison, N. B. (2012). There isn't wifi in heaven! Negotiating visibility on Facebook memorial pages. *Journal of Broadcasting & Electronic Media, 56*, 378–400.

Mashable. (2010, August 5). Google: There are 129,864,880 books in the entire world. Retrieved October 22, 2019, from https://mashable.com/2010/08/05/number-of-books-in -the-world

Maslowska, E., Smit, E. G., & van den Putte, B. (2016). It is all in the name: A study of consumers' responses to personalized communication. *Journal of Interactive Advertising, 16*(1), 74–85.

Matsa, K. E. (2017, June 16). Network news fact sheet. Pew Research Center. Retrieved June 20, 2018, from http://www.journalism.org/fact-sheet/network-news

Matsa, K. E. (2017, July 13). Local TV news fact sheet. Pew Research Center. Retrieved June 20, 2018, from http://www.journalism.org/fact-sheet/local-tv-news

Matthews, H. (2018, June 15). 27 online dating statistics and what they mean for the future of dating. DatingNews.com. Retrieved July 3, 2019, from https://www.datingnews.com/ industry-trends/online-dating-statistics-what-they-mean for-future

McAllister, M. P., & Orme, S. (2017). The impact of digital media on advertising: Five cultural dilemmas. In P. Messaris & L. Humphreys (Eds.), *Digital media: Transformations in human communication* (2nd ed., pp. 71–78). New York: Peter Lang.

McCaffrey, P. (Ed.) (2010). *The news and its future.* New York: H. W. Wilson.

McCombs, M. (2005). A look at agenda-setting: Past, present and future. *Journalism Studies, 6*(4), 543–557. doi:10.1080/14616700500250438

McGuire, W. J. (1990). Dynamic operations of thought systems. *American Psychologist, 45*, 504–512.

McGregor, S. C., Mourão, R. R., Neto, I., Straubhaar, J. D., & Angeluci, A. (2017). Second screening as convergence in Brazil and the United States. *Journal of Broadcasting & Electronic Media, 61*(1), 163–181.

McIlwraith, R. D. (1998). "I'm addicted to television": The personality, imagination, and TV watching patterns of self-identified TV addicts. *Journal of Broadcasting & Electronic Media, 42*, 371–386.

McIntosh, W. D., Schwegler, A. F., & Terry-Murray, R. M. (2000). Threat and television viewing in the United States, 1960–1990. *Media Psychology, 2*, 35–46.

McLeod, A. (2019, May 30). New website Credder aims to fight fake news, promote real journalism. Retrieved May 30, 2019, from https://www.mintpressnews.com/like-yelp-but -for-news-new-website-credder-aims-to-fight-fake-news-promote-real-journalism/258874

McLeod, J. M., Ward, L. S., & Tancill, K. (1965). Alienation and uses of mass media. *Public Opinion Quarterly, 29*, 583–594.

Mead, G. H. (1934). *Mind, self, and society.* Chicago: University of Chicago Press.

Mediakix (2017, September 14). How the internet became home to hundreds of millions of blogs in less than 25 years. Retrieved June 20, 2018, from https://mediakix.com/2017/09/ how-many-blogs-are-there-in-the-world.

Metzger, M. J., & Suh, J. J. (2017). Comparative optimism about privacy risks on Facebook. *Journal of Communication, 67*(2), 203–232.

Mihailidis, P. (2015). Media literacy and mediated communities: Emerging perspectives for digital culture. In M. Shumow (Ed.), *Mediated communities: Civic voices, empowerment and media literacy in the digital era* (pp. 15–29). New York: Peter Lang.

Milkovich, D. (2018, December 3). 13 alarming cyber security facts and stats. Retrieved September 7, 2019, from https://www.cybintsolutions.com/cyber-security-facts-stats

Mills, C. W. (1956). *The power elite.* New York: Oxford University Press.

Mills, H. (2018). Avatar creation: The social construction of "beauty" in Second Life. *Journalism & Mass Communication Quarterly, 95*(3), 607–624.

Moeller, J., Kühne, R., & De Vreese, C. (2018). Mobilizing youth in the 21st century: How digital media use fosters civic duty, information efficacy, and political participation. *Journal of Broadcasting & Electronic Media, 62*(3), 445–460.

Moeller, J., Shehata, A., & Kruikemeier, S. (2018). Internet use and political interest: Growth curves, reinforcing spirals, and causal effects during adolescence. *Journal of Communication, 68*(6), 1052–1078.

Moon, S. J., & Hadley, P. (2014). Routinizing a new technology in the newsroom: Twitter as a news source in mainstream media. *Journal of Broadcasting & Electronic Media, 58*(2), 289–305.

Moraga-Gonzalez, J.-L., & Wildenbeest, R. (2012). Comparison sites. In M. Peitz & J. Waldfogel (Eds.), *The Oxford handbook of the digital economy* (pp. 224–253). New York: Oxford University Press.

Moran, G., & Muzellec, L. (2017). eWOM credibility on social networking sites: A framework. *Journal of Marketing Communications, 23*(2), 149–161.

Moran, G., Muzellec, L., & Nolan, E. (2014). Consumer moments of truth in the digital context. *Journal of Advertising Research, 54*(2), 200–204.

Morgan, S. E., Movius, L., & Cody, M. J. (2009). The power of narratives: The effect of entertainment television organ donation storylines on the attitudes, knowledge, and behaviors of donors and nondonors. *Journal of Communication, 59*, 135–151.

Moy, P., Torres, M., Tanaka, K., & McCluskey, M. R. (2005). Knowledge or trust? Investigating linkages between media reliance and participation. *Communication Research, 32*, 59–96.

Nabi, R. L., & Oliver, M. B. (Eds.) (2009). *Media processes and effects.* Los Angeles: Sage.

NCTV says violence on TV up 16%. (1983, March 22). *Broadcasting Magazine,* p. 63.

Nansen, B., Kohn, T., Arnold, M., van Ryn, L., & Gibbs, M. (2017). Social media in the funeral industry: On the digitization of grief. *Journal of Broadcasting & Electronic Media, 61*(1), 73–89.

Napper, P., & Rao, A. (2019). *The power of agency.* New York: St. Martin's Press.

National Television Violence Study (1999). *Annual report, volume 3.* Thousand Oaks, CA: Sage.

Nee, R. C., & De Maio, M. (2019). A "presidential look"? An analysis of gender framing in 2016 persuasive memes of Hillary Clinton. *Journal of Broadcasting & Electronic Media, 63*(2), 304–321. https://doi-org.proxy.library.ucsb.edu:9443/10.1080/08838151.2019.1620561

Nekmat, E., Gower, K. K., Zhou, S., & Metzger, M. (2019). Connective-collective action on social media: Moderated mediation of cognitive elaboration and perceived source credibility on personalness of source. *Communication Research, 46*(1), 62–87. https://doi.org.proxy.library.ucsb.edu:9443/10.1177/0093650215609676

Neubaum, G., & Krämer, N. C. (2017). Monitoring the opinion of the crowd: Psychological mechanisms underlying public opinion perceptions on social media. *Media Psychology, 20*(3), 502–553.

Neubaum, G., & Krämer, N. C. (2018). What do we fear? Expected sanctions for expressing minority opinions in offline and online communication. *Communication Research, 45*(2), 139–164. https://doi.org.proxy.library.ucsb.edu:9443/10.1177/0093650215623837

Neuman, W. R., Marcus, G. E., & MacKuen, M. B. (2018). Hardwired for news: Affective intelligence and political attention. *Journal of Broadcasting & Electronic Media, 62*(4), 614–635.

Newbury, C. (2019, November 4). 33 Facebook stats that matter to marketers in 2020. Hoot-suite. Retrieved January 11, 2019, from https://blog.hootsuite.com/facebook-statistics/#usage

Newzoo. (2017). Global games market report. https://newzoo.com/insights/articles/newzoos-key-developments-in-2017

Nguyen, M. H., van Weert, J. C. M., Bol, N., Loos, E. F., Tytgat, K. M. A. J., van de Ven, A. W. H., & Smets, E. M. A. (2017). Tailoring the mode of information presentation: Effects on younger and older adults' attention and recall of online information. *Human Communication Research, 43*(1), 102–126. https://doi-org.proxy.library.ucsb.edu:9443/10.1111/hcre.12097

Nielsen. (2018). Juggling act: Audiences have more media at their disposal and are using them simultaneously. https://www.nielsen.com/us/en/insights/news/2018/juggling-act-audiences-have-more-media-at-their-disposal-and-are-using-them-simultaneously.html

Normand, J.-M., Giannopoulos, E., Spanlang, B., & Slater, M. (2011). Multisensory stimulation can induce an illusion of larger belly size in immersive virtual reality. *PLoS One, 6*(1), e16128.

NumberOf.net (2015). Number of users on Twitter. Retrieved January 28, 2015, from http://www.numberof.net/number-of-users-on-twitter

Nyaole-Kowuor, R. (2015). Civic voices in the digital era: Opportunities and challenges in Kenya. In M. Shumow (Ed.), *Mediated communities: Civic voices, empowerment and media literacy in the digital era* (pp. 55–74). New York: Peter Lang.

Omoniyi, T. (2018). Digital evangelism: Varieties of English in unexpected places. In A. Rosowsky (Ed.), *Faith and language practices in digital spaces* (pp. 135–157). Bristol, UK: Multilingual Matters.

Oliver, M. B. (2008). Tender affective states as predictors of entertainment preference. *Journal of Communication, 58,* 40–61.

Olson, J. M., & Stone, J. (2005). The influence of behavior on attitudes. In D. Albarracin, B. T. Johnson, & M. P. Zanna (Eds.), *The handbook of attitudes* (pp. 223–271). Mahwah, NJ: Erlbaum.

O'Neal, S. (2016). The personal-data tsunami and the future of marketing: A moments-based marketing approach for the new people-data economy. *Journal of Advertising Research, 56*(2), 136–141.

PageFair. (2017). The state of the blocked web: 2017 global adblock report. https://pagefair.com/downloads/2017/01/PageFair-2017-Adblock-Report.pdf

Pandharipande, R. V. (2018). Online satsang and online puja: Faith and language in the era of globalization. In A. Rosowsky (Ed.), *Faith and language practices in digital spaces* (pp. 185–208). Bristol, UK: Multilingual Matters.

Papacharissi, Z., & Mendelson, A. L. (2007). An exploratory study of reality appeal: Uses and gratifications of reality TV shows. *Journal of Broadcasting & Electronic Media, 51,* 355–370.

Pariser, E. (2011). *The filter bubble: What the internet is hiding from you.* New York: Penguin.

Park, C. S., & Kaye, B. K. (2018). News engagement on social media and democratic citizenship: Direct and moderating roles of curatorial news use in political involvement. *Journalism & Mass Communication Quarterly, 95*(4), 1103–1127.

Park, C. S., & Kaye, B. K. (2019). Mediating roles of news curation and news elaboration in the relationship between social media use for news and political knowledge. *Journal of Broadcasting & Electronic Media, 63*(3), 455–473. https://doi-org.proxy.library.ucsb.edu:9443/10.1080/08838151.2019.1653070

Parks, M. R., & Floyd, K. (1996). Making friends in cyberspace. *Journal of Communication, 46*(1), 80–97.

Parra-Arnau, J., Achara, J. P., & Castelluccia, C. (2017). MyAdChoices: Bringing transparency and control to online advertising. *ACM Transactions on the Web, 11*(1), 1–41.

Partridge, C. (2004). *The re-enchantment of the West: Alternative spiritualities, sacralization, popular culture, and occulture*. London: T. & T. Clark.

Penney, J. (2017). Social media and citizen participation in "official" and "unofficial" electoral promotion: A structural analysis of the 2016 Bernie Sanders digital campaign. *Journal of Communication, 67*(3), 402–423.

Pettegree, A. (2014). *The invention of news: How the world came to know about itself*. New Haven, CT: Yale University Press.

Petty, R. E., & Cacioppo, J. T. (1986). *Communication and persuasion: Central and peripheral routes to attitude change*. New York: Springer Verlag.

Pew Research Center. (2014, November 6). Religion and electronic media: One-in-five Americans share their faith online. https://www.pewforum.org/2014/11/06/religion-and-electronic -media

Pew Research Center's Journalism Project Staff. (2014, March 26). Key indicators in media & news. Retrieved on January 31, 2015, from http://www.journalism.org/2014/03/26/state-of -the-news-media-2014–key-indicators-in-media-and-news

Pew Research Center for People & the Press. (2012, September 27). *In changing news landscape, even television is vulnerable: Trends in news consumption, 1991–2012*. Retrieved March 24, 2013, from http://www.people-press.org/2012/09/27/in-changing-news-landscape-even -television-is-vulnerable

Pincus, H., Wojcieszak, M., & Boomgarden, H. (2017). Do multimedia matter? Cognitive and affective effects of embedded multimedia journalism. *Journalism & Mass Communication Quarterly, 94*(3), 747–771. https://doi.org/10.1177/1077699016654679

Post, S. (2019). Polarizing communication as media effects on antagonists: Understanding communication in conflicts in digital media societies. *Communication Theory, 29*(2), 213–235. https://doi-org.proxy.library.ucsb.edu:9443/10.1093/ct/qty022

Potter, W. J. (1999). *On media violence*. Thousand Oaks, CA: Sage.

Potter, W. J. (2009). *Arguing for a general framework for mass media scholarship*. Thousand Oaks, CA: Sage.

Potter, W. J. (2012). *Media effects*. Los Angeles: Sage.

Potter, W. J. (2019). *Media literacy* (9th ed.). Los Angeles: Sage.

Potter, W. J., & Ware, W. (1987). An analysis of the contexts of antisocial acts on prime-time television. *Communication Research, 14*, 664–686.

Purcell, K., & Rainie, L. (2014, December 8). Americans feel better informed thanks to the internet. Retrieved January 31, 2015, from http://www.pewinternet.org/2014/12/08/better-informed

Raine, L., & Wellman, B. (2012). *Networked: The new social operating system*. Cambridge, MA: MIT Press.

Rains, S. A., Tsetsi, E., Akers, C., Pavlich, C. A., & Appelbaum, M. (2019). Factors influencing the quality of social support messages produced online: The role of responsibility for distress and others' support attempts. *Communication Research, 46*(6), 866–886. https://doi-org .proxy.library.ucsb.edu:9443/10.1177/0093650218796371

Ray, A., Ghasemkhani, H., & Kannan, K. N. (2017). Ad-blockers, advertisers, and internet: The economic implications of ad-blocker platforms. In *Proceedings of the 2017 International Conference on Information Systems*. Atlanta, GA: Association for Information Systems.

Reagan, J. (1996). The "repertoire" of information sources. *Journal of Broadcasting & Electronic Media, 40*, 112–121.

Recuber, T. (2017). Digital discourse analysis: Finding meaning in small online spaces. In J. Daniels, K. Gregory, & T. M. Cottom (Eds.), *Digital sociologies* (pp. 47–60). Bristol, UK: Policy Press.

Reichelt, J., Sievert, J., & Jacob, F. (2014). How credibility affects eWOM reading: The influences of expertise, trustworthiness, and similarity on utilitarian and social functions. *Journal of Marketing Communications, 20*(1–2), 65–81.

Reinecke, L., Aufenanger, S., Beutel, M. E., Dreier, M., Quiring, O., Stark, B., Wölfling, K., & Müller, K. W. (2017). Digital stress over the life span: The effects of communication load and internet multitasking on perceived stress and psychological health impairments in a German probability sample. *Media Psychology, 20*(1), 90–115.

Reinhard, C. D., & Dervin, B. (2014). Comparing novice users' sense-making processes in virtual worlds: An application of Dervin's sense-making methodology. In U. Plesner & L. Phillips (Eds.), *Researching virtual worlds: Methodologies for studying emergent practices* (pp. 121–144). New York: Routledge.

Reiss, S., & Wiltz, J. (2004). Why people watch reality TV. *Media Psychology, 6*, 363–378.

Retail: Amazon sellers get a devil's bargain. (2019, August 2). *The Week.*

Revers, M. (2014). The Twitterization of news making: Transparency and journalistic professionalism. *Journal of Communication, 64*, 806–826. doi: 10.1111/jcom.12111

Reviews: Not every star shines so bright. (2019, June 14). *The Week.*

Rhodes, N., Potocki, B., & Masterson, D. S. (2018). Portrayals of intimate partner violence in music videos: Effects on perceptions of IPV warning signs. *Media Psychology, 21*(1), 137–156.

Richardson, G. W., Jr. (2019). Screaming at Obama: The Tea Party and the Affordable Care Act. In G. W. Richardson Jr. (Ed.), *Social media and politics: A new way to participate in the political process* (Vol. 2, pp. 173–197). Santa Barbara, CA: Praeger.

Riggs, K. E. (1996). Television use in a retirement community. *Journal of Communication, 46*(1), 144–156.

Riordan, M. A., & Trichtinger, L. A. (2017). Overconfidence at the keyboard: Confidence and accuracy in interpreting affect in e-mail exchanges. *Human Communication Research, 43*(1), 1–24. https://doi.org/10.1111/hcrc.12093

Robinson, N. W., Zeng, C., & Holbert, R. L. (2018). The stubborn pervasiveness of television news in the digital age and the field's attention to the medium, 2010–2014. *Journal of Broadcasting & Electronic Media, 62*(2), 287–301.

Rosenstein, A. W., & Grant, A. E. (1997). Reconceptualizing the role of habit: A new model of television audience activity. *Journal of Broadcasting & Electronic Media, 41*, 324–344.

Rosowsky, A. (2018). Virtual allegiance: Online "bay'ah" practices within a worldwide Sufi order. In A. Rosowsky (Ed.), *Faith and language practices in digital spaces* (pp. 209–233). Bristol, UK: Multilingual Matters.

Rossi, B. (2017, June 6). How virtual worlds are teaching better lessons. InformationAge. Retrieved June 30, 2019, from https://www.information-age.com/virtual-worlds-teaching -better-lessons-123466625

Rubenking, B., & Lang, A. (2014). Captivated and grossed out: An examination of processing core and sociomoral disgusts in entertainment media. *Journal of Communication, 64*, 543–565. doi: 10.1111/jcom.12094

Rutz, O. J., Bucklin, R. E., & Sonnier, G. P. (2012). A latent instrumental variables approach to modeling keyword conversion in paid search advertising. *Journal of Marketing Research, 49*(3), 306–319.

Rutz, O. J., & Trusov, M. (2011). Zooming in on paid search ads: A consumer-level model calibrated on aggregated data. *Marketing Science, 30*(5), 789–800.

Ryan, M. (2009). The sociotechnical infrastructures of virtual worlds. In D. Heider (Ed.), *Living virtually: Researching new worlds* (pp. 23–44). New York: Peter Lang.

Sabra, J. B. (2017). "I hate when they do that!" Netiquette in mourning and memorialization among Danish Facebook users. *Journal of Broadcasting & Electronic Media, 61*(1), 24–40.

Sah, Y. J., Ratan, R., Tsai, H.-Y. S., Peng, W., & Sarinopoulos, I. (2017). Are you what your avatar eats? Health-behavior effects of avatar-manifested self-concept. *Media Psychology, 20*(4), 632–657.

Sahni, N. S., Wheeler, C., & Chintagunta, P. (2018). Personalization in email marketing: The role of noninformative advertising content. *Marketing Science, 37*(2), 236–258.

Salami, L. O. (2018). Ifa, the word and the virtual world: A study of the perceptions of and attitudes toward Ifa religious tradition on the internet. In A. Rosowsky (Ed.), *Faith and language practices in digital spaces* (pp. 71–90). Bristol, UK: Multilingual Matters.

Saleem, M., Wojcieszak, M. E., Hawkins, I., Li, M., & Ramasubramanian, S. (2019). Social identity threats: How media and discrimination affect Muslim Americans' identification as Americans and trust in the U.S. government. *Journal of Communication, 69*(2), 214–236.

Sapolsky, B. S., & Tabarlet, J. (1990). *Sex in prime-time television: 1979 vs. 1989.* Unpublished manuscript, Department of Communication, Florida State University, Tallahassee.

Sawin, T. (2018). Re-parishing in social media: Identity-based virtual faith communities and physical parishes. In A. Rosowsky (Ed.), *Faith and language practices in digital spaces* (pp. 19–44). Bristol, UK: Multilingual Matters.

Sawyer, K. (2007). *Group genius: The creative power of collaboration.* Cambridge, MA: Basic Books.

Sayre, S., & King, C. (2003). *Entertainment & society: Audiences, trends, and impacts.* Thousand Oaks, CA: Sage.

Schmidt, E., & Cohen, J. (2013). *The new digital age: Reshaping the future of people, nations and business.* New York: Knopf.

Schmierbach, M., Xu, Q., Oeldorf-Hirsch, A., & Dardis, F. E. (2012). Electronic friend or virtual foe: Exploring the role of competitive and cooperative multiplayer video game modes in fostering enjoyment. *Media Psychology 15,* 356–371.

Schmitt, K. L., Woolf, K. D., & Anderson, D. R. (2003). Viewing the viewers: Viewing behaviors by children and adults during television programs and commercials. *Journal of Communication, 53,* 265–281.

Schramm, W., Lyle, J., & Parker, E. B. (1961). *Television in the lives of our children.* Stanford, CA: Stanford University Press.

Schudson, M. (2003). *The sociology of news.* New York: Norton.

Schultze, U. (2014). Understanding cyborgism: Using photo-diary interviews to study performative identity in Second Life. In U. Plesner & L. Phillips (Eds.), *Researching virtual worlds: Methodologies for studying emergent practices* (pp. 53–75). New York: Routledge.

Schwarz, C. (2015). Ticket to die: The tragedy at Once station and the civic use of social media in Argentina. In M. Shumow (Ed.), *Mediated communities: Civic voices, empowerment and media literacy in the digital era* (pp. 33–54). New York: Peter Lang.

Scott, D. M. (2013). *The new rules of marketing and PR* (4th edition). Hoboken, NJ: Wiley.

Scott, M. (2016, May 30). Rise of ad-blocking software threatens online revenue. *New York Times.* https://www.nytimes.com/2016/05/31/business/international/smartphone-ad-blocking-software-mobile.html

Seargeant, P., & Tagg, C. (2018). Critical digital literacy education in the "fake news" era. In D. Reedy & J. Parker (Eds.), *Digital literacy unpacked* (pp. 179–189). London: Facet Publishing.

Sears, D. O., & Freedman, J. L. (1967). Selective exposure to information: A critical review. *Public Opinion Quarterly, 31*(2), 194–213. https://doi.org/10.1086/267513

Segijn, C. M., & Eisend, M. (2019). A meta-analysis into multiscreening and advertising effectiveness: Direct effects, moderators, and underlying mechanisms. *Journal of Advertising, 48*(3), 313–332. https://doi-org.proxy.library.ucsb.edu:9443/10.1080/00913367.2019.1604009

Segijn, C. M., Voorveld, H. A. M., & Smit, E. G. (2016). The underlying effects of multiscreening. *Journal of Advertising, 45*(4), 391–402.

Segijn, C. M., Voorveld, H. A., Vandeberg, L., Pennekamp, S. F., & Smit, E. G. (2017). Insight into everyday media use with multiple screens. *International Journal of Advertising, 36*(5), 779–797.

Shaw, A., & Hargittai, E. (2018). The pipeline of online participation inequalities: The case of Wikipedia editing. *Journal of Communication, 68*(1), 143–168.

Shafer, D. M. (2014). Investigating suspense as a predictor of enjoyment in sports video games. *Journal of Broadcasting & Electronic Media, 58*(2), 272–288.

Shah, D., Cho, J., Eveland, W. P., Jr., & Kwak, N. (2005). Information and expression in a digital age: Modeling internet effects on civic participation. *Communication Research, 32,* 531–565.

Shah, D. V., McLeod, J. M., & Yoon, S. H. (2001). Communication, context, and community: An exploration of print, broadcast, and Internet influences. *Communication Research, 28,* 464–506.

Shermer, M. (2002). *Why people believe weird things: Pseudoscience, superstition, and other confusions of our time* (2nd edition). New York: Henry Holt.

Sherry, J. L. (2001). The effects of violent video games on aggression: A meta-analysis. *Human Communication Research, 27,* 409–431.

Sherry, J. L. (2004). Flow and media enjoyment. *Communication Theory, 14,* 328–347.

Shin, W., & Kim, H. K. (2019). What motivates parents to mediate children's use of smartphones? An application of the theory of planned behavior. *Journal of Broadcasting & Electronic Media, 63*(1), 144–159.

Shin, J., & Thorson, K. (2017). Partisan selective sharing: The biased diffusion of fact-checking messages on social media. *Journal of Communication, 67*(2), 233–255.

Shumow, M. (2015). Revolutions and reality: Community action in an era of state intrusion and corporatization of digital networks. In M. Shumow (Ed.), *Mediated communities: Civic voices, empowerment and media literacy in the digital era* (pp. 193–205). New York: Peter Lang.

Siebert, T. (2006, September 7). Marketing to college students: Go Web! Media Daily News. Retrieved October 30, 2006, from http://publications.mediapost.com/index/cfm?fuseaction=Articles.san&s=47799&NId=23107&p=216556

Siemens, J. C., Smith, S., & Fisher, D. (2015). Investigating the effects of active control on brand recall within in-game advertising. *Journal of Interactive Advertising, 15*(1), 43–53.

Signorielli, N. (1990). Television's mean and dangerous world: A continuation of the cultural indicators perspective. In N. Signorielli & M. Morgan (Eds.), *Cultivation analysis: New directions in media effects research* (pp. 85–106). Newbury Park, CA: Sage.

Simon, H. A. (1971). Designing organizations for an information-rich world. In M. Greenberger (Ed.), *Computers, communications, and the public interest.* Baltimore, MD: Johns Hopkins University Press.

Simon, J. P. (2014). Production, consumption and innovative business models. In G. De Prato, E. Sanz, & J. P. Simon (Eds.), *Digital media worlds: The new economy of media* (pp. 41–56). London: Palgrave Macmillan.

Simonov, A., Nosko, C., & Rao, J. M. (2018). Competition and crowd-out for brand keywords in sponsored search. *Marketing Science, 37*(2), 200–215.

Singel, R. (2010, October 27). Web gives birth to banner ads. *Wired.* https://www.wired.com/2010/10/1027hotwired-banner-ads

Slater, M. D. (2003). Alienation, aggression, and sensation seeking as predictors of adolescent use of violent film, computer, and website content. *Journal of Communication, 53,* 105–121.

Slater, M. D., Henry, K. L., Swaim, R. C., & Cardador, J. M. (2004). Vulnerable teens, vulnerable times: How sensation seeking, alienation, and victimization moderate the violent media content-aggressiveness relation. *Communication Research, 31,* 642–668.

Smith, L. R., Pegoraro, A., & Cruikshank, S. A. (2019). Tweet, retweet, favorite: The impact of Twitter use on enjoyment and sports viewing. *Journal of Broadcasting & Electronic Media, 63*(1), 94–110.

Smythe, D. W. (1954). Reality as presented on television. *Public Opinion Quarterly, 18,* 143–156.

Soldat-Jaffe, T. (2018). Yiddish Wikipedia: History revisited. In A. Rosowsky (Ed.), *Faith and language practices in digital spaces* (pp. 113–131). Bristol, UK: Multilingual Matters.

Söllner, J., & Dost, F. (2019). Exploring the selective use of ad blockers and testing banner appeals to reduce ad blocking. *Journal of Advertising, 48*(3), 302–312. https://doi-org.proxy .library.ucsb.edu:9443/10.1080/00913367.2019.1613699

Song, Y., & Mela, C. F. (2011). A dynamic model of sponsored search advertising. *Marketing Science, 30*(3), 447–468.

Souza, A. (2018). Facebook: A medium for the language planning of migrant churches. In A. Rosowsky (Ed.), *Faith and language practices in digital spaces* (pp. 45–67). Bristol, UK: Multilingual Matters.

Sparks, G. G. (2015). *Media effects research: A basic overview* (5th ed.). Boston: Cengage Learning.

Sruoginis, K. (2017). Digital trends: Consumer usage of digital and its influence on ad revenue; Half year 2017 update. Interactive Advertising Bureau. https://www.iab.com/wp-content /uploads/2017/12/Digital-Trends-Consumer-Usage-of-Digital-and-its-Influence-on-Ad -Revenue.pdf

Statista (2018, June 9). Percentage of U. S. population who currently use any social media from 2008 to 2017. Retrieved June 9, 2018, from https://www.statista.com/statistics/273476 /percentage-of-us-population-with-a-social-network-profile

Statista. (2019, August 9). Percentage of U.S. population with a social media profile from 2008 to 2019. Retrieved February 6, 2020, from https://www.statista.com/statistics/273476 /percentage-of-us-population-with-a-social-network-profile

Stocking, G. (2018, June 6). Digital news fact sheet. Pew Research Center. https://www.jour nalism.org/fact-sheet/digital-news

Strand, D. L. (2014). Presence in virtual worlds: Mediating a distributed, assembled and emergent object of study. In U. Plesner & L. Phillips (Eds.), *Researching virtual worlds: Methodologies for studying emergent practices* (pp. 34–52). New York: Routledge.

Sung, Y. H., Kang, E. Y., & Lee, W.-N. (2018). Why do we indulge? Exploring motivations for binge watching. *Journal of Broadcasting & Electronic Media, 62*(3), 408–426.

Sussman, S., Lisha, N., & Griffiths, M. D. (2011). Prevalence of the addictions: A problem of the majority or the minority? *Evaluation and the Health Professions, 34,* 3–56.

Swant, M. (2016, May 10). Twitter says users now trust influencers nearly as much as their friends. *Adweek.* http://www.adweek.com/digital/twitter-says-users-now-trust-influencers -nearly-much-their-friends-171367

Talavera, M. (2015, July 14). 10 reasons why influencer marketing is the next big thing. *Adweek.* http://www.adweek.com/digital/10-reasons-why-influencer-marketing-is-the-next -big-thing

Tamborini, R., Grall, C., Prabhu, S., Hofer, M., Novotny, E., Hahn, L., Klebig, B., Kryston, K., Baldwin, J., Aley, M., & Sethi, N. (2018). Using attribution theory to explain the affective dispositions of tireless moral monitors toward narrative characters. *Journal of Communication, 68*(5), 842–871.

Tefertiller, A. (2018). Media substitution in cable cord-cutting: The adoption of web-streaming television. *Journal of Broadcasting & Electronic Media, 62*(3), 390–407.

Teixeira, T., Wedel, M., & Pieters, R. (2012). Emotion-induced engagement in internet video advertisements. *Journal of Marketing Research, 49*(2), 144–159.

Terlutter, R., & Capella, M. L. (2013). The gamification of advertising: Analysis and research directions of in-game advertising, advergames, and advertising in social network games. *Journal of Advertising, 42*(2/3), 95–112.

The basics of selling on eBay. (2007). *Student guide*. San Jose, CA: eBay.

The new tech bubble. (2011, May 14). *The Economist*, p. 13.

Thompson, C. (2019, September). The weird joys of world-building. *Wired*, pp. 26, 28.

Toff, B., & Nielsen, R. K. (2018). "I just google it": Folk theories of distributed discovery. *Journal of Communication, 68*(3), 636–657.

Tokunaga, R. S., & Quick, J. D. (2018). Impressions on social networking sites: Examining the influence of frequency of status updates and likes on judgments of observers. *Media Psychology, 21*(2), 157–181.

Tokunaga, R. S., Wright, P. J., & Roskos, J. E. (2019). Pornography and impersonal sex. *Human Communication Research, 45*(1), 78–118. https://doi-org.proxy.library.ucsb.edu:9443/10.1093/hcr/hqy014

Trusov, M., Bucklin, R. E., & Pauwels, K. (2009). Effects of word-of-mouth versus traditional marketing: Findings from an internet social networking site. *Journal of Marketing, 73*, 90–102.

Tsfati, Y., & Cappella, J. N. (2005). Why do people watch news they do not trust? The need for cognition as a moderator in the association between news media skepticism and exposure. *Media Psychology, 7*, 251–271.

Turkle, S. (2011). *Alone together: Why we expect more from technology and less from each other*. New York: Basic Books.

Turow, J., Hennessy, M., & Draper, N. (2015). The tradeoff fallacy: How marketers are misrepresenting American consumers and opening them up to exploitation. Report from the Annenberg School for Communication, University of Pennsylvania. https://www.asc.upenn.edu/sites/default/files/TradeoffFallacy_1.pdf

Turow, J., Hennessy, M., & Draper, N. (2018). Persistent misperceptions: Americans' misplaced confidence in privacy policies, 2003–2015. *Journal of Broadcasting & Electronic Media, 62*(3), 461–478.

Tuten, T. L., & Solomon, M. R. (2018). *Social media marketing* (3rd ed.). Los Angeles: Sage.

Tversky, A., & Kahneman, D. (1973). Availability: A heuristic for judging frequency and probability. *Cognitive Psychology, 4*, 207–232.

Valente, A. (2019, July 2). The 10 most expensive games ever made, ranked. TheGamer. Retrieved February 9, 2020, from https://www.thegamer.com/most-expensive-games-ever-made

Valenzuela, S., Puente, S., & Flores, P. M. (2017). Comparing disaster news on Twitter and television: An intermedia agenda setting perspective. *Journal of Broadcasting & Electronic Media, 61*(4), 615–637.

Vandenbosch, L., Driesmans, K., Trekels, J., & Eggermont, S. (2017). Sexualized video game avatars and self-objectification in adolescents: The role of gender congruency and activation frequency. *Media Psychology, 20*(2), 221–239.

Vandenbosch, L., & van Oosten, J. M. F. (2017). The relationship between online pornography and the sexual objectification of women: The attenuating role of porn literacy education. *Journal of Communication, 67*(6), 1015–1036.

Vandenbosch, L., van Oosten, J. M. F., & Peter, J. (2018). Sexually explicit internet material and adolescents' sexual performance orientation: The mediating roles of enjoyment and perceived utility. *Media Psychology, 21*(1), 50–74.

Vandewater, E. A., Lee, J. H., & Shim, M.-S. (2005). Family conflict and violent electronic media use in school-aged children. *Media Psychology, 7*, 73–86.

Van Damme, E. (2010). Gender and sexual scripts in popular US teen series: A study on the gendered discourses in *One Tree Hill* and *Gossip Girl*. *Catalan Journal of Communication & Cultural Studies, 2*(1), 77–92. https://doi.org/10.1386/cjcs.2.1.77_1

van Oosten, J. M. F., Peter, J., & Vandenbosch, L. (2017). Adolescents' sexual media use and willingness to engage in casual sex: Differential relations and underlying processes. *Human Communication Research, 43*(1), 127–147. https://doi-org.proxy.library.ucsb.edu:9443/10.1111/hcre.12098

Van Reijmersdal, E. A., Rozendaal, E., & Buijzen, M. (2012). Effects of prominence, involvement, and persuasion knowledge on children's cognitive and affective responses to advergames. *Journal of Interactive Marketing, 26*(1), 33–42.

van't Riet, J., Hühn, A., Ketelaar, P., Khan, V.-J., Konig, R., Rozendaal, E., & Markopoulos, P. (2016). Investigating the effects of location-based advertising in the supermarket: Does goal congruence trump location congruence? *Journal of Interactive Advertising, 16*(1), 31–43.

Vermeir, I., Kazakova, S., Tessitore, T., Cauberghe, V., & Slabbinck, H. (2015). Impact of flow on recognition of and attitudes towards in-game brand placements: Brand congruence and placement prominence as moderators. *International Journal of Advertising, 33*(4), 785–810.

Video games. (2019, August 23). Microsoft teams with "Ninja." *The Week*.

Vincent, C. S., & Straub, S. (2017). Structures of dissent: Social media resistance journalism, and the mobilization of poverty activism. In G. W. Richardson Jr. (Ed.), *Social media and politics: A new way to participate in the political process* (Vol. 2, pp. 1–19). Santa Barbara, CA: Praeger.

Vishwanath, A., Harrison, B., & Ng, Y. J. (2018). Suspicion, cognition, and automaticity model of phishing susceptibility. *Communication Research, 45*(8), 1146–1166. https://doi.org.proxy.library.ucsb.edu:9443/10.1177/0093650215627483

Vivienne, S., & Burgess, J. (2012). The digital storyteller's stage: Queer everyday activists negotiating privacy and publicness. *Journal of Broadcasting & Electronic Media, 56*, 362–377.

Vogels, E. A., & O'Sullivan, L. F. (2018). Porn, peers, and performing oral sex: The mediating role of peer norms on pornography's influence regarding oral sex. *Media Psychology, 21*(4), 669–699.

Vyvey, T., Castellar, E. N., & Van Looy, J. (2018). Loaded with fun? The impact of enjoyment and cognitive load on brand retention in digital games. *Journal of Interactive Advertising, 18*(1), 72–82. https://doi-org.proxy.library.ucsb.edu:9443/10.1080/15252019.2018.1446370

Waddell, T. F., & Sundar, S. S. (2017). #thisshowsucks! The overpowering influence of negative social media comments on television viewers. *Journal of Broadcasting & Electronic Media, 61*(2), 393–409.

Walker, D. (2010). Experiencing flow: Is doing it together better than doing it alone? *Journal of Positive Psychology, 5*, 3–11.

Walther, J. B., DeAndrea, D., Kim, J., & Anthony, J. C. (2010). The influence of online comments on perceptions of antimarijuana public service announcements on YouTube. *Human Communication Research, 36*(4), 469–492.

Walther, J. B., Kashian, N., Jang, J.-W., Shin, S. Y., Dai, Y., & Koutamanis, M. (2018). The effect of message persistence and disclosure on liking in computer-mediated communication. *Media Psychology, 21*(2), 308–327.

Wang, H., & Sparks, C. (2019). Chinese newspaper groups in the digital era: The resurgence of the party press. *Journal of Communication, 69*(1), 94–119.

Webster, J. G., & Phalen, P. F. (1997). *The mass audience: Rediscovering the dominant model.* Mahwah, NJ: Erlbaum.

Weeks, B. E., Kim, D. H., Hahn, L. B., Diehl, T. H., & Kwak, N. (2019). Hostile media perceptions in the age of social media: Following politicians, emotions, and perceptions of media bias. *Journal of Broadcasting & Electronic Media, 63*(3), 374–392. https://doi-org .proxy.library.ucsb.edu:9443/10.1080/08838151.2019.1653069

Wegener, D. T., & Carlston, D. E. (2005). Cognitive processes in attitude formation and change. In D. Albarracin, B. T. Johnson, & M. P. Zanna (Eds.), *The handbook of attitudes* (pp. 493–542). Mahwah, NJ: Erlbaum

Wheelock, A. (2015, May 4). 5 virtual worlds for engaged learning. *ISTE Blog.* https://www.iste .org/explore/In-the-classroom/5-virtual-worlds-for-engaged-learning

Williams, D. (2006). Groups and goblins: The social and civic impact of an online game. *Journal of Broadcasting & Electronic Media 50*, 651–670.

Williams, L. (2019). Platforms with purpose: Clicktivism and crowfunding campaigns in the era of *Citizens United.* In G. W. Richardson Jr. (Ed.), *Social media and politics: A new way to participate in the political process* (Vol. 2, pp. 21–41). Santa Barbara, CA: Praeger.

Williams, T. M., Zabrack, M. L., & Joy, L. A. (1982). The portrayal of aggression on North American television. *Journal of Applied Social Psychology, 12,* 360–380.

Williams-Grut, O. (2017, December 20). The cryptocurrency market is now doing the same daily volume as the New York Stock Exchange. Retrieved June 8, 2018, from http://mar kets.businessinsider.com/currencies/news/daily-cryptocurrency-volumes-vs-stock-market -volumes-2017-12-1011680451

Winkler, T., & Buckner, K. (2006). Receptiveness of gamers to embedded brand messages in ad- vergames: Attitudes towards product placement. *Journal of Interactive Advertising, 7*(1), 37–46.

Winn, M. (1977). *Plug in drug: Television, computers and family life.* New York: Penguin.

Winter, S., Krämer, N. C., Benninghoff, B., & Gallus, C. (2018). Shared entertainment, shared opinions: The influence of social TV comments on the evaluation of talent shows. *Journal of Broadcasting & Electronic Media, 62*(1), 21–37.

Wojdynski, B. (2016). The deceptiveness of sponsored news articles: How readers recognize and perceive native advertising. *American Behavioral Scientist, 60*(12), 1475–1491.

Wright, P. J., & Tokunaga, R. S. (2018). Pornography consumption, sexual liberalism, and support for abortion in the United States: Aggregate results from two national panel studies. *Media Psychology, 21*(1), 75–92.

Wright, P. J., Tokunaga, R. S., Kraus, A., & Klann, E. (2017). Pornography consumption and satisfaction: A meta-analysis. *Human Communication Research, 43*(3), 315–343. https://doi -org.proxy.library.ucsb.edu:9443/10.1111/hcre.12108

Wyer, R. S., Jr., & Albarracin, D. (2005). Belief formation, organization, and change: Cogni- tive and motivational influences. In D. Albarracin, B. T. Johnson, & M. P. Zanna (Eds.), *The handbook of attitudes* (pp. 273–322). Mahwah, NJ: Erlbaum.

Xu, L., Chen, J., & Whinston, A. (2011). Price competition and endogenous valuation in search advertising. *Journal of Marketing Research, 48*(3), 566–586.

Xu, Q., & Armstrong, C. L. (2019). #SELFIES at the 2016 Rio Olympics: Comparing self- representations of male and female athletes from the U.S. and China. *Journal of Broadcasting & Electronic Media, 63*(2), 322–338. https://doi-org.proxy.library.ucsb.edu:9443/10.1080/ 08838151.2019.1621138

Xu, W. W., & Feng, M. (2014). Talking to the broadcasters on Twitter: Networked gatekeep- ing in Twitter conversations with journalists. *Journal of Broadcasting & Electronic Media, 58*(3), 420–437.

Yang, F., & Shen, F. (2018). Effects of web interactivity: A meta-analysis. *Communication Research, 45*(5), 635–658. https://doi.org.proxy.library.ucsb.edu:9443/10.1177/00936502 17700748

Yang, F., Zhong, B., Kumar, A., Chow, S.-M., & Ouyang, A. (2018). Exchanging social support online: A longitudinal social network analysis of irritable bowel syndrome patients' interactions on a health forum. *Journalism & Mass Communication Quarterly, 95*(4), 1033–1057.

Yaveroglu, I., & Donthu, N. (2008). Advertising repetition and placement issues in on-line environments. *Journal of Advertising, 37*(2), 31–43.

Yee, N. (2002, October). Ariadne—Understanding MMORPG addiction. http://www.nick yee.com/hub/addiction/home.html

Yeykelis, L., Cummings, J. J., & Reeves, B. (2018). The fragmentation of work, entertainment, e-mail, and news on a personal computer: Motivational predictors of switching between media content. *Media Psychology, 21*(3), 377–402.

Ying, L., Korneliussen, T., & Grønhaug, K. (2009). The effect of ad value, ad placement, and ad execution on the perceived intrusiveness of web advertisements. *International Journal of Advertising, 28*(4), 623–638.

Yoo, C. Y. (2009). Effects beyond click-through: Incidental exposure to web advertising. *Journal of Marketing Communications, 15*(4), 227–246.

Yoo, S.-C., & Eastin, M. S. (2017). Contextual advertising in games: Impacts of game context on a player's memory and evaluation of brands in video games. *Journal of Marketing Communications, 23*(6), 614–631.

Young, M. (2017). *Ogilvy on advertising in the digital age.* New York: Bloomsbury.

Yu, R. P., Ellison, N. B., & Lampe, C. (2018). Facebook use and its role in shaping access to social benefits among older adults. *Journal of Broadcasting & Electronic Media, 62*(1), 71–90.

Yuan, E. J., & Webster, J. G. (2006). Channel repertoires: Using peoplemeter data in Beijing. *Journal of Broadcasting & Electronic Media, 50*, 524–36.

Zajonc, R. B. (1968). Attitudinal effects of mere exposure. *Journal of Personality and Social Psychology, 9*(2) 1–27.

Zanjani, S. H. A., Diamond, W. D., & Chan, K. (2011). Does ad-context congruity help surfers and information seekers remember ads in cluttered e-magazines? *Journal of Advertising, 40*(4), 67–84.

Zephoria Digital Marketing. (2018, May). The top 20 valuable Facebook statistics. Retrieved June 8, 2018, from https://zephoria.com/top-15-valuable-facebook-statistics

Zhang, Y., Dixon, T. L., & Conrad, K. (2010). Female body image as a function of themes in rap music videos: A content analysis. *Sex Roles, 62*(11/12), 787–797. https://doi .org/10.1007/s11199-009-9656-y

Zheng, N. (2009). When geography matters in a virtual world: In-game urban planning and its impact on the Second Life community. In D. Heider (Ed.), *Living virtually: Researching new worlds* (pp. 93–110). New York: Peter Lang.

Zillmann, D. (1991). Television viewing and physiological arousal. In J. Bryant & D. Zillmann (Eds.), *Responding to the screen: Reception and reaction processes* (pp. 103–133). Hillsdale, NJ: Lawrence Erlbaum.

Zubayr, C. (1999). The loyal viewer? Patterns of repeat viewing in Germany. *Journal of Broadcasting & Electronic Media, 43*, 346–363.

Zubcsek, P. P., Katona, Z., & Sarvary, M. (2017). Predicting mobile advertising response using consumer colocation networks. *Journal of Marketing, 81*(4), 109–126.

Index

Made in the USA
Las Vegas, NV
03 February 2021